Treasures of Texas
NATIONAL HISTORIC LANDMARKS OF THE LONE STAR STATE

TRISTAN G. SMITH

4880 Lower Valley Road • Atglen, PA 19310

Other Schiffer Books on Related Subjects:

Texas Hill Country: A Scenic Journey, Eric Pohl, 978-0-7643-5392-5

254: A Photographer's Journey through Every Texas County, Ronn Varnell and Lance Varnell, 978-0-7643-6163-0

Copyright © 2025 by Tristan G. Smith

Library of Congress Control Number: 2024941289

All rights reserved. No part of this work may be reproduced or used in any form or by any means—graphic, electronic, or mechanical, including photocopying or information storage and retrieval systems—without written permission from the publisher.

The scanning, uploading, and distribution of this book or any part thereof via the Internet or any other means without the permission of the publisher is illegal and punishable by law. Please purchase only authorized editions and do not participate in or encourage the electronic piracy of copyrighted materials.

"Schiffer," "Schiffer Publishing, Ltd.," and the pen and inkwell logo are registered trademarks of Schiffer Publishing, Ltd.

Designed by Beth Oberholtzer
Cover design by Jack Chappell
Images by Tristan G. Smith unless otherwise noted.
Type set in Arno Pro/Gotham Narrow/Odibee Sans/Baka Too
Aesthetic Contemporary printable seamless pattern, (c) by ann1195, courtesy of shutterstock.com

ISBN: 978-0-7643-6910-0
ePub: 978-1-5073-0548-5

Printed in India

Published by Schiffer Publishing, Ltd.
4880 Lower Valley Road
Atglen, PA 19310
Phone: (610) 593-1777; Fax: (610) 593-2002
Email: info@schifferbooks.com
Web: www.schifferbooks.com

For our complete selection of fine books on this and related subjects, please visit our website at www.schifferbooks.com. You may also write for a free catalog.

Schiffer Publishing's titles are available at special discounts for bulk purchases for sales promotions or premiums. Special editions, including personalized covers, corporate imprints, and excerpts, can be created in large quantities for special needs. For more information, contact the publisher.

For Mom and Dad.
Thank you for instilling me with a sense
of exploration and adventure.

Contents

Introduction	6
National Historic Landmarks: A Brief History	8
Using This Guidebook	14

Forts & Military — 16

Presidio Nuestra Señora de Loreto de la Bahía (1749)	18
Fort Brown (1846)	22
Fort Belknap (1851)	26
Fort Davis (1854)	30
Fort Concho (1867)	34
Fort Richardson (1867)	38
Fort Sam Houston (1876)	42
Hangar 9, Brooks Air Force Base (1918)	46
Randolph Field Historic District (1931)	50

Battlefields & War — 54

The Alamo (March 1836)	56
San Jacinto Battlefield (March 1836)	60
Palo Alto Battlefield (May 8, 1846)	64
Resaca de la Palma Battlefield (May 9, 1846)	68
Palmito Ranch Battlefield (May 12, 1865)	72
USS *Texas* (1914)	76
HA-19 (1938)	80
USS *Lexington* (1942)	84
USS *Cabot* (1942)	88

Government — 92

Woodland (1848)	94
Governor's Mansion (1854)	98
Texas State Capitol (1885)	102
Lyndon Baines Johnson Boyhood Home (1901)	106
Samuel T. Rayburn House (1916)	110
John Nance Garner House (1920)	114
Dealey Plaza Historic District (1963)	118

Entertainment — 124

Majestic Theatre (1929)	126
Highland Park Shopping Village (1931)	130
Bastrop State Park (1933)	134
Fair Park Texas Centennial Buildings (1936)	138

Industry & Innovation — 144

- King Ranch (1852) — 146
- *Elissa* (1877) — 150
- JA Ranch (1879) — 154
- Lucas Gusher, Spindletop Oil Field (1901) — 158
- Walter C. Porter Farm (1933) — 162
- Space Environment Simulation Laboratory, Chambers A & B (1965) — 166
- Apollo Mission Control Center (1965) — 170

Texas Heritage — 174

- Spanish Governor's Palace (1722) — 176
- Mission Concepción (1731) — 180
- Espada Acequia (1731) — 184
- Treviño-Uribe Rancho (1851–71) — 188
- José Antonio Navarro House Complex (1855) — 192
- Rio Vista Bracero Reception Center (1942–64) — 196

Residential Life — 200

- Roma Historic District (1821) — 202
- Strand Historic District (1850) — 206
- East End Historic District (ca. 1886) — 210

Archeological Sites — 214

- Harrell Site — 216
- Hueco Tanks State Park & Historic Site — 220
- Landergin Mesa — 224
- Lower Pecos Canyonlands Archeological District — 228
- Lubbock Lake Landmark — 232
- Plainview Site — 236

Terms You May Need to Know — 240
Bibliography — 246
About the Author — 256

Introduction

You know those markers you see affixed to buildings or on roadside pullouts when you travel out of town? I'm a nerd for those. There are databases that chart what each one says, and I can grab my phone (as a passenger, don't worry), check an app, and see what it says without even slowing down to look at it. That's no fun though—I like stopping. Even if just to see the empty field in front of me, or to take in the soundscape in the historic district I've entered, or to smell the flowers in the wind in a neighborhood of a historic home deemed worthy of interpretation. But even though I love stopping, I'll never be able stop for them all—there are too many of them and not enough time. In addition to the national ones, if you add in markers posted by state programs, city programs, and some counties with programs . . . well, you get the point.

Since the passage of the National Historic Preservation Act, which established the National Register of Historic Places (NRHP), in 1966, more than one and a half million properties have been added, over 95,000 of them listed individually (the remaining being contributing resources within historic districts). Out of those 95,000, there is a more elite group. These listed properties are National Historic Landmarks (NHLs) and have been recognized by the government as having outstanding historical significance. Only 2,500 of those 95,000 places listed in the NRHP are recognized as a National Historic Landmark. That's less than 3 percent. Now *that* is a number I can stop for. In 1935, Congress passed the Historic Sites Act, authorizing the interior secretary to formally record and organize historic properties so there was a record of designated properties with national historical significance. This came under the authority of the National Park Service, and, over the next few decades, surveys such as the Historic American Buildings Survey compiled information about these significant properties in a program called the Historic Sites Survey.

Most of these would become national historic sites. The first national historic site designation was made for the Salem Maritime National Historic Site in March 1938 in Massachusetts.

The National Park System took on the administration of the survey data in 1960, and out of that rose the National Register of Historic Places in 1966, with the NHL program folded in. On October 9, 1960, ninety-two properties were announced as designated NHLs by the secretary of the interior, although the Sergeant Floyd Monument in Sioux City, Iowa, had been officially designated earlier in June. About half of the landmarks are privately owned. When one of the properties or districts gets added, it often triggers the activation of local preservation laws. So, in 1980, legislation was amended so listing procedures required an owner agreement to the designations.

Now, when I was a kid, other than a couple of trips to Florida on an airplane, we primarily took road trips. I grew up in the Kansas City, Missouri, area. Sitting right in the middle of the nation, we were within proximity to interstates and highways that led throughout the country. While we mostly stuck to locations within a few hours of home (including that arch in St. Louis), we traveled the hell out of those few hours and saw a lot. Much of it included historic sites of some kind.

My mom was the family historian, a role I've mainly taken over, and my dad, who passed away in March 2021, had started out with ambitions of being a history teacher before life got in the way. On those trips, we stopped at historic sites, read historic markers, walked the grounds, visited the gift shop if there was one, and moved on to the next. I've brought that habit with me as an adult now living in Texas. On the road trips of my childhood, my parents liked to share the history of the places we visited with everyone in the family. I do too when I travel now, and I like to bring other people along with me or get them excited enough to want to go on a trip to see sites on their own.

That's why you are sitting here, holding this book in your hands. I want you to get excited about what you can see in Texas. There are so many sites in the Lone Star State that have changed the fabric of the American landscape, altered the path the country was on, improved or worsened life for others. America has a fascinating story to tell—including all the good *and* the bad. When you move away from the broadest picture that you get in school, you start to learn just how many places and events outside of those bigger stories are being told, but few listen to. My hope with this book is to spur you to visit a new place, to explore a place you've already been with a new perspective, or even to introduce you to a place you haven't heard about before.

The history of Texas stretches back tens of thousands of years, at least in the historical record we are looking at. Most of these sites chart a journey from Spanish Texas to the present. The American story doesn't begin in 1776 in New England; it doesn't necessarily start with pilgrims or Christopher Columbus. Search throughout Texas, and you'll see a wide panoramic view of Texan and American history—and a great example of what it means to live in this melting pot we call the United States.

As you explore Texas, you're never really farther away than about four hours from one NHL (Fort Davis) to another (Fort Concho), with the rest much closer to each other than that. San Antonio / Béxar County plays host to the most NHLs, with nine locations. The Brownsville area / Cameron County counts four, plus one that has been removed (don't worry; you may not be able to go see it, but it's listed in this book). Then Houston / Harris County has four, while Dallas / Dallas County has three. The rest are scattered throughout the rest of the state. Some sites are more accessible than others, with no really insurmountable obstacles. Others, especially the protected archeological sites, are completely inaccessible to the general public.

I hope you enjoy this book. Historic sites mean a lot to me, and I hope that they either mean a lot to you now or will become important fixtures in your life. Look, everyone has a story . . . so, too, does every place. Get curious. Go explore. Take someone and talk about it. Pick a place. Stand there. Get a full view of your surroundings. Close your eyes. Listen. Smell. Touch. Try to capture a feeling of what this site was like when it was in its prime. If you can do that with each of these places you visit, then you've made the efforts of those federal employees back in the 1930s–1960s who started designating these sites worth it.

—*Tristan G. Smith*

National Historic Landmarks:
A Brief History

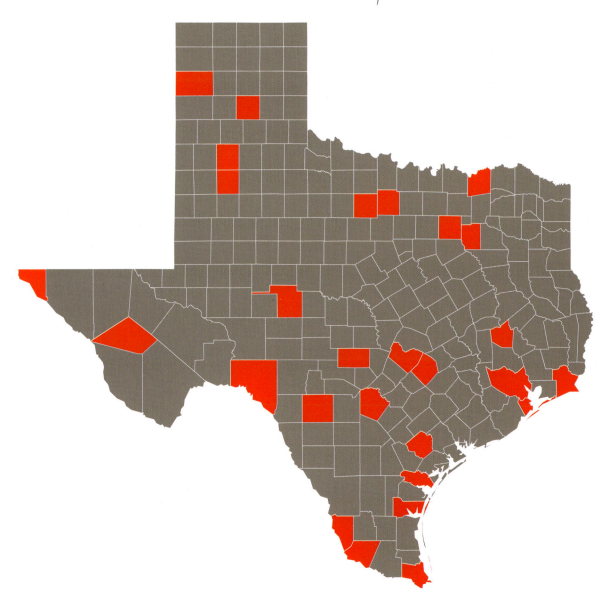

Texas county map with counties with National Historic Landmarks marked in red

8 TREASURES OF TEXAS

So, what is a National Historic Landmark, and what sets it apart from a place listed on the country's National Register of Historic Places (NRHP)? Well, in the simplest terms, an NHL can be a building, a district, an object, a site, or a structure that has officially been recognized by the US government for having outstanding historical significance. Within this, a National Historic Landmark District may include contributing properties that are buildings, sites, or objects and might also include noncontributing properties. The contributing properties within the district may or may not be listed separately as well. Out of the over 90,000 places listed on the NRHP, roughly 2,500 of them have been recognized as NHLs, or about 3 percent—creating a fairly excluding club.

Let's travel back to the Great Depression. Prior to 1935, efforts to preserve the cultural heritage locations of national importance were done piecemeal through the United States Congress. That year, Congress passed the Historic Sites Act, authorizing the interior secretary to formally record and organize the historic properties in the United States that had "national historical significance." It also gave the National Park Service the authority to administer these historically significant federally owned properties.

For the following decades, surveys such as the Historic American Buildings Surveys would amass information on these properties, leading to appropriate designations. The first designation came as a national memorial. In December 1935, the Gateway Arch National Park (then called the Jefferson National

The Jefferson National Expansion Memorial, or Gateway Arch, in St. Louis, Missouri, seen here during its 1965 construction, was built as a monument to westward expansion. It was added to the NHL list in 1987 but as a national memorial in 1935. *Courtesy of the National Archives and Records Administration*

Expansion Memorial) in St. Louis was issued. The first designation of a national historic site was made for the Salem Maritime National Historic Site in March 1938.

Once the National Park Service took on the administration of the survey data in 1960, the National Historic Landmark Program began to get some formalization. In

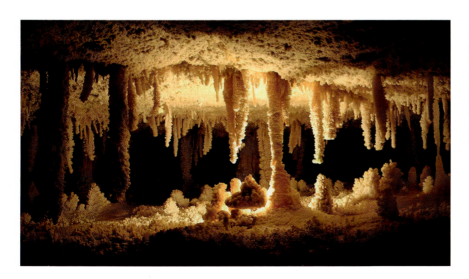

Similar to National Historic Landmarks, there are also twenty designated National Natural Landmarks. The program began in 1965 with the addition of Sutton County's Caverns of Sonora, seen here, and the Odessa Meteor Crater in Ector County.

National Historic Landmarks: A Brief History

Starting in 1935, surveys would amass information about historic properties, most of which would become national historic sites. The first was the Salem Maritime National Historic Site in 1938, which includes the customhouse seen here around 1880. Some locations become landmarks. *Courtesy of the New York Public Library Digital Collection*

October 1960, ninety-two properties were announced as designated NHLs, starting with the Sergeant Floyd Monument in Sioux City, Iowa. In 1966, the National Register of Historic Places was established; encompassed within it was the National Historic Landmark Program. Each had rules and procedures for inclusion and designation.

The Ins and Outs of the NHL

National Historic Landmarks earn their designation through the US secretary of the interior by meeting a list of criteria. These sites must be where events of national historical significance occurred. They can be places where prominent persons lived or worked. They may have embraced the ideals that helped shape the nation (for good or bad). They might serve as outstanding examples of design or construction. A place might characterize a certain way of life, emblematic for a location, site, or culture. Additionally, it might be an archeological site that has, or is still yet able, to yield information.

Over 2,500 NHLs have been designated, with multiple locations generally being added each year. Most but not all of these sites are located within the United States. These sites are located in all fifty states and the District of Columbia, with some located in US commonwealths and territories, associated states, and a few in foreign states. Additionally, over a hundred ships or shipwrecks have also been designated as NHLs. Three states—Pennsylvania, Massachusetts, and New York—account for nearly 25 percent of the nation's NHLs. Three cities within those states (Philadelphia, Boston, and New York City) all separately have more NHLs than forty of the fifty states, with New York City having more NHLs than all but five states.

Roughly half of the NHLs are privately owned. Because the system recognizes these properties, to be added to the NHL listings, a property owner must agree to a location being involved, and the owner may

The first official landmark, declared in 1960, is the Sergeant Floyd Monument, seen here under construction. This Sioux City, Iowa, monument to the only Lewis and Clark Expedition death overlooks the Missouri River valley. The 100-foot white sandstone obelisk was completed in 1901 and replaced the stolen original cedar post. *Courtesy of the US Army Corps of Engineers*

Including *HA-19*, Battleship *Texas*, the *Elissa*, and USS *Lexington*, there are 133 NHLs that are ships, shipwrecks, or shipyards. The *Philadelphia*, a 1776 Continental navy gunboat, was sunk in battle that October. It is on display at the National Museum of American History.

architectural or historical significance. Historic sites can also be designated as state archeological landmarks, but those must first be listed in the National Register. Additionally, many cities throughout the state have preservation programs, laws, rules, and regulations that can help provide protection and assistance when it comes to preserving landmarks and sites that these locales deem important on more of a microlevel.

Also, just because a site receives the honor of National Historic Landmark status does not necessarily mean that the status will last forever. This recognition does not prevent changes being made to the property that can completely alter its character. When a property object, resulting in the secretary of the interior being able to designate a site only as eligible for designation. The program relies on suggestions for new designations from the National Park Service, which also assists in maintaining the landmarks. If the site is not already listed on the National Register of Historic Places, an NHL is automatically added to the NRHP upon designation. Potential landmarks may be identified through theme studies or special studies undertaken by the National Park Service, providing a comparative analysis of properties associated with a specific area of American history, such as civil rights or women's history.

This is all at the national level. There are also efforts on state and local levels to protect or raise awareness about the historical importance of sites. Established in 1953, the Texas Historical Commission, the state agency for historic preservation, awards Recorded Texas Historic Landmark (RTHL) designation to buildings at least fifty years old that are deemed to have

Independence National Historic Park, added in October 1966, is the most visited. The district in Philadelphia includes Independence Hall (seen here around 1900), the Liberty Bell, the First and Second Banks of the United Sates, and a re-created City Tavern, among other sites. *Courtesy of the National Archives*

National Historic Landmarks: A Brief History **11**

Under the 1966 National Historic Preservation Act, both landmarks and historic sites became administered by the National Park Service. The first property listed on the National Register was the Old Slater Mill, a historic district seen here in 1910, in Pawtucket, Rhode Island. *Courtesy of the National Archives*

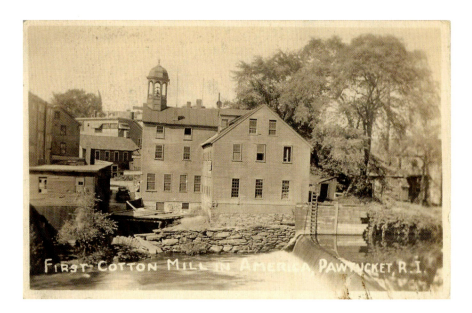

New York City has the most National Historic Landmarks of any city and more than all but five states. Its sites include the Dakota Apartments, seen here around 1890, famed as a home to numerous artists, actors, and musicians. John Lennon was murdered outside the building in 1980. *Courtesy of the Library of Congress*

Formerly the chancery of the United States diplomatic mission to Morocco, the American Legation in Tangier, established in 1821, was the first American public property abroad and is the only NHL located in a foreign country. *Courtesy of the Library of Congress*

undergoes enough alteration that it loses its ability to convey its national significance, a withdrawal of status is considered; this is done either at the request of the owner or on the initiative of the secretary of the interior.

There are four criteria used as a justification for removal: the property has ceased to meet criteria for designation (the qualities that made it eligible have been lost or destroyed), additional information demonstrates that it does not actually possess sufficient significance for continued listing, a professional error was made in the designation process, or there was a prejudicial procedural error in the process (or a combination of these). Loss of integrity is the most common reason for withdrawal and generally deals with alteration, addition, or demolition.

Designation as a landmark does lend some assistance to property owners. It may provide the site with additional protections from development and make the property eligible for preservation grants and technical preservation assistance. Since most landmarks are privately owned, they are generally governed by local preservation laws. The designation does not prohibit under federal law or regulations any actions taken by the property owner with respect to the property, especially if they wish that federal funding, licensing, or permits are not involved.

In Texas there are fifty-one current NHLs and one former landmark. The landmarks in Texas are distributed across twenty-nine of the state's 254 counties; the highest concentration, nine sites, is located in Béxar County. This book will give readers an overview of the National Historic Landmarks in Texas, providing for each a brief but comprehensive history of the location, details on what made it important enough to receive the designation, and, when appropriate, the information to visit or view the site.

National Historic Landmarks: A Brief History 13

Using This Guidebook

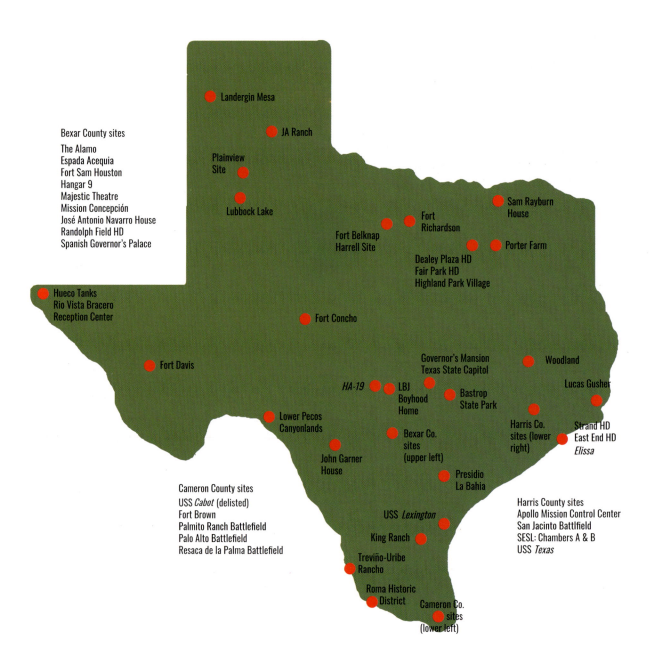

Illustration of all NHL site locations in Texas

14   TREASURES OF TEXAS

This guidebook is divided into eight history-focused areas within Texas's history. Each section begins with some general overview and information about each of these historical segments, followed by descriptions of each site located within that focus by date of importance. The state map and table of contents in the front of the book will help readers find specific sites. Color-coded symbols at the top of each page indicate the relevant topic areas.

Site Information

Here you will find basic information about each site. I've included the physical address. If there are multiple points of interest, the location of each is noted. I also list the site's phone number and website where appropriate. Additionally, you will find the important dates in the life of each of these sites. It might be the date it was built, a point in time when it was deemed pivotal (for example, I use the Battle of the Alamo as the important date, but its history stretches well before the 1836 battle), or possibly a time frame or era. Below that are the dates the site was listed on various registers for preservation, from local to national and—in one instance—international.

Site Descriptions

The short essays in these sections provide some historical overview and background on each site. Here you will learn about what each site's tie is to a national narrative, or why the site or district was deemed important enough to land itself on the NHL register. I've tried to pull the sites together into common themes or foci; however, many of these sites could easily overlap into multiple categories, so I have chosen what seemed to be the most pertinent points of importance in each site's history and placed them correspondingly (only in a few cases, because it was the closest I could get without having a solitary site listed on its own).

Site Visitor Information

This section at the end of each description gives a brief summary of site location and information on whether it's accessible to the public and, if so, what the operating schedule is and if there is camping or other facilities on-site. Before visiting one of these parks or sites, checking the websites individually or calling ahead for updated park schedules and recent changes is highly recommended, since there are many factors included in the altering of opening and operating schedules that a book like this cannot foresee. Remember, regulations at these locations are aimed at protecting the historical resources for current and future generations as well as providing a pleasant and safe experience for visitors. To preserve these sites, please refrain from removing plants, minerals, wildlife, and any artifacts. Please don't litter or damage any park grounds or facilities, and be courteous to others.

Forts & Military

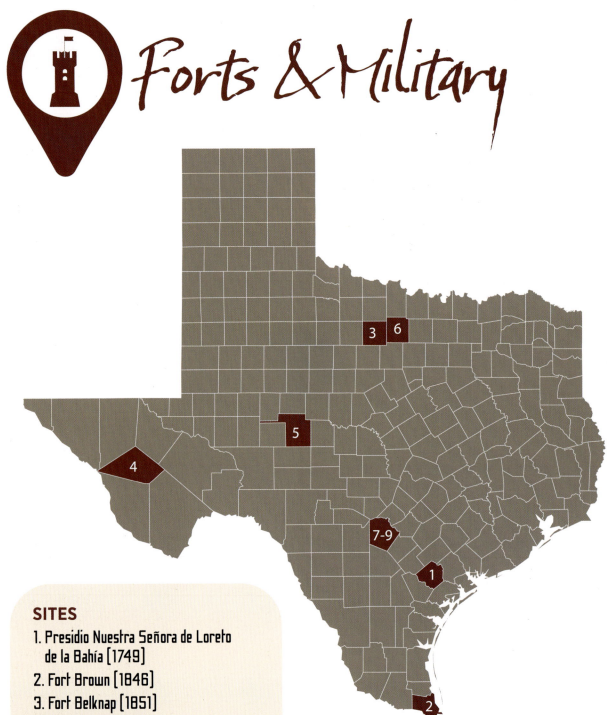

SITES
1. Presidio Nuestra Señora de Loreto de la Bahía (1749)
2. Fort Brown (1846)
3. Fort Belknap (1851)
4. Fort Davis (1854)
5. Fort Concho (1867)
6. Fort Richardson (1867)
7. Fort Sam Houston (1876)
8. Hangar 9, Brooks Air Force Base (1918)
9. Randolph Field Historic District (1931)

The military and forts in Texas have a long history. Throughout the history of the land that is now Texas, Spaniards, Mexicans, Texans, Americans, Native Americans, and more established over thirty forts and presidios. These fortified places served as logistic bases for supplies, retreats for much-needed rest and the recuperation of soldiers, and a way to protect nearby trails, civilians, and settlements who lived within their barricades.

In more modern times, military fortresses and equipment project national might, strength, and protection. Some patrolled the open spaces of the West Texas frontier, an open and vast stretch of sand, dirt, and plants, while others trained and housed soldiers during times of national and international conflicts, as well as our peaceful interludes. Most of the forts in this section had been abandoned by the twentieth century, before going on to be used for a variety of purposes. Partially because of the arid climate and varied postmilitary use, several forts remain in excellent condition, and a few are still in operation today.

All of these sites are little changed and provide a glimpse into twentieth-century modern warfare and the soldier way of life, giving visitors a sense of the rough and isolated, but well-ordered, life in the wilderness ... tamed only by their walls and function.

Presidio Nuestra Señora de Loreto de la Bahía

217 US-183
Goliad, TX 77963
361-645-3752
https://thc.texas.gov/historic-sites/presidio-la-bahia

Important Dates

Built: **1749**
Added to National Register of Historic Places:
    December 24, 1967
Designated a National Historic Landmark:
    December 24, 1967
Designated a Recorded Texas Historic
    Landmark: **1969**

Presidio la Bahía was originally constructed by the Spanish army in 1747 atop the ruins of a failed 1721 French fort and later moved to this location. It was the site of the Battle of Goliad in October 1835 and of the Goliad Massacre the following March.

18   TREASURES OF TEXAS

Site Description

Now part of Goliad State Park and Historic Site, the Presidio la Bahía ("Fort on the Bay") is an exemplary site interpreting the geopolitical tensions in the region and the emergence of the ranching culture in Texas. The Spanish began colonizing South Texas as early as the late seventeenth century. Colonization of the area was politically and economically advantageous for the Spaniards, who set about saving the souls of the Native American tribes while creating a supply of native labor and deterring the French in Louisiana from gaining a foothold in the area.

Mission Nuestra Señora de la Bahía del Espíritu Santo de Zúñiga, also called Mission Espíritu Santo, was first established in 1722 by Franciscan priests and was moved three times over the years, eventually landing near present-day Goliad. Encounters with the Karankawa would force the relocations of both Spanish explorer Álvar Núñez Cabeza de Vaca in 1528 and then French explorer René-Robert Cavelier, Sieur de La Salle's Fort Saint Louis near Port Lavaca in 1685. Built directly on top of LaSalle's failed Fort St. Louis, the Presidio la Bahía and the Mission Espíritu Santo de Zúñiga were constructed in 1721. Unable to grow enough crops or attract the local tribes to convert, the mission moved again in 1726.

Above: The historic Presidio la Bahía at Goliad seen from outside its walls in 1912. A dirt road winds past the mission on the left. *Courtesy of UNT Libraries, The Portal to Texas History*

Below: This aerial shot, taken in 2021 by William Hicks, shows a cannon turret, the protective walls, living space, and Our Lady of Loreto Chapel at the presidio. *Courtesy of UNT Libraries, The Portal to Texas History*

Forts & Military 19

This time, the missionaries traveled some 26 miles inland to present-day Victoria, along the Guadalupe River, home to the Tamique and Aranama people. This iteration, too, would eventually be relocated. During the fall of 1749, Mission Espíritu Santo and Presidio Nuestra Señora de Loreta de Bahía moved to present-day Goliad, one on each bank of the San Antonio River. These two settlements helped protect El Camino la Bahía, a major trade route to the north and east. The first settlement buildings were jacals, constructed of wattle and daub. More permanent stone structures followed, including a *convento* and a living area for the families at the mission, a granary, and a forge.

Life and work at the mission and presidio for the multiple resident tribes provided protection from raids. Additionally, the skills they received while working there resulted in a society adept as horse riders and ranchers. The mission would grow and become one of the first cattle ranches in the region. By 1788, the mission's agricultural haul included a variety of crops and counted over 15,000 head of cattle, reaching a height of 40,000 at its peak, with the incorporation of herds from other missions.

As raids from the Lipan Apache and Comanche became more problematic at Mission Espíritu Santo, the priests began arming the native peoples living there. The raids—along with desertion and disease—contributed to a population decline at the mission in the late eighteenth century, resulting in a secularization of the mission land in 1794.

Just days following the start of the Texas Revolution, in October 1835, Texian insurgents attacked Presidio la Bahía. They managed to take the Mexican garrison in only thirty minutes, renaming it Fort Defiance. During the siege of the Alamo, Texian commander William B. Travis repeatedly requested reinforcements, but a relief mission was abandoned. Following the fall of the Alamo, General Houston ordered Fannin to abandon la Bahía. Fannin took his time and a week later suffered for it. Following the Battle of Coleto, la Bahía was captured;

Fannin's garrison was rounded up and imprisoned in the presidio. On March 27, the Texians were marched outside the presidio walls and executed. The event is now known as the Goliad Massacre.

Once Texas became a state, the mission would fall into disrepair. The next few decades saw many of the buildings used for a variety of purposes, and stones were offered for reuse in newer buildings, causing an eventual dismantling of the mission. Restoration efforts began when the Texas State Park System took control of the site, utilizing the efforts of Civilian Conservation Corps (CCC) crews to rebuild much of the mission, including the chapel and granary. Additional structure rehabilitation and the addition of exhibits came during the 1970s.

Today, visitors to Goliad State Historic Park will find the reconstructed Spanish colonial-era mission of Nuestra Señora de Espíritu Santo de Zúñiga and the ruins of the 1750s Mission Rosario State Historic Site (open by appointment only). The park also has a museum at the Zaragoza Birthplace State Historic Site. La Bahía is owned by the Catholic Diocese of Victoria but operates as a public museum. Directly adjacent, a short walk away, is the Fannin Memorial Monument that commemorates the Goliad Massacre of 1836.

> **Visitor Information**
>
> HOURS: Daily 10 a.m.–5 p.m., last admission at 4:30 p.m.
> *Admission fee charged*
>
> In addition to the historic sites, visitors to the park can take advantage of camping, picnicking, hiking, fishing, swimming, and nature exploration. The park offers a floating dock and river access for kayaks and canoes and is a takeout point for the Goliad Paddling Trail.

Above: Taken in 1912, this photograph shows the interior of the church at Presidio la Bahía. Shot down the aisles between the pews, the image provides a view of the church altar at the other end. *Courtesy of UNT Libraries, The Portal to Texas History*

Left: The Fannin Memorial Monument is located a short distance from the walls of Presidio la Bahía. It marks the common burial site of Colonel Fannin and his men following their execution after their capture by the Mexican army at the 1836 Battle of Coleto Creek.

Forts & Military   21

Fort Brown

80 Fort Brown
UT-Brownsville and Texas Southmost Junior College campuses
Brownsville, TX 78520
956-541-5560
https://www.nps.gov/paal/learn/historyculture/siegeofforttexas.htm

Important Dates

Built: **1846**
Added to National Register of Historic Places:
October 15, 1966
Designated a National Historic Landmark:
December 19, 1960

Champion Hall served as the medical laboratory and isolation ward at Fort Brown until World War I. It was completed in 1869 during the rebuilding of the fort by Captain William Alonzo Wainwright and then known as the Post Hospital Annex and medical laboratory. *Courtesy of the Library of Congress*

Site Description

Sitting at the southernmost tip of the state, Fort Brown was established as a star-shaped earthen breastwork fort. Standing along the Rio Grande River, across from the Mexican port of Matamoros, it was activated on March 28, 1846. The fort was constructed as Camp Taylor, also known as "Fort Texas," to house eight hundred men; it featured a moat and a drawbridge. In May 1846, General Zachary Taylor left fifty men to defend the fort, under the command of Major Jacob Brown. The Mexican forces, under General Mariano Arista, sought to drive General Taylor from the territory and sent a massive force to attack. Taylor began his return upon hearing the bombardment, encountering forces at Palo Alto on May 8 and Resaca de la Palma the next day. While the fort withstood the attack, Major Brown lost his life. The next week, he was memorialized with the renaming of the fort in his honor.

In the lower Rio Grande valley, especially in the immediate vicinity of Fort Brown, is where American armies would first engage Mexican troops, demonstrating the United States' position as an emerging world power. While the Mexican-American War is most closely identified with Fort Brown, this fort has been directly connected to the training of troops during the Civil War, the Spanish-American War, and the Pancho Villa border activity of 1913–1917, as well as conflicts between Mexican paramilitaries and Brownsville citizens in 1859. Additionally, in 1882, during the height of a yellow fever outbreak, Dr. William Crawford Gorgas was assigned to the fort's hospital, studying the disease for several years. He would later serve as US surgeon general.

Relations between those in town and those at the fort were not always genial. In 1906, a unit of the famed African American buffalo soldiers arrived at Fort Brown. Their presence built resentment among many of the white residents of Brownsville. That strained tension came to a head on August 13 and 14, when a group of unidentified people raided Brownsville, wounding one white man and killing another. Despite the backing of officers and clear alibis, the buffalo soldiers were blamed. A subsequent US Army investigation brought down a guilty charge, resulting in every single one of the 168 soldiers being discharged without honor. The army finally conducted another investigation in 1972 that resulted in honorable discharges for the soldiers. By this time, however, only two of the soldiers were alive. Regardless of this about-face, the army continued to withhold the deceased soldiers' pensions from their descendants.

The fort continued to be well used whenever a cavalry regiment of the army was stationed at Fort Brown. The 124th Cavalry Regiment of the Texas National Guard went into active military training following the attack on Pearl Harbor and was sent to the China-Burma-India theater. The fort was transferred to the United States Army Air Force Training Command,

Since Fort Brown was deactivated in 1945, it has lent itself better to historic preservation than most of its frontier counterparts. Many of the original buildings, seen here around 1910, still exist and are now part of the campuses of University of Texas at Brownsville and Texas Southmost Junior College. *Courtesy of the Texas Escapes, Dan Whatley Collection*

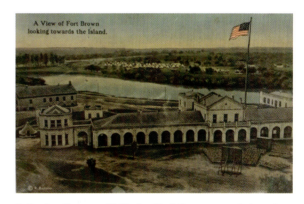

Following the war with Mexico, Fort Brown expanded nearby the original earthworks and would play a role in the Civil War, as a training ground during the Spanish-American War, and again as a point of mobilization during the Mexican Revolution. *Courtesy of the Texas Escapes, Dan Whatley Collection*

Above: Only remnants of the Fort Brown earthworks remain. Today they form the boundary of the Fort Brown Memorial Golf Course and its adjacent driving range. These remains are those of the only such fort in the United States for the US-Mexican War.

Left: Sarah Bowman or Borginnes, the Heroine of Fort Brown, was a legendary camp follower who distinguished herself by refusing to join the other women in an underground magazine. She operated the fort's mess for nearly a week before shots pierced her sunbonnet and knocked a tray from her hands. *Courtesy of the Library of Congress*

which used the garrison for flexible gunnery tasks. On February 1, 1946, Fort Brown was inactivated and in April was turned over to the Army Corps of Engineers. Two years later, the City of Brownsville and Texas Southmost Junior College acquired Fort Brown, preserving and studying the site and achieving its National Historic Landmark status in 1960.

The National Historic Landmark consists of three discontiguous districts. One includes the original earthen fortification, the second features the fort's remaining historic cavalry barracks, while the third

Three former post areas are included in the discontinuous landmark district. These areas include the 1846 earthworks, a cavalry barracks constructed in 1848, and a collection of buildings erected between 1868 and 1870. This latter collection includes a hospital, barracks, a commissary, a colonel's house, officers' quarters, and a morgue.

Visitor Information

HOURS: Open during campus daytime hours. Interior access to buildings requires university permission.
Admission fee charged

consists of a handful of surviving historic buildings dating back to 1868. The different districts reflect three distinct phases of construction. The first phase began in 1846, with the original construction. The second began in 1848, with the construction of the Brownsville Barracks and the beginnings of a permanent post along the southwest side of the lagoon. The third phase of construction along the north side of that lagoon began in late 1867, which constitutes the majority of the landmark's contributing buildings.

During the second phase of construction, the post was occupied by a garrison of one to four companies, except for a short evacuation in 1859. Confederate troops occupied Fort Brown on March 20, 1861. Prior to abandoning the fort to Union troops, the Confederates burned the fort on March 20, 1863. Union general Nathaniel Banks's men would occupy the fort until 1864. Confederate forces, under the leadership of General James E. Slaughter and the return of Colonel Ford, took control of the area and held the post until the end of the war, when Union general Egbert Brown moved in.

Additional permanent buildings were begun in 1867, only to be destroyed by a hurricane in October that fall. The third phase got underway on the lagoon's north side later that year under the direction of Major William Wainwright. Another hurricane destroyed many buildings at the fort in 1933, necessitating the remodeling of others.

Fort Belknap

5385 FM 61
Newcastle, TX 76372
940-846-3222

Important Dates

Built: **1851**
Added to National Register of Historic Places:
  October 15, 1966
Designated a National Historic Landmark:
  December 19, 1960

Located near Newcastle, Fort Belknap was the northernmost fort in a line from the Rio Grande to the Red River. Prior to the Civil War, the post was abandoned due to redistribution of federal troops to the north and an unreliable water source.

Site Description

As Texas grew in popularity with potential settlers, the settlers' need for protection also grew. Fort Belknap would become the northern anchor of a chain of forts founded to protect the Texas frontier from the Red River to the Rio Grande. This post was one without defensive works, serving more as a base of operations. From here, troops pursued raiding bands of Kiowa and Comanche, with mounted expeditions occasionally carrying the war from the fort as far north as the Kansas plains. Fort Belknap and its brothers gave confidence to the settlers, who came in such numbers that counties quickly were organized. Belknap would become the hub of a network of roads stretching in every direction, most notably the Butterfield Overland Mail Route from St. Louis to San Francisco.

Other forts in the frontier fort system were Forts Griffin, Concho, Richardson, Chadbourne, Stockton, Davis, Bliss, McKavett, Clark, McIntosh, Inge, and Phantom Hill in Texas, with Fort Sill in Oklahoma (then Indian Territory). Subposts, or intermediate stations, were also used and included Bothwick's Station on Salt Creek (between Forts Richardson and Belknap), Camp Wichita near Buffalo Springs (between Fort Richardson and Red River Station), and Mountain Pass (between Forts Concho and Griffin).

The US Army established Fort Belknap 3 miles south of present-day Newcastle in Young County on June 24, 1851, under the command of Brevet Brigadier General William G. Belknap. The commanding officer, Captain C. L. Stephenson, Fifth Infantry, found no water in the 6-foot-deep shafts dug at the location where the Newcastle water tower now stands. The lack of water caused him to move the fort 2 miles south, where adequate water was found in the springs by the Brazos River. The current well was dug in 1857 under the direction of Captain Gabriel R. Paul of the Seventh Infantry. The first buildings erected were jacals, some of which were later replaced with stone.

Abandoned prior to the Civil War, the fort was mainly used for safety and shelter from storms. Despite being briefly occupied in 1867, the fort was effectively out of commission. By 1936, the fort had been gradually dismantled for its materials, so that only the magazine and part of the cornhouse remained. *Courtesy of the Library of Congress*

Primarily a base of operations, Fort Belknap was the center of a network of frontier roads, including the Butterfield Overland Mail Route. Seen here around 1869, this Concord wagon is being protected by buffalo soldiers. *Courtesy of the National Archives & Records Administration*

The fort was a four-company post. Among those companies stationed at Fort Belknap were some from the 5th and 7th US Infantry, the 2nd US Dragoons, and the 2nd and 6th US Cavalry, while notable officers included Captain Randolph B. Marcy and Lieutenant George B. McClellan, who explored the Canadian River together, finding the headwaters of the Red River. In early 1861, believing war to be imminent, General David E. Twiggs ordered Colonel William H. Emory to gather all federal troops and move them north to Fort Leavenworth, Kansas, effectively abandoning the post. On February 9, General Twiggs, in San Antonio, surrendered all United States forts and military equipment in Texas. Families remaining in Young County would gather in the fort's abandoned buildings, especially when seeking shelter from storms.

While abandoned prior to the Civil War, the fort was occupied occasionally by state troops of the Frontier Regiment under Colonel James M. Norris. Major Starr, with troops of the 6th US Cavalry, reoccupied the fort on April 28, 1867. When Fort Griffin was founded in Shackelford County, Fort Belknap was abandoned for good in September 1867. The fort was gradually dismantled for building materials; by 1936, only the fort's magazine and part of the cornhouse remained.

During the Texas centennial in 1936, Senator Benjamin G. O'Neal and local citizens restored and rebuilt some of the buildings, mostly on their

In the 1930s, portions of Fort Belknap were rebuilt and restored, many on their original foundations. Starting in 2019, the fort underwent a renovation to update the museum housed in the commissary building, seen here.

original foundations. During the 1970s, the Fort Belknap Archives, with help from the Young County Commissioners Court, rebuilt Infantry Quarters Number Four to house the records of North Texas. Since the restoration, Fort Belknap has become a cultural and recreational center. In 2019, the fort underwent a renovation project. This process updated the museum, housed in the commissary building, and built a new support structure for the grape arbor, which includes the largest mustang grape vine known to exist.

Visitor Information

HOURS: March to November: Monday through Saturday, 9 a.m.–5 p.m.; Sunday, 1:30–5 p.m.; closed Wednesdays. Closed for lunch, 12–1:30 p.m.
No entrance fee

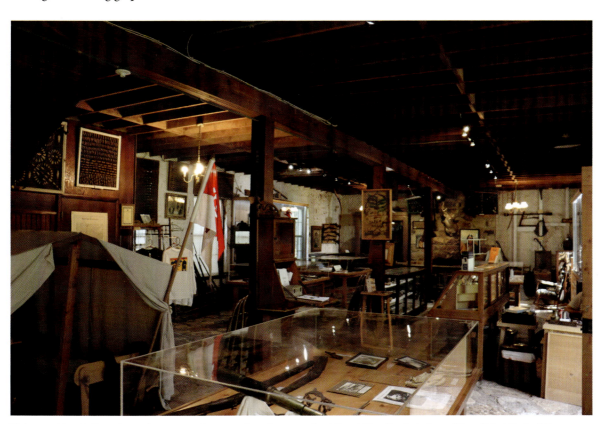

Visitors to Fort Belknap have the opportunity to explore the grounds of the old frontier fort. A small handful of the buildings are open, with the primary building serving as the fort's current museum building, where one can find numerous interpretive exhibits.

Forts & Military

Fort Davis

101 Lt. Flipper Drive
Fort Davis, TX 79734
432-426-3224
www.nps.gov/foda/index.htm

Important Dates

Built: **1854**
Added to National Register of Historic Places:
 October 15, 1966
Designated a National Historic Landmark:
 December 19, 1960
Designated a National Historic Site:
 September 8, 1961

Ruins of the officers' quarters. *Courtesy of UNT Libraries, The Portal to Texas History*

Fort Davis National Historic Site as seen from the ridge. *Courtesy of the National Park Service*

Site Description

Interested in locating a route through the Southwest that contained available water, the War Department founded Fort Davis on Limpia Creek. Established on the site of an earlier Indian village, the fort is tucked into a canyon at the eastern base of the Davis Mountains in far western Texas. It was established on land leased from San Antonio surveyor John James on the order of Secretary of War Jefferson Davis in 1854. Once established, the area attracted settlers, and the city of Fort Davis would be established to the fort's southwest, starting originally as the rough-and-tumble settlement of Chihuahua.

Fort Davis served as a key member of a line of forts that included Forts Griffin, Concho, Belknap, Chadbourne, Stockton, Richardson, Bliss, McKavett, Clark, McIntosh, Inge, and Phantom Hill in Texas, with Fort Sill in Oklahoma and a handful of intermediate stations along the routes stretching between San Antonio and El Paso. Thirteen regiments were garrisoned at Fort Davis and played a significant role in the defense and development of West Texas, guarding the Trans-Pecos segment toward California.

Named for the US secretary of war Jefferson Davis, seen here in a photograph taken prior to his Civil War defection for the Confederacy. *Courtesy of the National Archives and Records Administration*

Forts & Military 31

With the end of the war with Mexico in 1848 came a vast admission of new land, and westward expansion to the Pacific coast was a certainty. This, coupled with the discovery of gold in California in 1849, would send thousands of migrants, mail and wagon trains, and prospectors to the West. Seeking to avoid the snow, winter weather, and mountainous terrain that the northerly routes contained, they would push their way over southern trails. Fort Davis was there to protect these routes, most importantly the Trans-Pecos portion of the San Antonio–El Paso Road and the Chihuahuan Trail, while also controlling activities on the southern stem of the Great Comanche War Trail and Mescalero Apache war trails.

However, this route was not without peril. Indian trails leading south into Mexico intersected the El Paso Road, and Apache and Comanche raids were common until the Civil War. The US military found it necessary by 1854 to construct a fort in West Texas to protect this route. That October, Brevet General Persifor F. Smith, then commanding the Department of Texas, personally selected the site of Fort Davis both for its attractive climate and proximity to water. He named the post after Jefferson Davis. Within days, six companies of the Eighth US Infantry, under Lieutenant Colonel Washington Seawell, arrived at Painted Comanche Camp to build and garrison the new post.

When hostilities between the North and South reached a tipping point toward war, the US troops evacuated Fort Davis under orders from Brigadier General David E. Twiggs and were quickly replaced by Confederate cavalry forces under Colonel John R. Baylor in April 1861. Confederate troops occupied the fort for about a year before retreating to San Antonio after failing to take New Mexico for the Confederacy. For five years, Fort Davis sat abandoned, with wood from its buildings being taken for fuel.

Following the war, in June 1867, federal troops returned to reoccupy the site and begin construction of a new post, led by Lieutenant Colonel Wesley Merritt. This improved major installation could house more than six hundred men and contained more than sixty

Fort Davis ruins, quartermaster depot, storehouse. *Courtesy of UNT Libraries, The Portal to Texas History*

adobe and stone structures by the mid-1880s. For nearly twenty years, from 1867 to 1885, the post was garrisoned primarily by units composed of white officers and Black enlisted soldiers (known as the "buffalo soldiers") of the 9th and 10th US Cavalry regiments and the 24th and 25th US Infantry regiments.

Those stationed at Fort Davis during this latter period compiled a notable record of military achievements against the Apache and Comanches. In September 1879, Apache chief Victorio and Mescalero Apache warriors began a series of attacks in the area west of Fort Davis. Colonel Benjamin H. Grierson led his troops from Fort Davis and other posts against these raiders. Following several intense engagements, Victorio retreated into Mexico, where he and many of his followers were killed in a battle with Mexican troops in October 1880.

Following this campaign, life at Fort Davis settled down and became more routine. Large numbers of cattlemen began moving into the area; the soldiers were kept busy drilling on the parade ground, patrolling the surrounding area, and repairing roads and damaged telegraph lines. As a military fort, by this point the usefulness of Fort Davis had come to an end. Fort Davis was ordered abandoned in 1891.

Today, the 460-acre site is preserved as Fort Davis National Historic Site. The site includes twenty-four restored stone and adobe structures and over a hundred ruins and foundations of early Fort Davis. Five of the historic buildings have been restored and refurbished to their 1880 appearance. There is a museum and visitor center, and the lieutenant's quarters and post hospital are open daily along with audio programs, videos, self-guided tours, and, in the summer, living history demonstrations. Fort Davis is widely regarded as one of the best remaining examples of a US Army fort in the southwestern United States.

Visitor Information

HOURS: 8 a.m.–5 p.m. daily. Closed holidays.
Admission fee charged

View of Officers' Quarters from a nearby hiking trail in the surrounding parkland. *Courtesy of UNT Libraries, The Portal to Texas History*

Fort Concho

630 South Oakes Street
San Angelo, TX 76903
325-657-4444
https://fortconcho.com

Important Dates

Built: **1867**
Added to National Register of Historic Places:
   October 15, 1996
Designated a National Historic Landmark:
   July 4, 1961
Designated a Texas State Antiquities Landmark:
   January 1, 1986

Headquarters Building, seen here, was constructed in 1875, nearly a decade into the fort's operation. Four of the rooms on the ground floor—the court-martial room, the orderly's room, the adjutant's office, and regimental HQ—have been remodeled to their original appearance.

Site Description

Located in San Angelo, Fort Concho is a former US Army installation established in November 1867. Located at the confluence of the North and South Concho Rivers, along the Butterfield Overland Mail Route and the Goodnight-Loving Trail, the fort was an active military base for over two decades. It served as the principal base of the Fourth Cavalry from 1867 to 1875 and then the "buffalo soldiers" of the 10th Cavalry until 1882.

Following the Mexican War and the discovery of gold in California, American settlers began crossing West Texas in large numbers. To protect them, the army ordered the construction of a string of forts, including Fort Chadbourne in 1852. That fort would become a station along the Butterfield Overland Mail Route in 1858. The Civil War brought the use of these trails to a near standstill. Following the war, immigrants began returning, many of them cattle herders following routes such as the Goodnight-Loving Trail, along the old Butterfield route, in 1866.

When raids on the trails began to pick up, the army was ordered to reoccupy the prewar Texas billets. In May 1867, Fort Chadbourne was reoccupied. Due to a lack of water, the army replaced the fort with a new installation that held a good proximity to the guarded trade routes and grazing lands and had an abundance of water. It was located at the junction of the branches of the Concho River, roughly 50 miles south of Fort Chadbourne. Construction began on Fort Concho in March 1868.

Progress was slow because all materials to build the fort needed to be shipped in. Civilian masons and carpenters were employed to help build the post, but the assistant quartermaster of the Department of Texas, Captain David Porter, was overseeing the construction of three forts and often was not present to direct the

Visitors to Fort Concho are welcome to enter most of the historic buildings. Here, the enlisted men's quarters interprets life at Fort Concho in the mid- to late nineteenth century.

Established in 1867, Fort Concho was built to protect the nearby frontier settlements, patrol and map West Texas, and put down hostile threats in the area. *Courtesy of UNT Libraries, The Portal to Texas History*

Forts & Military 35

Constructed primarily of native limestone, Fort Concho's forty-plus buildings covered more than 1,600 acres. Today, the site encompasses most of the former army post and includes twenty-four original and restored fort structures. Here are the ruins to one of the original buildings.

construction. After much bickering and leadership change, Captain Joseph Rendlebrock, quartermaster of the 4th Cavalry, was charged with completing the fort in August 1868. By the end of the year, his crew had completed the commissary, the quartermaster's store, and a wing of the hospital. Over the next eight years, the fort would add multiple officers' residences and regimental barracks, a permanent guardhouse, stables, the rest of the hospital, a magazine, a bakery, several storehouses, workshops, a parade ground, a stone command structure, and, finally in early 1879, the schoolhouse-chapel. By 1889, the fort was an eight-company installation with thirty-nine permanent buildings.

Outside of construction, the garrison would patrol, scout, and escort cattle herds and wagon trains on the San Antonio–El Paso Road. In March 1871, the Department of Texas was created and the action at the fort escalated to confrontation. Punitive expeditions were ordered, with garrisons establishing subposts, including a reoccupied Fort Chadbourne and, on the Middle Concho, Camp Charlotte. Raids from the Comanche and Kiowa increased throughout 1871, culminating in battles in 1872 at the Battle of the North Fork, where 116 women and children were captured and temporarily interned at Fort Concho's quartermaster's corral before transport to Oklahoma. Then, on June 27, 1874, came the start of the Red River War at Adobe Walls. The Comanches were chased over the following year to their base of operation in the Palo Duro Canyon. It was destroyed on September 28, with army forces continuing to patrol throughout the winter, preventing any rebuilding of supplies and forcing the Comanches' return to the reservation.

By 1875, Fort Concho was one of the main US Army bases in Texas. The garrison continued to patrol the frontier, escort wagons and settlers, and mount expeditions. Trouble with tribes continued to plague settlers and soldiers of the 4th Cavalry and later the 10th Cavalry throughout the rest of the 1870s. Eventually, the Mescalero Apache would get driven into Mexico and destroyed by the US Army in October 1880. The final battle of the American Indian Wars was fought in Texas on January 27, 1881, when Texas Rangers defeated what was left of the Ojo Caliente and Mescalero Apache.

The 10th Cavalry would be replaced at Fort Concho in 1882, by the 16th Infantry. Ten days before their arrival, the Concho flooded, destroying the town of Ben Ficklin and damaging San Angelo. The soldiers

36 TREASURES OF TEXAS

> **Visitor Information**
>
> HOURS: Monday–Saturday, 9 a.m.–5 p.m., and Sunday, 1 p.m.–5 p.m. Guided tours are offered at 10 a.m., 11:30 a.m., 1:30 p.m., and 3 p.m. *Admission fee charged*

In June 1889, the last soldiers marched away, and Fort Concho was deactivated. Seen here is the hospital, built from 1868 to 1870.

spent much of their first week providing aid. After recovering, San Angelo prospered while Fort Concho wilted under poor maintenance. The fort would serve primarily as a base for troops awaiting transfer elsewhere, and, when Fort McKavett was abandoned in June 1883, the garrison moved to Fort Concho. With the advent of barbed wire, the soldiers were primarily patrolmen along the roads. Eventually the soldiers left the fort for new outposts, and K Company lowered the flag for the final time on June 20, 1889.

While there was an initial movement in the early years of the twentieth century to parcel off the fort's land and sell it, attempts were made to salvage the fort as a park. Eventually the eastern third of the parade ground and other pieces of property were donated to the City of San Angelo in 1913. The site was designated, in 1924, as a state historic site and, in 1929, was joined by a new Fort Concho Museum. The museum effort saved the original headquarters building and helped develop and expand public ownership of the museum. Eventually the purchase, renovation, and reconstruction of some of the fort's original buildings were underway. Originally the project included the schoolhouse-chapel, two enlisted men's barracks, and the acquisition of an office building. Other original fort buildings, such as barracks, officers' quarters, and the old commissary, were at least partially restored and used as exhibits by 1980. Additional efforts over the years have brought the Fort Concho Museum collection to over 35,000 artifacts, furnished the interior of some of the buildings, restored additional buildings (including sixteen original structures), completed six reconstructions, and stabilized a ruin, making Fort Concho one of the best-preserved frontier forts in the United States.

Fort Concho served as regimental headquarters for some of the most famous frontier units, such as the 4th Cavalry and 10th Cavalry. Elements of all four regiments of the famed buffalo soldiers were stationed here, as were Ranald Mackenzie, Benjamin Grierson, and William "Pecos Bill" Shafter.

Forts & Military   37

Fort Richardson

228 State Park Road 61
Jacksboro, TX 76458
940-567-3506
https://tpwd.texas.gov/state-parks/fort-richardson

Important Dates

Built: **1867**
Designated a National Historic Landmark:
  November 27, 1963
Added to National Register of Historic Places:
  October 15, 1966
Designated a Texas State Historic Site: **1968**
Designated a Texas State Antiquities Landmark:
  January 1, 1983

The largest remaining structure on the site today is the post hospital, seen here. After being abandoned, it was used as an Indian school before falling into disrepair. Renovations began in 1973; today, visitors can tour seven restored original buildings, two replica buildings, the ruins, and the parade ground.

Site Description

Among the chain of Texas forts protecting the North Texas frontier during conflicts between settlers and Native Americans, Fort Richardson was the northernmost. Following the Civil War, Fort Belknap was abandoned due to a lack of water, with Fort Richardson taking its place in 1867. This fort was instrumental in quelling the Kiowa-Comanche conflicts of the post–Civil War period. Close to the Oklahoma border, Fort Richardson acted as overseer and protector during President Ulysses Grant's Peace Policy programs. Constructed in 1867, the fort was named in honor of Union general Israel B. Richardson, who died during the Civil War at the Battle of Antietam. As was the case with many frontier army installations, Fort Richardson facilitated white immigration and settlement. The chain of forts protected and encouraged settlement in north-central and West Texas; others included Forts Griffin, Concho, Belknap, Chadbourne, Stockton, Davis, McKavett, Clark, McIntosh, Inge, and Phantom Hill in Texas, as well as Fort Sill in Oklahoma. Additional subposts, or intermediate stations, included Bothwick's Station on Salt Creek between Fort Richardson and Belknap, Camp Wichita near Buffalo Springs between Fort Richardson and Red River Station, and Mountain Pass between Fort Concho and Fort Griffin.

Originally, the site selected was near Buffalo Springs in Clay County, about 20 miles north of Fort Richardson. The location proved untenable, lacking adequate timber and water. With raids so frequent and devastating, an entire town, Henrietta, was abandoned due to a lack of security in 1862. The US 6th Cavalry Regiment moved south to the current location of the fort, beginning construction in 1867 and occupying it starting in late November. Fort Richardson would become the anchor of the frontier fort system and the

Kiowa chiefs Satanta and Big Tree, seen here in 1871, attacked a nearby freight-hauling wagon train. They were the first Native Americans to be tried in a Texas civil court and held at the fort. They were originally sentenced to hang, but the sentence was commuted to life in prison. *Courtesy of the Library of Congress*

Fort Richardson was the last army outpost in North Texas along the military road to Fort Sill. By 1872, it was listed as the largest US Army installation, with a population of 666 officers and men. Seen here is the installation's guardhouse. *Courtesy of Lawrence T. Jones III Texas Photographs, SMU Libraries*

Forts & Military 39

Looking across Fort Richardson's parade ground from the old entrance toward the hospital. Off to the right are the bakery, the guardhouse, and the fort's magazine. The historic site is located a short distance away.

last army outpost in North Texas along the military road to Fort Sill. By 1872, the fort had become the largest US Army installation in the United States, with a population of 666 officers and men. Units calling the fort home included the 4th and the 6th Cavalry Regiment and the US 11th Infantry Regiment. Portions of the 10th Cavalry Regiment and the 24th Infantry Regiment, both consisting of buffalo soldier regiments, also occupied the fortress.

Routine duties and everyday life at Fort Richardson were difficult. Patrols along the frontier from Clay and Jack Counties west to Palo Duro Canyon were long and arduous. Battles with the Comanche and Kiowa were commonplace as the cavalry and infantry units

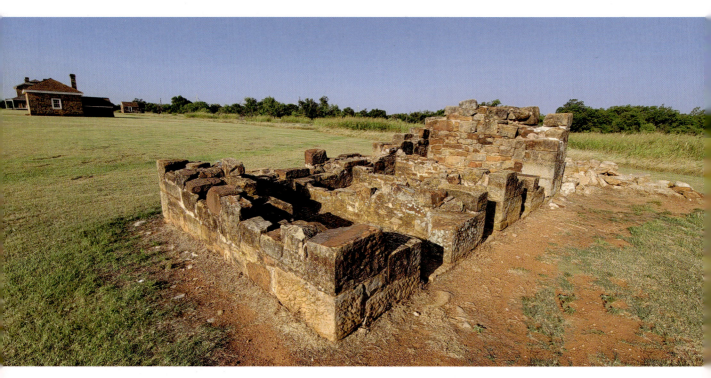

General William T. Sherman stayed at Fort Richardson in 1871, having arrested Kiowa chiefs Satanta and Big Tree for their role in the Warren Wagon Train Raid. They would have been held here, in the fort's jail—barely large enough for a person to lie down in.

sought to prove their ability to repel attacks and protect the settlers.

From 1870 to 1875, the region surrounding Fort Richardson suffered more than any other part of Texas from Kiowa and Comanche raids. North Texas, as a result, was nearly depopulated because of it. Nearby, in 1871, a wagon train led by Henry Warren was ambushed and massacred. General William T. Sherman had just passed over the route, the old Butterfield trail. News of the event impressed upon him the dire situation facing North Texas. Sherman ordered Colonel Ranald S. Mackenzie out of Fort Richardson to track down the perpetrators. At Fort Sill Reservation, leaders Satanta, Satank, and Big Tree were arrested and sent to Jacksboro, a settlement only a half mile north of the fort, for a nonmilitary trial. While en route to Jacksboro, according to the official report, Satank tried to escape and was shot and killed in the process. The trial resulted in Satanta and Big Tree being sentenced to hanging, later commuted to time in prison. It was the first time Native Americans were tried in a nonmilitary court and was the beginning of the end of the Peace Policy, which had placed the responsibility for the southwestern tribes under Quaker Indian agents.

Troops from Fort Richardson participated in the Red River War of 1874–75 and in the Battle of Palo Duro Canyon in September 1874. Victory at Palo Duro ended the Red River War with Quanah Parker's Comanches and Red Warbonnet's Kiowas. With the conclusion of the war in 1875, the power the Kiowas and Comanches held over North Texas had broken. With troops having captured so much of their provisions, the tribes were forced to move back to reservations in Oklahoma before winter set in. With the tribes displaced, the need for Fort Richardson was gone. By May 1878, Fort Richardson was abandoned by the military.

For a short time afterward, the fort was used as an Indian school, but mostly the fort went unused. Since its abandonment, many of Fort Richardson's fifty-five buildings fell into disrepair. The Texas Parks and Wildlife Department acquired the property in 1969. Of the original buildings at Fort Richardson, only a small handful remained standing. Extensive archeological investigations of the site were conducted, identifying a number of the fort's original buildings and sites. In 1973, it opened as a state historic site.

Visitor Information

PARK HOURS: 8 a.m.–5 p.m. daily. Historic buildings are open for self-guided tours on Saturday and Sunday from 10 a.m. to 4 p.m. *Admission fee charged*

Ranger-guided walking tours of the fort are offered Tuesday through Friday at 10 a.m. and 2 p.m. The tours take about two hours and are approximately 1 mile in length.

In addition to visiting the historic fort, activities include picnicking, camping, hiking, biking, horseback riding, wading in Lost Creek, swimming at Lost Creek Reservoir, and fishing.

Today, the site is called Fort Richardson State Park, Historic Site and Lost Creek Reservoir State Trailway. Visitors can tour seven restored original buildings: the post hospital, officers' quarters, powder magazine, morgue, commissary, guardhouse, and bakery. Two replica buildings, the enlisted men's barracks and the officers' barracks, house the site's Interpretive Center.

A newer modern entrance for Fort Richardson is located just off Highway 281 in Jacksboro. Today, the site is called Fort Richardson State Park, Historic Site and Lost Creek Reservoir State Trailway.

Forts & Military 41

Fort Sam Houston

892 Hood Street
San Antonio, TX 78208
210-221-9205
www.jbsa.mil

Important Dates

Built: **1876**
Added to National Register of Historic Places:
 May 15, 1975
Designated a National Historic Landmark:
 May 15, 1975

The clock tower at Fort Sam Houston. Nearby is where Geronimo and his captured compatriots were housed on the lawn.

42 TREASURES OF TEXAS

Site Description

Fort Sam Houston, a major military installation in the northeast section of San Antonio, was established in the 1870s. However, the United States Army has had a presence in the city since the days of the Republic of Texas. Originally, when the fort opened in 1876, it covered just 40 acres. Today, it covers over 50 square miles. Structures survive from multiple periods of the post's history, reflecting a varying collection of architectural styles.

Originally, the army's first establishment near the city of San Antonio was Camp Almus, which included the Alamo property as a quartermaster depot. Since that time, city leaders attempted to secure the establishment of a permanent United States military installation, finally prevailing in the 1870s, on land northeast of the city. Today, Fort Sam Antonio has not only a national impact, but a global one.

Since 1879, Fort Sam Houston has been the focal point of military operations in the region. Between 1885 and 1891, sixty buildings designed by Alfred Giles were added to the site, making Fort Sam Houston the second largest base in the US Army. In 1890, the post in San Antonio was officially designated in honor of General Sam Houston. Fort Sam has sustained other area installations regularly, played a major role in international military conflicts, and houses the headquarters of multiple military entities.

It has played a significant role in numerous military operations and activities. In 1886, Apache chief Geronimo and his captured warriors were held in

Inside the historic landmark's museum and visitor center. Exhibits here track the storied history of the fort and its residents.

the quadrangle prior to his exile to Florida. Fort Sam supplied the Rough Riders when they rendezvoused in San Antonio in 1898, furnished most of the men and material for General John J. Pershing's campaign against Pancho Villa in 1916, and provided training facilities for thousands of troops during World War I. In 1910, Fort Sam Houston acquired the first airplane hangar in the Department of Texas, and during the next few years, Lieutenant Benny Foulois conducted aerial

Photograph of Fort Sam Houston (located at Northeast San Antonio) in San Antonio, Texas. *Courtesy of UNT Libraries, The Portal to Texas History*

Looking from the residential homes along the parade ground toward the historic clock tower and beyond.

trials that would lead to the establishment of the Signal Corps aviation section and new infantry tactics that would carry out the army's first airborne maneuvers in World War II. Future president Dwight D. Eisenhower was stationed at Fort Sam twice. Prior to World War I, he would meet his future wife, Mamie Doud, and then would be stationed here again before becoming general of the army at the beginning of World War II. Their home is on the National Register of Historic Places.

During the Base Realignment and Closure Act of 2005, multiple military operations moved to the fort and served as the headquarters for Joint Base San Antonio. The base includes ten military headquarters, subpost Camp Bullis, the Fort Sam Houston National Cemetery, and three primary schools, and it supports National Guard and Army Reserve units, plus Junior and Senior Reserve Officer Training Corps units. While the quadrangle houses the original post buildings, many of the historic officers' quarters, barracks, and other buildings remain in use.

Besides the quadrangle, which was completed in 1879, there are four groups of buildings that were erected at the fort in the late nineteenth and twentieth centuries: the staff post, infantry post, artillery post, and cavalry post, all of which are connected visually with only a few outlying buildings having no particular historical significance. The fort's historic area includes the following listings as well as a number of infantry post officers' quarters (thirteen buildings), infantry

Photograph of the clock tower at Fort Sam Houston near San Antonio, Texas, taken in 1890. *Courtesy of UNT Libraries, The Portal to Texas History*

44   TREASURES OF TEXAS

post barracks (twelve buildings), infantry post bachelor officers' quarters, staff post officers' quarters (fourteen buildings), the old staff post hospital, artillery post officers' quarters (eighteen buildings), cavalry post officers' quarters (seventeen buildings), artillery post and cavalry post barracks (fourteen buildings), a veterinary hospital, and stables. Other historic buildings reside on base but outside this historic district and include the cemetery, the Eisenhowers' home prior to World War I, and a German prisoner-of-war campsite.

Quadrangle (Building 16)

Constructed from 1876 to 1879, this was the first building erected at Fort Sam Houston. Made of gray

Numerous soldiers on horseback in the field near the quadrangle at Fort Sam Houston near San Antonio, Texas. The photograph was taken from the nearby historic tower. *Courtesy of UNT Libraries, The Portal to Texas History*

limestone, the building houses offices, shops, sheds, and warehouse space. A centrally located, arched gateway in the south facade provides access to the courtyard.

Watchtower (Building 40)

Measuring in at 15 feet square and 90 feet high, the watchtower was completed sometime in 1876 or 1877 and houses a watchman's room, a 6,400-gallon water tank, and a clock that has a face on all four tower sides.

Infantry Post HQ (Building 616)

Built of yellow brick in 1886, the two-story structure is the only one retaining the white-painted gingerbread trim that once decorated all post quarters.

Sallport Building (Building 613)

Built of yellow brick and decorated with gray limestone, this three-story structure is situated in the center of the "U" formed by barracks 601–612. It was completed in 1887 as a band barracks and converted into a guardhouse in 1893. The building and the adjoining barracks were designed by well-known Texas architect Alfred Giles.

Infantry Post Bell Tower Barracks (Building 646)

This 1893 two-story yellow brick building once had a three-story bell tower at the south end. The bell and the third story of the tower have been removed, but a veranda remains.

Pershing House (Building 6)

Also known as the staff post commanding officer's quarters, this irregularly shaped, two-story limestone residence was built in 1881 and has seen less extensive alteration. The eleven-room, six-and-a-half-bath house is unique in appearance among the buildings on Fort Sam. A number of general officers have resided here, including F. D. Grant (son of Ulysses S.) and John J. Pershing.

One of the many officers' buildings surrounding the parade grounds outside the historic walled quadrangle

Cavalry Post Officer's Quarter (Building 179)

One of a number of two-story red-brick buildings erected in 1909. General Dwight D. Eisenhower occupied quarters 179 in 1941 shortly before becoming general of the army. It is on the National Register of Historic Places.

"Gift" Chapel (Building 2200)

Citizens of San Antonio donated the funds and the land for this Second Renaissance Revival structure. It was completed in 1909 and dedicated by President William H. Taft. Among the noteworthy features are a copper dome, a parapet that completely extends around the roofline, and twenty-two stained-glass windows (added between 1929 and 1931).

Visitor Information

Because it is a working US military base, access to Fort Sam Houston is limited. However, much of the historic portion of the fort is open to the public, including the historic quadrangle, the "Gift" Chapel, and the Fort Sam Houston Museum. Visitors may also view the Pershing House and visit Fort Sam Houston Cemetery.

Visitors who are not in possession of military IDs, Department of Defense civilian or contractor IDs, or previously issued and active base access passes must enter JBSA–Fort Sam Houston through the following visitor control centers:

WALTERS STREET VISITOR CENTER HOURS: Monday–Friday, 6 a.m.–5 p.m.; closed weekends and holidays
BROOKE ARMY MEDICAL CENTER (BAMC)/I-35 HOURS: Open 24/7

Hangar 9, Brooks Air Force Base

8081 Inner Circle Road
San Antonio, TX 78235
210-534-1000

Important Dates

Built: **1918**
Added to National Register of Historic Places:
 May 21, 1970
Designated a National Historic Landmark:
 December 8, 1976
Designated a Recorded Texas Historic
 Landmark: **1967**

Hangar 9 is now used as an event showcase location for San Antonio. Despite this, its exterior and interior have remained historically accurate and preserved.

Site Description

Brooks Air Force Base, located about 7 miles southeast of San Antonio, was one of thirty-two US Army Air Service training camps established in 1918 after the United States' entry into World War I. Hangar 9 now stands as the only World War I–era aircraft hangar listed in the National Register of Historic Places—an impressive feat for a building constructed as a temporary structure. It was established as Gosport Field but changed to Signal Corps Aviation School, Kelly Field No. 5, on December 5, 1917. The army established the facility to train flying instructors in the Gosport system, calling the site Gosport Field. This method, developed by the Royal Air Force, had an instructor speaking to a student pilot through a tube, correcting the trainee in flight. Following the death of Cadet Sidney Johnson Brooks Jr. in a training accident, the army renamed the facility Brooks Field on February 4, 1918. By the end

Photograph of several airplanes and cars in front of Hangar 9 at Brooks Field in San Antonio, Texas, ca. 1920–25. *Courtesy of UNT Libraries, The Portal to Texas History*

Photograph of the Brooks Air Force Base Hangar 9 in San Antonio, Texas, ca. 1960s. *Courtesy of UNT Libraries, The Portal to Texas History*

Forts & Military   47

of that year, Brooks Field housed sixteen hangars, with Hangar 9 reputedly being the oldest existing hangar in the US Air Force. It is today the Edward H. White II Memorial Museum.

After World War I, in 1919, the army replaced the pilot school with a balloon and airship school. However, following a series of accidents, the army closed this school in 1922. Until 1931, Brooks served as the primary flying school for the Army Air Corps, training more than 1,400 pilots. Notable instructors included Charles Lindbergh, Jimmy Doolittle, and Claire L. Chennault. In 1926, the School of Aviation Medicine was transferred to Brooks from Hazelhurst Field. Both the flying school and the aviation medicine school were moved in 1931 to nearby Randolph Field (now Randolph Air Force Base).

As the country inched back toward war on a global stage, procedures at the field ratcheted up. In 1928, Brooks began training paratroops, and, on Thanksgiving the following year, the first mass paratroop drop in US armed forces history took place there. This experiment confirmed the practicality of using tactical paratrooper warfare, which would see implementation during World War II. The United States Air Force Security Service (USAFSS) provided communications training for radio intercept operators, Russian-language analysts, and cryptanalysts. Brooks served as a center for aerial-observation training in the 1930s, and in 1940 a special school for combat observers began. On January 1, 1941, the army established an Air Corps Advanced Flying School to teach pilots of single-engine aircraft aerial-observation skills. This training continued until

This aerial view of Brooks Field, Texas, features planes lined up in a curved row among the base's buildings and roads, ca. 1920–1930s. *Courtesy of UNT Libraries, The Portal to Texas History*

A modern version of Hangar 9, showcasing the size needed to fit even the earliest airplanes for the Army Air Force.

1943, when Brooks began training pilots for the new B-25 bomber for use in the war.

The base's training function came to a halt in 1945, following the addition of a tactical unit under the Third Air Force. In 1948, when the air force was officially separated from the army, the Department of Defense changed the name of the base to Brooks Air Force Base, and it became home to the 259th Air Base, the 2577th Air Force Reserve Flying Training Center, the 2577th Air Base Group, and the 3790th Air Base Group, as well as many other units since.

Beginning during the summer of 1959, Brooks transitioned from a flight-training base to a center for medical research, development, and education. The School of Aviation Medicine returned, and the base became headquarters for the Aerospace Medical Center in October. On June 23, 1960, all flying at Brooks came to a halt. With the growth of the US space program, the aviation medicine school became the United States Air Force School of Aerospace Medicine in 1961 and became part of the Aerospace Medical Division the following year. The center played a major role in the national space program, including involvement in the development of the capsule that carried Sam, the monkey, into outer space on December 4, 1959. Researchers at Brooks continued to study space medicine and added many contributions to the advancement of manned flight.

In 1995, the Department of Defense decided to close the base, but it managed to avoid being shuttered. In 2002, the facility was renamed the Brooks City-Base but again was recommended for closure in 2005. It officially closed on September 15, 2011. Today it is one of forty former installations managed by the Air Force Civil Engineer Center (AFCEC) in San Antonio. The former base has since been transformed by the Brooks Development Authority into a master planned community with a state-of-the-art hospital. It was restored in 1969 to become the United States Air Force Museum of Aerospace Medicine. The museum features displays on the early history of Brooks Field and an extensive collection of photographs and equipment related to aviation and aerospace medicine.

> **Visitor Information**
>
> Hangar 9 is closed to the general public. It is available as an events venue.

Texas Historical Marker showcasing the importance of Hangar 9 and Brooks Air Force Base to the history of San Antonio, Texas, and the country.

Forts & Military   49

Randolph Field Historic District

Randolph Air Force Base
Located off Pat Booker Road
San Antonio, TX 78150
210-652-2838
www.jbsa.mil/Information/
Gate-Hours-Visitor-Information/
JBSA-Randolph-Visitor-Info/

Important Dates

Opened: **November 2, 1931**
Added to National Register of Historic Places:
   July 8, 1996
Designated a National Historic Landmark:
   August 7, 2001

Joint Base San Antonio is home and headquarters to the 12th Flying Training Wing. The 12 FTW consists of three flying groups and a maintenance directorate spanning more than 1,600 miles from San Antonio to Pensacola, Florida, and the US Air Force Academy in Colorado. *Photo by Rich McFadden, United States Air Force*

50 TREASURES OF TEXAS

The administration building, known more commonly as "the Taj Mahal," was finished in 1931. Its tower stands at 170 feet tall atop a Spanish Colonial Revival–style base building. *Courtesy of UNT Libraries, The Portal to Texas History*

Site Description

The Randolph Field Historic District encompasses the central portion of Randolph Air Force Base, near San Antonio. Built between 1929 and 1931, Randolph Field was innovative in its design using the principles of the Garden City movement. The site includes a unique and well-preserved collection of mission revival and art deco architecture, and it was the first permanent flight-training facility of the US Army Air Corps, later the US Air Force, in September 1947.

The United States Army Air Service provided the aerial warfare capability of the United States during World War I; however, such a service was still in its infancy, despite the leaps and bounds in technology and effectiveness throughout the war. Most of the facilities established during the war were disbanded once the war was over. Some flight-training operations

Randolph Field's administration building, known officially as "Building 100" but better known as "the Taj Mahal," seen here in 1942, opened in 1931. The tower conceals a 500,000-gallon water storage tank, and its beacon can be seen by aircraft up to 50 miles away. *Courtesy of the Library of Congress*

Forts & Military 51

Aerial image taken by the United States Army Air Corps in September 1931 that shows the administration building and other district buildings. *Courtesy of UNT Libraries, The Portal to Texas History*

were maintained at a variety of the temporary facilities throughout the nation into the early 1920s, while the debate over the status of the air corps as part of the US Army took place.

In 1926, the War Department decided to centralize flight-training operations, and a site about 15 miles northeast of San Antonio was identified in 1927. Construction at Randolph Field began in 1928, continuing until completion by the end of 1931. The completed "West Point of the Air" became the site of unique air corps schools for flying training and aviation medicine, as well as a landmark in airfield planning and design. Additionally, administrative headquarters at Randolph Field, including the Air Corps Training Center and the Army Air Forces Central Flying Training Command, were keystrokes in the organizational structure of the Army Air Forces; they played pivotal roles in the transition of the Army Air Corps' forty-year campaign to become an independent branch of the US armed forces. The base would serve as headquarters of the Air Education and Training Command as well as the Air Force Personnel Center, and it housed the headquarters for the 12th Flying Training Wing.

Early plans called for a circular central element, originally divided by function. The final plan for the base was drafted by George B. Ford, who incorporated the idea of the circular plan and combined it with principles of the Garden City movement, in which the circle contains residences while the functional and operational parts of the base were located outside the circle. When completed, it had taken nearly five years to construct the five-hundred-plus buildings and the 30 miles of roadways that make up the base named for Captain William Millican Randolph. Captain Randolph, a native Texan, Texas A&M graduate, and member of the committee assigned to select a name for this new airfield, was killed on February 17, 1928, when his AT-4 crashed on takeoff from Gorman Field in Texas.

This type of design addressed a large army concern. It was thought that the impact of long taxi distances would result in increased exposure of the aircraft to dust and therefore result in higher maintenance costs. To solve this problem, Ford placed rows of hangars parallel to the field's two runways, which were oriented to maximize the benefits of prevailing winds. This design also included the very prominent administration building, known affectionately as "the Taj Mahal." This building is approached from the main base entrance and includes a 170-foot tower that embeds the base's water tower.

Most of Randolph Field's residential buildings are designed in the mission revival style. Their orientation in circular bands eliminated the procession of architecture that is typically found on military bases. There is individual variation among the buildings, with wings placed on different ends, and the exterior stucco has been given different coloring. Found within Randolph Fields' 405 acres are 350 contributing buildings, sites, and structures along with forty-seven noncontributing ones. Architectural styles featured are the mission revival, Spanish Colonial Revival, and streamline moderne styles.

In addition to the residential buildings and the Taj Mahal, one will find a number of iconic buildings. Remaining virtually untouched from the time it was built in 1934 is JBSA-Randolph S main chapel. Buildings 499, 492, and 663 once served as barracks for enlisted personnel of the Army Air Corps. However, extensive renovations throughout the twentieth century have left only Building 633 as a contributing member to the historic district designation. It once housed at least 250 to 300 personnel and consisted of an administration section, reception area, chow hall, kitchen, and living quarters. Adjacent to the barracks is a swimming pool, listed in early records as an "auxiliary water storage tank" in order to avoid the impression that the Army Air Corps was building a country club rather than trying to take the edge off the hot and humid summers.

By the early 1990s, the base hosted over eight thousand personnel, including more than three thousand civilian workers. On October 1, 2010, Randolph AFB merged with Lackland Air Force Base and the US Army's Fort Sam Houston to form Joint Base San Antonio. Most recently, major renovations came to the base commissary and the main entrance to the base, which leads to "the Taj."

Visitor Information

HOURS: March to November: Saturday–Thursday, 8 a.m.–4:30 p.m., and Friday, 8 a.m.–6:30 p.m. December to February: 8 a.m.–4:30 p.m. daily.
Admission fee charged

Constructed in the image of San Antonio's Missions Concepción and San José, the main chapel was constructed in 1934 and is located on Washington Circle across from the administration building ("the Taj Mahal"). It has largely remained unchanged and was the last building constructed during the base's initial construction phase. *Photo by Sean Worrell, United States Air Force*

Forts & Military   53

SITES
1. The Alamo (March 1836)
2. San Jacinto Battlefield (March 1836)
3. Palo Alto Battlefield (May 8, 1846)
4. Resaca de la Palma Battlefield (May 9, 1846)
5. Palmito Ranch Battlefield (May 12, 1865)
6. USS *Texas* (1914)
7. *HA-19* (1938)
8. USS *Lexington* (1942)
9. USS *Cabot* (1942)*

*delisted in 2001

The lands of Texas have been contested for centuries. Well before the Spanish and other European settlers arrived, the land that would eventually make up the Lone Star State was the setting of numerous battles and skirmishes between the Indigenous tribes that sought to make the land their home. As Anglo settlers moved in, Texas played a role in some of the United States' great conflicts, including the Mexican-American War, the Civil War, the Spanish-American War, both world wars, and, most notably, the Texas Revolution. Eventually, these sites were decommissioned and given a new life as floating museums or as artifacts telling a more complete narrative of a moment in time.

Visiting these sites, many directly on the land where battles in these wars were fought, offers an opportunity to encounter the sometimes bloody history that helped shape Texas.

The Alamo

300 Alamo Plaza
San Antonio, TX 78516
210-225-1391
https://www.thealamo.org

Important Dates

Built: **1718**
Period of Importance:
    February 23–March 6, 1936 *(battle)*
Designated a National Historic Landmark:
    December 19, 1960
Added to National Register of Historic Places:
    October 15, 1966
US Historic District *(Contributing Property: Alamo Plaza Historic District)*: **July 13, 1977**
Texas State Antiquities Landmark: **June 28, 1983**
UNESCO World Heritage Site: **2015**

The Alamo has welcomed over four million visitors annually since 2002. The chapel and long barracks, as well as the grounds, are open to the public. There are numerous artifacts on display, and another complex building and a large mural are on-site as well.

The Alamo courtyard walkway with a colonnade is just one of many features to be found along the grounds of the old mission. In 2015, it was designated as a World Heritage Site by the United Nations. The San Antonio Missions, a group including the Alamo and four other missions, became the first World Heritage Site in Texas and one of twenty-three in the United States.

Site Description

The Alamo is synonymous with Texas history. Originally a Spanish mission, it was first referred to as San Antonio de Padua, and later San Antonio de Valero Mission in honor of Saint Anthony de Padua and the Duke of Valero, the Spanish viceroy. Authorized by the viceroy of Mexico in 1716, Fray Antonio de Olivares brought with him Indian converts and the records from San Francisco Solano Mission to establish the mission on May 1, 1718.

Following a devastating hurricane that destroyed many of the existing buildings, the mission moved to its current site in 1724, with the cornerstone of the chapel being laid on May 8, 1744. The original chapel suffered a structural collapse in the mid-1750s. While reconstruction efforts began in earnest in 1758, they were never completed. The goal of the mission was for the purpose of Christianizing and educating the Indians; however, it would also serve as a fortress. Activity began to trail off after 1765, and the mission was secularized in 1793. Eventually the mission closed, and the buildings were abandoned.

The oldest known photo of the Alamo (ca. 1849), prior to its reconstruction in 1850 by the army, which built out the walls and added the famous stone arch that visitors see today.
Courtesy of the Briscoe Center for American History

Battlefields & War 57

The Alamo in use as a US Army depot, with three covered wagons pulled by horses in the foreground. The former *convento* and long barracks, which the army used as a warehouse, is partially visible on the left. *Courtesy of UNT Libraries, The Portal to Texas History*

In 1803, the Second Flying Company of San Carlos de Parras, a company of Spanish soldiers from Alamo de Parras, Coahuila, Mexico, occupied the abandoned mission's buildings as barracks for a number of years, possibly giving rise to the more popular name "the Alamo." Spanish and Mexican forces would occupy the mission site almost continuously from 1803 to December 1835, when General Martín Perfecto de Cos surrendered the fortress to Texan forces following the Siege of Béxar, early in the Texas Revolution.

The Alamo, along with the Presidio la Bahía, served as the only true outposts along the two roads leading out of Mexico and into Texas. Serving as a frontier picket guard, they were to alert the Texas settlements of an enemy advance. Following the siege, many of the men returned home to their families. Without speedy reinforcements, the best the forces could do was likely to stall opposing forces on the frontier

James Walker Fannin Jr. took command at Goliad for the Texians, while James Clinton Neill received command at the Alamo in Béxar. Preparations were made, eventually reinforcements were sent, and the old mission—located on the outskirts of town—began to roughly resemble a fort. Neill did his best and installed roughly twenty artillery pieces of various calibers on the walls of the Alamo. Throughout January and early February 1836, the Alamo saw the arrival of James Bowie, William Travis, David Crockett, and their accompanying forces.

When Santa Anna's Centralist army arrived on February 23, he surprised the Texans, who didn't expect his arrival until March 15. The Texans holed up in the Alamo, with word dispatched for provisions and reinforcements. In response to a request to surrender the Alamo, Travis replied with a cannonball. For twelve days, Santa Anna assaulted the fortified mission. The following day, despite the Texans being on their last supplies and facing sure defeat, Santa Anna stormed the Alamo, taking the walls, proceeding past the defensive perimeter, and taking the fighting into the dim rooms of the long barracks, overwhelming the Texan forces. Travis was among the first to die, while Bowie, sick and confined to his bed, was killed. The chapel was the last to fall. The assault lasted no more than ninety minutes. By eight o'clock that morning, every fighting man defending the Alamo was dead—killed in battle or executed at capture, their bodies stacked and burned. While victorious, between four hundred and six hundred Mexican soldiers were killed or wounded.

Over the next 125 years, the Alamo would go through a series of hardships to become the tourist attraction and national landmark that visitors see today, some of which continues behind the scenes to this day. Mexican soldiers who remained at the mission following the battle for the next two months repaired and fortified the complex, then undid all their progress upon Santa Anna's defeat and capture at the Battle of San Jacinto. Only a few buildings survived, with the chapel left in ruins. Most of the long barracks was still standing, and the building that contained the south wall gate and several rooms was mostly intact.

The mission would again be used, variously by the Texians and Mexican army, from 1836 to 1842 as a fort. Pieces of debris would be sold to tourists, and it was common, and allowed, for San Antonio residents to cart off wagonloads of stone from the fort for use elsewhere or as souvenirs. The Roman Catholic Church regained the sanctuary in 1841, but by 1845 it was still abandoned and overgrown and had become home to a colony of bats. The Mexican-American War brought the US Army back in 1846, which used part of the complex for its quartermaster's department. While the city, the army, and the church would fight over ownership, the convent building was restored, the grounds cleared, and the walls rebuilt. A new roof was added to the chapel, and the bell-shaped facade, or campanulate, was added to its front. The complex would eventually contain a supply depot, offices, storage facilities, a blacksmith shop, and stables.

The Confederacy would take over the Alamo during the Civil War, before its control reverted to the US Army following the war. The army would abandon the Alamo in 1876 and move to Fort Sam Houston. The church sold the convent to Horace Grenet, who would construct a new building on the grounds and use it, and the convent, for a wholesale grocery operation.

When rail service first began in 1877, the city attempted to market the Alamo as a tourist site. The church would later sell the chapel in 1883 to the state, which placed a manager at the site who gave tours. The state, however, made no efforts to restore the chapel, nor was there an effort to celebrate the fiftieth anniversary of the battle. Management and ownership over the site became even more contentious over the next half century and beyond. By World War II, the upper walls of the long barracks from the convent were removed (leaving only the one-story walls of the west and south portions of the building) and a wall was constructed, as was a museum, and several nonhistoric buildings on the property were razed. When the HemisFair was hosted by San Antonio in 1968, the long barracks were roofed and turned into a museum. Few structural changes have taken place since that time. A state law transferred custodianship from the Daughters of the Republic of Texas to the Texas General Land Office in 2015.

As of 2022, the Alamo welcomed nearly two million visitors a year. Visitors can tour the chapel and the long barracks (containing a small museum with paintings, weapons, and other artifacts from the Texas Revolution era), and there are additional artifacts in another complex building. In 2015, the state purchased three additional historic buildings on Alamo Plaza, with the hopes for an expansion program that enhances the overall visitor experience in the future.

Visitor Information

HOURS: Daily 9 a.m.–5:30 p.m.
No admission fee

You will need a free timed ticket to enter the Alamo church.

The Alamo chapel today. In 1849, the US Army began renting the facility for use as a quartermaster's depot (remnants of which remain) until 1876, when Fort Sam Houston opened. The army sold the chapel to the state, and, while there were occasional tours, no effort was made to restore it.

San Jacinto Battlefield

3523 Independence Parkway South
La Porte, TX 77571
281-479-2431
https://thc.texas.gov/historic-sites/san-jacinto-battleground-state-historic-site

Important Dates

Period of Importance:
March 19–20, 1836 (battle)
Added to National Register of Historic Places:
October 15, 1966
Designated a National Historic Landmark:
December 19, 1960

Seen from across the reflecting pond is the site of the San Jacinto Monument and Battlefield. On a clear day, visitors can see the surrounding battlefield and all the way to Houston in one direction and the coast in the opposite.

60   TREASURES OF TEXAS

Site Description

The San Jacinto Battleground State Historic Site includes the location of the Battle of San Jacinto and the accompanying monument and museum, and until 2021 it also served as the site of the museum ship USS *Texas*. It is located off the Houston Ship Channel near Houston. The most prominent feature is the San Jacinto Monument, where visitors can take an elevator to an observation deck for a view of Houston and the ship channel and look down toward the battlefield.

Following the Battle of the Alamo, Mexican forces occupied the Alamo, and on March 19–20, General James Fannin surrendered during the Battle of Coleto in Goliad. In response, for the Texians, the Battle of the Alamo became a symbol of resistance and a rallying cry for independence. General Sam Houston, realizing that his army was the last hope for an independent Texas, was aware that his ill-trained—and similarly ill-disciplined—force would likely be good for only one battle. He managed to avoid engagement, retreating 120 miles across the Navidad and the Colorado Rivers, losing numerous troops who complained that Houston was a coward. They camped for two weeks while they rested and recovered, then drilled at Groce's Landing on the Brazos River on March 31. Determined that the rebellion was at an end and set to block the Texian army's retreat and end the war once and for good, Mexican general and president Antonio López de Santa Anna headed toward present-day Houston. The two forces arrived at Lynch's Ferry within hours of each other. The Texians' camp was in a wooded area along the banks of Buffalo Bayou, with great cover but no room for retreat. Santa Anna made camp in a plain near the San Jacinto River in a spot that was bordered by woods on one side and marsh and lake on the other and was extremely vulnerable.

On April 21, 1836, the Texas militia of roughly eight hundred men under Sam Houston launched a surprise attack against the 1,500-man force under Santa Anna. The Mexicans were routed, with 650 killed and hundreds taken prisoner. The Texians lost eleven, with thirty others, including Houston, wounded. The Battle of San Jacinto is regarded as one of the most one-sided victories in military history. Santa Anna was captured the following day, and General Martín Perfecto de Cos was captured on April 24. The fight lasted just eighteen minutes. In exchange for his freedom, in mid-May, Santa Anna signed a treaty in Velasco recognizing Texas's independence. Immediately following the Battle of San Jacinto, the land (which was then privately owned) became almost sacred ground as plans came together for a formal monument.

The beginnings of the San Jacinto Battleground State Historic Site date back to the early 1880s. In

Battle of San Jacinto veterans gathered for a reunion at the Texas Veterans Association convention in Belton in 1883.
Courtesy of UNT Libraries, The Portal to Texas History

Survivors of the Battle of San Jacinto at a meeting of the Texas Veterans Association at Galveston around 1880.
Courtesy of UNT Libraries, The Portal to Texas History

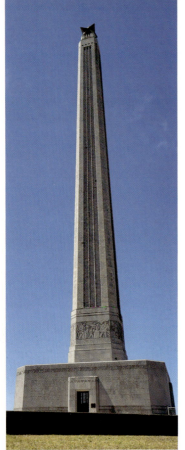

Above, left: Photograph of the obelisk portion of the San Jacinto Monument taken from the ground below. *Courtesy of UNT Libraries, The Portal to Texas History*

Above, right: Standing 10 feet taller than its Washington counterpart, the 567-foot San Jacinto Monument is topped with a 220-ton star.

preparation for the fiftieth anniversary of the Texas Revolution, the State of Texas purchased 10 acres along Buffalo Bayou. A push for more appropriations came through the Daughters of the Republic of Texas, and, in 1897, legislation was passed to establish a public park, with an additional 336 acres of land purchased. Improvements at the site came in 1907, when it was officially named San Jacinto State Park, becoming the first official state park in Texas. Additional improvements came in preparation for the 1928 Democratic National Convention in Houston.

The largest addition to the site was the erection of the San Jacinto Monument, which includes, within its base, the San Jacinto Museum of History. The monument is the world's tallest war memorial, standing 15 feet taller than the Washington Monument, and it honors all those who fought for Texas's independence. Plans for constructing the monument finally came together at San Jacinto's one-hundred-year anniversary, following the establishment of the state park and accompanying improvements. Help came from President Franklin D. Roosevelt's secretary of commerce, Jesse H. Jones, a prominent Houstonian and adept fundraiser.

The monument was designed by architect Alfred C. Finn, engineer Robert J. Cummins, and Jesse H. Jones, and its construction ran from 1936 to 1939. At 570 feet, it is one of the finest examples of moderne (art deco) architecture in the United States and has been

Peppered throughout the battlefield's grounds are historic markers that interpret the site's importance to the overall battle for Texas independence but also the role of each location during the day's hectic activity. All sites can be reached easily by car or on foot.

62   TREASURES OF TEXAS

recognized as a National Historic Civil Engineering Landmark. The museum located in the base greets visitors through giant bronze doors emblazoned with the six flags of Texas. The 125-foot square base features text panels highlighting events leading up to and culminating with the Texas Revolution. Following the octagonal shaft past the observation level culminates with a 220-ton star made from stone, steel, and concrete. The museum's exhibits focus on the history of Texan culture, including Mayan, Spanish, and Mexican influences; the history of the Texas Revolution; the Republic of Texas; and some of the important figures in Texas history. The 160-seat Jesse H. Jones Theatre for Texas Studies presents a thirty-five-minute movie, which lasts longer than the battle itself, titled *Texas Forever!! The Battle of San Jacinto*.

One of the largest projects designed to protect the battlefield and monument came through improvements to the site's seawall in 2016. The project was drastically needed, since drilling for oil and underground water had led to severe land subsidence and erosion along the bay area shoreline, with roughly 100 acres of the battleground becoming submerged under the bay.

Visitor Information

HOURS: Battleground: 9 a.m.–6 p.m. daily; Monument and Museum of History: Friday–Sunday, 9 a.m.–6 p.m.; Monument Observation Floor: Friday–Sunday, 9 a.m.–5:30 p.m.
Admission fee charged

Photograph of a man standing between tall metal gates leading to the San Jacinto battlefield. *Courtesy of UNT Libraries, The Portal to Texas History*

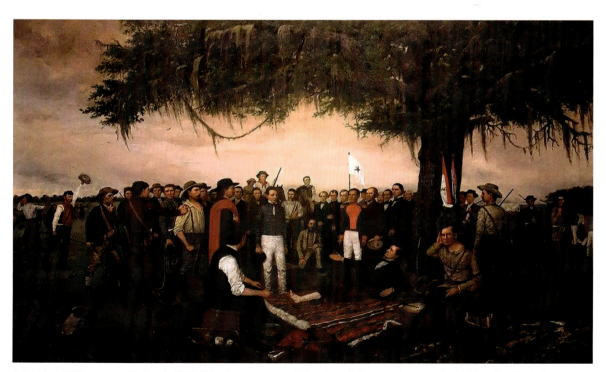

Painted by William Henry Huddle in 1886, this oil-on-canvas painting depicts the morning after the battle, when Santa Anna, disguised and dressed in the white paints of a private, is brought to the wounded General Sam Houston for an official surrender.

Battlefields & War   63

Palo Alto Battlefield

7200 Paredes Line Road
Brownsville, TX 78526
956-541-2785, ext. 333
https://nps.gov/paal/index.htm

Important Dates

Period of Importance: **May 8, 1846** *(battle)*
Added to National Register of Historic Places:
   October 15, 1996
Designated a National Historic Landmark:
   December 19, 1960
Designated a National Historic Site:
   November 19, 1978
Delisted as a National Historic Site:
   March 30, 2009
Designated a National Historic Park:
   March 30, 2009

Interpretive signs and trails wind through the battlefield at Palo Alto. Seen here, the Mexican Battle Line Trail puts visitors in the footsteps of the Mexican army. Battle of Palo Alto, Mexican Line.

The battlefield site at Palo Alto preserves the first major battleground in the Mexican-American War. The United States' victory in the battle fought on May 8, 1846, made an invasion of Mexico possible.

Site Description

Located near the city of Brownsville, Texas, the Palo Alto Battlefield National Historical Park preserves the grounds of the May 8, 1846, Battle of Palo Alto. This was the first major conflict in a border dispute that precipitated the Mexican-American War. The US Army victory in this battle made the invasion of Mexico possible.

Mexico and the United States had drifted closer and closer to war, dating back to 1845, when the United States annexed the Republic of Texas as a new state. The Mexicans had lost their war with the Texans in 1836, losing their bid to keep the Texians from breaking away and becoming the independent nation they were clamoring for. Since that loss, Mexico refused to recognize the independence of Texas, nor would it recognize the Rio Grande as an international boundary. Fearing a Mexican response to the annexation, President James K. Polk, in January 1846, ordered General Zachary Taylor to move his forces into Texas to defend the border at the Rio Grande.

A last-minute effort to settle the dispute diplomatically failed. As a result, Taylor was ordered to

This 1851 painting by Carl Nebel shows the action of the Mexican-American War battle at Palo Alto. *Courtesy of the National Park Service*

take his force to the Rio Grande. Mexican general Mariano Arista viewed this action as a hostile invasion of Mexican territory. On April 25, 1846, Arista took his soldiers across the river and attacked, resulting in a skirmish now known as the Thornton Affair and defeating the Americans.

Battlefields & War 65

General Zachary Taylor, depicted in this painting, was the leader of American forces at the Battle of Palo Alto. More than two hundred Mexican troops were killed or wounded, widely attributed to the effectiveness of the US artillery. Conversely, the US Army suffered approximately fifty casualties. *Courtesy of the Library of Congress*

Following the skirmish, Arista's troops began to cross the Rio Grande. On May 3, Arista's roughly 3,700 troops, most of the Army of the North, began to attack the American outpost at Fort Texas. Taylor had prepared Fort Texas to withstand a siege and moved most of his forces to protect his supply base at Fort Polk, near Point Isabel, some 23 miles northeast of Brownsville. The fort was garrisoned with five hundred men, four 18-pound field guns, and a field battery. Hearing the distant report of cannon fire, Taylor marched his Army of Occupation—roughly 2,300 soldiers—south to relieve the siege on May 7 with just over two thousand men and a two-hundred-wagon supply train. Arista, upon learning of his approach, diverted many of his units away from the siege to meet the oncoming force, with the intent to block them, but Taylor's scouts sighted the force at noon on May 8.

The two forces met on May 8—three days before the formal declaration of war on Mexico by the United States. Arista ordered two cavalry charges, first against the American right flank and then later against the left. Both proved unsuccessful. Poor training and inferior armaments undermined any advantage the Mexican army might have had in its size of force. The US "light" artillery was more mobile and accurate than that of Arista, tipping the scales in favor of the superior American artillery. That evening at dusk, both armies retired from the field of battle to camp for the night. Under the darkness of night and into the morning, Arista withdrew farther south. Taylor sent a 220-man battalion to reconnoiter the Mexican positions. The Battle of Resaca de la Palma would follow later that morning, and General Zachary Taylor would emerge from the war a national hero.

The National Park Service has acquired a little more than a third of the authorized land for the park, including the 300-acre southern core battlefield tract, which served as the location for Mexican forces during the battle. Private owners still control roughly 2,000 acres of the battlefield. The land has been altered somewhat since the time of the battle due to the high concentration and proliferation of honey mesquite.

The historic site portrays the battle and war and discusses the causes and consequences of the battle from the perspectives of both the United States and Mexico. The visitor center features exhibits and a fifteen-minute video about the war, while a half-mile trail, which includes interpretive panels, leads to an overlook of the battlefield. The Palo Alto Battlefield National Historic Site was redesignated a National Historic Park in 2009. During this process, the park was expanded and brought into the fold the Resaca de la Palma Battlefield, a separate 34 acres located inside the Brownsville city limits.

Visitor Information

HOURS: 8 a.m.–5 p.m. daily. Park trails close at 4:30 p.m.; all gates are locked at 5 p.m.
Visitor Center: 8 a.m.–5 p.m. daily
No entrance fees

The Battle of Palo Alto is marked with numerous markers, including this Texas Historical Marker. The battlefield location long served the area as a historic site but in 2009 was redesignated a National Historical Park, and it has been expanded to include the Resaca de la Palma Battlefield, highlighted elsewhere in this book.

Located near the center of the battlefield, the Palo Alto Battlefield Overlook provides a great view of the battlefield's expanse. On the afternoon of the battle, artillery rounds would have flown at this very location. *Courtesy of the National Park Service*

Battlefields & War **67**

Resaca de la Palma Battlefield

1024 Paredes Line Road
Brownsville, TX 78521

Palo Alto Battlefield National Historical Park Visitor Center
7200 Paredes Line Road
Brownsville, TX 78526

Important Dates

Period of Importance: **May 9, 1846** (*battle*)
Designated a National Historic Landmark:
 December 19, 1960
Added to National Register of Historic Places:
 October 15, 1966

NOTE: The battlefield location is *not* located at the Resaca de la Palma State Park. The battlefield is incorporated into, but is a separate unit of, the Palo Alto Battlefield National Historic Site. The Resaca de la Palma Battlefield is actually located approximately 6.5 miles south of the Palo Alto Battlefield and 3.5 miles north of downtown Brownsville.

The 1846 Battle of Resaca de la Palma undeveloped battlefield remnants have been preserved and are part of the Palo Alto Battlefield National Historical Park. Sites crucial to the Mexican-American War are littered throughout the area. Here, the site of Fort Polk is interpreted near the Rio Grande in Brownsville.

The Resaca de la Palma Battlefield is a separate unit of the Palo Alto Battlefield National Historical Park. It occupies a bend in the Resaca de la Palma, an oxbow-like body of water. It has been minimally developed and today features a small parking area, walking trail, and interpretive signage.

Site Description

On May 8, 1846, on the coastal prairie at Palo Alto, General Mariano Arista's Ejército del Norte ("Army of the North") engaged the US troops under General Zachary Taylor in a six-hour-long artillery battle. The Mexicans fell as the superior US cannons pounded the lines, causing hundreds of casualties. When nightfall came, it brought the battle to a close. General Arista decided to fall back and seek a position where the enemy guns might cause less damage. He chose to make a stand at Resaca de la Palma, just a few miles north of Matamoros, Tamaulipas. Also known as Resaca de Guerrero, the location was an old, dry river channel, or *resaca*, of the Rio Grande, one of many long, water-filled ravines left behind by the shifting course of the winding river.

During the night, Arista established new positions in the resaca, which crossed the road between Matamoros and Port Isabel, blocking it with artillery

This 1854 Currier and Ives print depicts General Zachary Taylor at the battle. In March 1846, Taylor established an army post on the banks of the Rio Grande, raised the American flag, and proclaimed the river as the southern boundary of the newly annexed state. Mexico disagreed. *Courtesy of the National Park Service*

Battlefields & War   69

At the time of its National Historic Landmark designation in 1960, only 50 acres of the battlefield had been left mostly unscathed. It had been used as a citrus orchard and polo field and, at one point, had been filled in, the channel of which has since been reestablished.

and placing infantry troops along banks of the resaca. The brush-covered ravine, about 5 miles south, provided the Mexican army with a strong defensive position and abundant cover. Cavalry troops were kept in the rear as a reserve force, hoping to force an infantry battle in the dense chaparral instead of the open-field artillery duel that did in the day before.

Taylor followed Arista from Palo Alto, leaving his wagon train safely entrenched at Palo Alto so he could focus all his attention on Arista's force. They arrived at Resaca de la Palma around 3 p.m. on May 9, and General Taylor immediately ordered a charge. American dragoons and light infantry fought with considerable difficulty against the Mexican artillery but eventually forced the Mexicans out of the resaca. Mexican resistance was stiff, counterattacking twice, but was beaten back both times. One US force found a path that led them over the waterway, around the most heavily fortified areas, and surprised the flank of the Mexican lines, finding inexperienced, demoralized, and underfed soldiers. They put up a valiant fight, but in less than an hour US forces emerged from the brush into the clearing housing General Arista's field headquarters.

Captain Charles May's dragoons seized the Mexican artillery blocking the resaca crossing while Captain Randolph Ridgely's artillery drew fire to expose Mexican positions. An initial charge drove many of the Mexican artillerymen from their guns, eventually resulting in the capture of the Mexican artillery commander, General Rómulo Díaz de la Vega, and several of his men. US infantry regiments entered the fight, taking the Mexican cannons, controlling the roadway, and effectively ending Mexican resistance, forcing a retreat.

The Mexican troops left so swiftly that they left behind all manner of baggage, including 474 muskets and carbines, eight pieces of artillery, Arista's correspondence and silver service, and the colors of the Tampico Battalion. Of the 1,700 Americans engaged in battle, only thirty-three were killed, with an additional eighty-nine wounded. Out of an estimated force of 4,000, Mexico officially recorded 154 killed, 205 wounded, and 156 missing, many of them likely drowning while trying to cross the Rio Grande at night. Taylor claimed to have buried two hundred Mexican dead.

The battle occurred just a day before news of the initial skirmish at Palo Alto reached Washington, DC. Upon learning that Mexican troops had crossed the Rio Grande and attacked US soldiers, President James K. Polk announced that Mexico had invaded US territory and "shed American blood upon American soil." Within days, on May 13, the United States declared war.

The impact on morale from the battle was enormous. US troops now had the confidence that they could defeat their foe anywhere and with any size of force. The loss threw the Mexican soldiers off balance by consecutive defeats. Mexican troops remained convinced that it was the US Army that had invaded Mexican soil, but their defeat at Resaca de la Palma prevented them from pressing that claim further. The Mexican army could not generate another push across the Rio Grande and, eventually, was unable to hold Matamoros. On May 18, the Mexican forces abandoned the city to a US occupation. The war continued for almost another two years, drawing to a close only after US troops occupied the Mexican capital. The Mexican officials found themselves negotiating a settlement that included recognition of the Rio Grande as the international boundary, and the sale of additional territories extending to the Pacific coast. The treaty, signed February 2, 1848, dictated that Mexicans occupying those lands now would gain rights as US citizens. That process had started shortly after Resaca de la Palma, since Mexican residents living north of the Rio Grande saw the writing on the wall: the United States was unlikely to lose its new foothold. Some fled to Mexico, but many stayed with their homes and property to become US citizens.

Today, the battlefield lies in the center of Brownsville. At the time of the site's 1960 National Historic Landmark designation, only a 50-acre fragment was relatively unscathed, having been used as a citrus orchard and polo field. The Resaca de la Palma itself was, at one time, filled in, but the channel has since been reestablished. Much of the dense brush has been cleared and developed, but a 34.4-acre portion of this important battlefield remains. In August 2011, Palo Alto Battlefield National Historic Park acquired the property as a second unit of the park. Visitors today are able to experience one of the few Mexican-American War battle sites on a landscape that is largely unchanged from 1846.

Visitor Information

The site does feature restroom facilities, a walking trail, interpretive waysides, and a picnic area. Gates to the battlefield are open Tuesday through Saturday, 9 a.m. to 3 p.m. For up-to-date information, call the site at 956-541-2785, ext. 333.

Leading the Mexican forces that day was General Mariano Arista, seen here in an 1851 painting by Édouard Pingret. The opening battles at Palo Alto and Resaca de la Palma were disastrous losses for Mexico. They resulted in Arista being court-martialed, but he was eventually acquitted. *Photo courtesy of D. R. Instituto Nacional de Antropología e Historia, Mexico*

Battlefields & War

Palmito Ranch Battlefield

Texas State Highway 4 and Palmito Hill Road
Brownsville, TX 78521
https://thc.texas.gov/historic-sites/palmito-ranch-battlefield

Important Dates

Period of Importance: **May 12–13, 1865** *(battle)*
Added to National Register of Historic Places:
   June 23, 1993
Designated a National Historic Landmark:
   September 25, 1997

The battle raged along the banks of the Rio Grande east of Brownsville, Texas. Located only a few miles from the southern tip of Texas, the landscape of the battlefield is flat and coastal in nature.

This marker, located on Texas State Highway 4, interprets the boundaries of the Palmito Ranch Battlefield. From this location, most of the action was waged right in front of the viewer, a short distance ahead.

Site Description

Depending on whom you ask, the Battle of Palmito Ranch, also known as the Battle of Palmito Hill, was the final battle of the Civil War. Fought along the banks of the Rio Grande, east of Brownsville, the men engaged on May 12 and 13, 1865. It took place more than a month after the general surrender of Confederate forces at Appomattox Court House, a fact that had been communicated to both commanders at Palmito and, therefore, could be classified as a postwar activity rather than the final battle.

Early on in the Civil War, the Union army occupied the border town of Brownsville, Texas, hoping to stifle support from Mexico across the Rio Grande and into the Confederate states. The occupation was short lived, and the Union force was unable to hold the city. They established a base at Brazos Santiago on Brazos Island from which to blockade the Rio Grande and Brownsville but could not manage to block the Mexican port of Bagdad. The Confederates would land supplies here, transport them 25 miles inland to Matamoros, and then ship them across the Rio Grande and into Brownsville.

Colonel John S. Ford, Confederate head of operations on the day of battle in 1865, as seen in this image by Louis de Planque. Palmito Ranch is considered by some as the final battle of the Civil War. *Courtesy of DeGolyer Library, SMU*

Battlefields & War   73

In an effort both to preserve the battlefield and invite visitors to the site, an interpretive pathway has been established. The path includes both monuments, such as the stone one on the right, and an interpretive center, which provides a more detailed look.

Then, in February 1865, the Union commander at Brazos Island, Col. Theodore H. Barrett, reported to his superiors that his base was secure from attack and that he could take Brownsville. They refused. Instead, Major General Lew Wallace sought and received Lt. General Ulysses S. Grant's permission to meet the Confederate commanders of the Brownsville area at Port Isabel on March 11, 1865, in the hopes of arranging a separate peace. During Wallace's meeting, he promised no retaliation against former Confederates so long as they took an oath of allegiance to the United States and promised that those who preferred to leave the country would have ample time to gather property and family before doing so.

An informal truce was arranged and sent by the Confederates up the chain of command while Wallace informed Grant that the rebels would soon be surrendering. Confederate major general John G. Walker denounced the terms and instead rebuked his subordinates for having even listened to them in the first place. Additionally, the commander of the Confederate Trans-Mississippi Department, Lieutenant General Edmund Kirby Smith, was not ready to abandon the Confederate cause either; on May 9, 1865, he told the governors of the western Confederate states that despite Lee's surrender, his own army remained and vowed to continue the fight.

Confederates in Texas were not unaware of the Confederacy's eastern fate. On May 1, 1865, a steamboat passenger heading up the Rio Grande toward Brownsville tossed a copy of the *New Orleans Times* to some Confederates at Palmito Ranch. The paper reported the news of Lee's surrender, Lincoln's assassination, and the surrender negotiations of Johnston and Sherman. With that news, several hundred soldiers left the army and returned home; however, those who remained were as resolute as General Smith and vowed to continue the fight.

The Federals, in the meantime, had received an erroneous report that the Southerners were preparing to evacuate Brownsville and move east of Corpus Christi. With this intelligence, Colonel Theodore H. Barrett dispatched an expedition composed of 250 men of the 62nd US Colored Infantry Regiment and fifty men of the 2nd Texas Cavalry Regiment under the command of Lieutenant Colonel David Branson to the mainland, on May 11, 1865, to attack reported rebel outposts and camps.

Early the following morning, on May 12, the expeditionary force surrounded the Confederate camp at White's Ranch but found no one present. Later that morning, people on the Mexican side of the river informed the Confederates of the Federals' whereabouts in the brush along the Rio Grande. Branson immediately led his men off to attack a Confederate camp at Palmito Ranch, scattering the rebel force.

Branson and his men remained at the site to feed themselves and their horses, but at 3 p.m. a sizable Confederate force appeared, hastening the Federals' march to retire to White's Ranch. Branson sent word of his precarious situation to Barrett, who responded by sending a two-hundred-man reinforcement from the 34th Indiana Volunteer Infantry. This augmented force, now commanded by Barrett, started out toward Palmito Ranch, skirmishing most of the way. A few miles from the ranch, the fighting escalated sharply. Barrett led his force back to a river bluff, where they could prepare dinner and camp for the night. At 4 p.m., a large Confederate cavalry force under Colonel John S. "Rip" Ford approached, and the Federals formed a battle line. The Union force was hammered with artillery, and Barrett ordered a retreat and eventual defeat, ending the battle.

Today, the area encompassing the battlefield remains relatively unchanged, and the site retains a great viewshed of the battlefield, especially from Boca Chica State Park and from Texas Highway 4. The marshy, windswept prairies, dotted with Spanish bayonet and prickly pears, are essentially the same as they were when encountered by the troops at the end of the war. The site covers more than 5,400 acres and was designated a National Historic Landmark in 1997. The area is best indicated by a large highway marker and radio audio option that details the history of the engagement on Texas State Highway 4, near where Palmito Ranch originally stood. The Civil War Trust and its partners have acquired and preserved an additional 3 acres of the battlefield.

> **Visitor Information**
>
> HOURS: Open daily, dawn to dusk. Unstaffed. *No entrance fees*
>
> NOTE: The site is not well marked but is indicated by a large highway marker telling the history of the battle. It sits on the Boca Chica Highway (TX-4) near where the Palmito Ranch originally stood. Traveling south on Palmito Hill Road will bring you to a Battlefield Interpretive Platform located in the core battlefield area. It provides visitors with a 360-degree view of the battlefield and has several low-profile wayside signs.

Union forces are seen here in occupation of Brownsville, Texas, in 1863. The fighting here would not cease until after the treaty was signed at Appomattox Court House. In May 1865, the Battle of Palmito Ranch was waged, finally bringing war stragglers to a close. *Courtesy of UNT Libraries, The Portal to Texas History*

USS *Texas*

Galveston, TX 77550
https://battleshiptexas.org

Important Dates

Ordered: **June 24, 1910**
Launched: **May 18, 1912**
Commissioned: **March 12, 1914**
Decommissioned: **April 21, 1948**
Added to National Register of Historic Places:
   December 8, 1976
Designated a National Historic Landmark: **December 8, 1976**

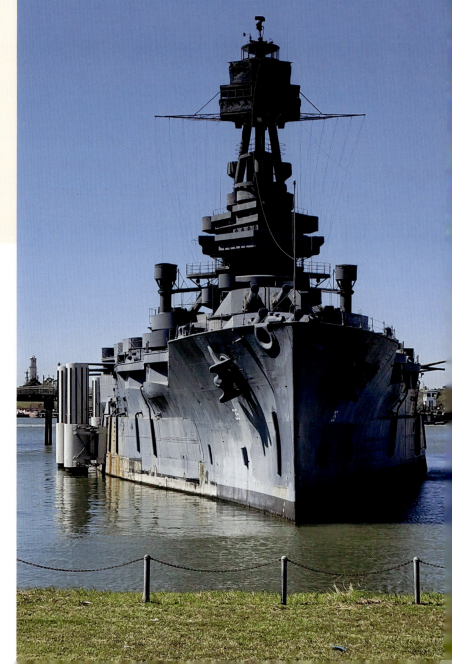

Following decommission, Battleship *Texas* became one of the first battleship museums and was docked off the ship channel in La Porte, across from the San Jacinto Battlefield and Monument.

Site Description

USS *Texas* (BB-35) is a former US Navy New York–class battleship. It was launched in 1912, commissioned in 1914, and finally decommissioned in 1948. It became the first permanent battleship memorial museum in the United States that same year; eight others have since received the same honor. It found a new anchorage along the busy Houston Ship Channel near the new San Jacinto Monument at San Jacinto State Park. Since that time, it has sat just across from the monument at Battleground Park.

Battleship *Texas* was the first of two New York–class battleships authorized on June 24, 1910. Bids for the new ship were accepted that fall, with the winning bid going to Newport News Shipbuilding Company. The contract, bid at $5.8 million excluding armor and armament, was signed on December 17, with plans delivered to the building yard one week later. Battleship *Texas* was first launched on May 18, 1912, sponsored by Claudia Lyon, daughter of Colonel Cecil Lyon, Republican national committeeman from Texas.

When it was commissioned in March 1914, it was considered the most powerful weapon in the world. Captain Albert W. Grant served in command with a main battery consisting of ten 14-inch Mark 1 guns, which could fire 1,400-pound armor-piercing shells to a range of 13 miles. Battleship *Texas* is credited with the introduction and innovation of advances in gunnery, aviation, and radar. Today, it is the last surviving dreadnought and is the only battleship in existence today that fought both in World Wars I and II.

Shortly after launch, in March 1914, *Texas* steamed its way to Veracruz to support the occupation of that Mexican city following the Tampico Incident. Its regular operations with the Atlantic Fleet began midyear and continued to January 1918, when it would cross the Atlantic to join the Grand Fleet in the North Sea.

Photograph of USS *Texas* being launched in Newport News, Virginia. *Courtesy of UNT Libraries, The Portal to Texas History*

Battlefields & War

On March 9, 1919, USS *Texas* became the first American warship to launch an airplane from its deck when Lieutenant Commander Edward O. McDonnell flew a Sopwith Camel from a fly-off platform constructed atop the no. 2 turret on the ship. *Courtesy of UNT Libraries, The Portal to Texas History*

In 2021, those caring for the preservation of Battleship *Texas* made the decision that it was in the best interest for the ship to be closed and fully repaired. Restoration work continued for the next four years, opening in 2025 at Galveston's Pier 20.

Texas would remain in the North Sea to the end of World War I, during times when it wasn't back in the States for repairs. One of the gun crews trained on *Texas* was assigned to the merchant vessel *Mongolia*. On April 19, the crew of *Mongolia* sighted a surfaced German U-boat. The gun crew on *Texas* opened fire on the U-boat, averting an attack on *Mongolia* and, in the process, firing the first American shots of the war. For most of the rest of the war, the ship was used entirely for convoy missions and occasional forays to reinforce the British squadron on blockade duty in the North Sea whenever German heavy units threatened.

At the end of the war, *Texas* was involved in the battleship divisions that met President Woodrow Wilson for the Paris Peace Conference. Following its service in the war, Battleship *Texas* returned to the states. Following overhaul, it resumed duty with the Atlantic Fleet early in 1919; its captain, Nathan Twining, successfully employed naval aircraft, showing the versatility of employing such equipment and leading the navy to add floatplanes to all the fleet's battleships and newer cruisers. *Texas* would later spend time with the Pacific Fleet before returning east in 1924 and returning to the shipyard in Newport News in 1924 for a major overhaul. There, the ship underwent modernization efforts to transition it from coal- to oil-fired boilers and received numerous other alterations, including turrets as well as upgrades to the stern, forecastle, bridge, and mainmast. Following the overhaul, it was designated the flagship of the US Fleet and resumed duty along the Eastern Seaboard, taking a few forays into the Pacific over the next decade. In 1937 it would return to the East Coast, become the flagship for the Atlantic Squadron, and see additional upgrades in anticipation to armed conflict.

Back in open waters well before the onset of World War II, Battleship *Texas* found itself back in the midst of war. Its first major combat operation came during Operation Torch's invasion of North Africa in October 1942, followed by action during preparations for D-Day and the landings at Normandy, the Battle of Cherbourg, Operation Dragoon for the invasion of southern France, and the Battles of Iwo Jima and Okinawa before arriving at Leyte in the Philippines until the Japanese surrender. *Texas* would spend the next few months bringing American troops home. In January 1946, the ship departed San Pedro, California, steamed through the Panama Canal, and arrived in Norfolk in preparation for inactivation. It was placed officially in reserve in Baltimore in June.

Funding issues would plague the battleship throughout its life when it came to repairs and restoration. Years of neglect in maintenance would result in cracks and gaps in coated surfaces, water intrusion, and steel deterioration. Projects over the years, however, would eventually round out, keeping the ship afloat. On August 1, 2020, operational control of the ship was transferred to the Battleship *Texas* Foundation. More than 36,000 items are part of the artifact collection and are being cared for by curators.

Visitor Information

Battleship *Texas* is currently moving for repairs and restoration. New location and opening date to be determined.

Modern view of Battleship *Texas*'s guns

Battlefields & War 79

HA-19 (Midget Submarine)

National Museum of the Pacific War
311 East Austin Street
Fredericksburg, TX 78624
830-997-8600
https://www.pacificwarmuseum.org

Important Dates

Launched: **1938**
Grounded: **December 7, 1941**
Added to National Register of Historic Places:
  June 30, 1989
Designated a National Historic Landmark:
  June 30, 1989

HA-19, on display in the Museum of the Pacific War, has its own dedicated room.

80   TREASURES OF TEXAS

Japanese midget submarine *HA-19* was involved in the attack on Pearl Harbor. Seen here sometime during a tour to sell war bonds during the later years of World War II, it was on display at the University of Texas. *Courtesy of UNT Libraries, The Portal to Texas History*

Site Description

The *HA-19*, also known as Japanese Midget Submarine "C" by the United States Navy, is a historic Imperial Japanese Navy type A Ko-hyoteki–class midget submarine that was part of the Japanese attack on Pearl Harbor on December 7, 1941. Today, the submarine is part of the collection and is displayed at the National Museum of the Pacific War in Fredericksburg.

HA-19 was built at the Kure Naval Dockyard in Kure, Hiroshima, Japan, in 1938. Its type 92 periscope was installed later, in May 1941. When submerged, it displaced 46 long tons. At just over 78 feet and almost 10 feet in height, *HA-19* could reach a speed of 23 knots on the surface and 19 knots when submerged. It carried with it armaments for two 17.7-inch torpedoes to be muzzle-loaded into tubes and one 300-pound scuttling charge.

In November 1941, *HA-19* was part of the Kido Butai, carried by its mother ship, a type C cruiser submarine, *I-24*. The two-man crew consisted of Ensign Kazuo Sakamaki and Chief Warrant Officer Kiyoshi Inagaki. On December 7, at 3:30 in the morning, *HA-19* was launched from its mother ship with a broken gyrocompass. With only four and a half hours to reach Pearl Harbor, the crew attempted to fix the compass en route. The sub's crew had orders to enter Pearl Harbor, Hawaii; attack the moored American warships with its two torpedoes; and then scuttle the submarine with explosives. Upon arrival, the crew was unable to enter the harbor due to navigational difficulties and ran the submarine aground, resulting in their capture by American forces.

When they approached the harbor entrance, their malfunctioning gyrocompass was still on the fritz. Impaired, the *HA-19* hit a reef three times before grounding on the right side of the entrance of Pearl Harbor at 8 a.m. Seventeen minutes later, with the main attack in full force, the stranded sub was spotted by USS *Helm*. Inagaki managed to make the submarine dive. It resurfaced at 8:19 a.m., and the destroyer spotted it again and fired, missing. The blast knocked *HA-19*

People viewing a Japanese submarine captured during World War II. The University of Texas at Austin Tower is in the background. *Courtesy of UNT Libraries, The Portal to Texas History*

off the reef and knocked Sakamaki unconscious. Once more, Inagaki dove to escape.

Upon Sakamaki regaining consciousness, the crew made another attempt to enter the harbor. The grounding damaged the vessel, and they found they could not fire one of its torpedoes. The sub slowly began to flood, and, as it did, the batteries began giving off fumes from being in contact with seawater. Once again, it hit the reef; the crew reversed for another attempt, and the sub grounded once more. They came free after adjusting the ballast, and on the final attempt, *HA-19* was depth-charged, damaging the periscope and effectively disabling its ability to fire the other torpedo.

Clearly at a loss, the crew decided to abort the attack and return to *I-24* near Lanai. The fumes from the batteries, however, overtook them, and *HA-19* was carried off by the currents. When they awoke it was night, and the crew planned to beach the sub at Waimānalo. The engine died, and the sub grounded on an offshore reef. Sakamaki ordered Inagaki to abandon ship, while he would set the explosive scuttling charge and follow him. The charge failed to detonate (possibly from being immersed in seawater). Sakamaki

HA-19 is housed at the Museum of the Pacific War in Fredericksburg. Outside the museum, the landscape includes features reminiscent of battleship and battlefield features. This is just outside the main entrance.

82   TREASURES OF TEXAS

managed to swim through the surf to shore. There, he collapsed only to be captured the following day. His crewmate, Inagaki, drowned, and his body washed ashore the next day.

HA-19 was given the American designation of "Midget C" because it was the third midget sub spotted by American forces. On December 8, the abandoned submarine was bombed by US Army aircraft; the bomb missed, and the sub broke free to wash ashore on the beach. In the days following, an army tractor pulled the sub out of the sea. The sub was built to be disassembled in three parts, so the army utilized this characteristic to dismantle it without destroying it. Upon transport to the Naval Submarine Base Pearl Harbor, it was examined, which yielded technical data and various documents.

In 1942, the army sent *HA-19* to the US mainland, where it went on war bond tours. The sub rounded out its tour at Navy Pier, Chicago, Illinois. From January 1947 to 1991, *HA-19* was on display in Key West, Florida. It spent time outside at Naval Station Key West and was loaned to the Key West Art and Historical Society, where it was displayed at the Key West Lighthouse and Military Museum. In 1990, the association administering the Key West Museum made the decision to focus strictly on the lighthouse and began divesting its military collections. In 1991, *HA-19* was moved to Fredericksburg, Texas, home of the National Museum of the Pacific War at the Admiral Nimitz State Historic Site. Sakamaki attended a historical conference that same year, finally reuniting with this submarine.

Visitor Information

HOURS: Wednesday–Sunday, 9 a.m.–5 p.m.
Admission fee charged

The war in the Pacific theater was dominated by US-Japanese conflicts. Seen here is the Japanese battle flag.

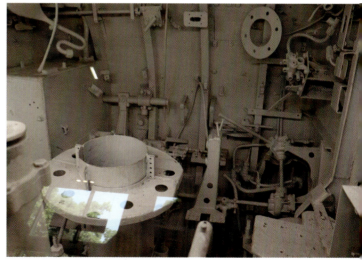

The dedicated *HA-19* Room backs up to the main lobby hallway, which also includes portholes for visitors to peer into the interior of the miniature Japanese submarine.

Exhibits throughout the museum give interpretations of the size, scope, reasoning, and impact of the Pacific theater of war.

USS *Lexington* (CV-16)

USS *Lexington* Museum
2914 North Shoreline Boulevard
Corpus Christi, TX 78402
800-523-9539
https://usslexington.com

Important Dates

Launched: **September 23, 1942**
Stricken: **November 8, 1991**
Added to National Register of Historic Places:
   July 31, 2003
Designated a National Historic Landmark:
   July 31, 2003

USS *Lexington* is an Essex-class aircraft carrier built during World War II for the navy. It became the fifth US Navy ship to bear the name in honor of the Battle of Lexington. Since 1992, the ship has operated as a museum and is docked in Corpus Christi.

USS *Lexington* in its original configuration and underway in November 1943. The Japanese referred to it as a "ghost" ship for its tendency to reappear after reportedly being sunk. This, coupled with the ship's dark blue camouflage scheme, led to its "Blue Ghost" nickname. *Courtesy the United States Navy*

Site Description

Nicknamed "the Blue Ghost," USS *Lexington* is an Essex-class aircraft carrier built during World War II for the United States Navy. Originally named *Cabot*, the new carrier was renamed during construction to commemorate the recently lost USS *Lexington* (CV-2), becoming the fifth navy ship to bear the name in honor of the Battle of Lexington. Since 1992, the ship has operated as a museum, docked in Corpus Christi.

Lexington was laid down as *Cabot* on July 15, 1941, by the Fore River Shipyard in Quincy, Massachusetts. The following May, USS *Lexington*, which was built in the same shipyard twenty years earlier, was sunk during the Battle of the Coral Sea. Shipyard workers requested and got approval from the navy secretary to change the name of *Cabot* to *Lexington*. The ship was launched in September 1942 and then commissioned on February 17, 1943, with Captain Felix Stump in command.

Lexington was immediately pressed into service and would see extensive travel throughout the Pacific War. For much of its service, it functioned as Admiral Marc Mitscher's flagship, leading the Fast Carrier Task Force through their battles across the Pacific. *Lexington* would receive eleven battle stars and the Presidential Unit Citation by the end of the war, participating in raids at Tarawa, Wake Island, and the Marshalls and in the Kwajalein Raid during 1943. During that final raid, it was struck by a torpedo but managed to make Pearl Harbor—and then on to Bremerton, Washington—for repairs.

The following year, *Lexington* returned to Majuro in time to be brought under Task Force 58 in March under Rear Admiral Marc Mitscher. During that year, the ship saw action at Hollandia, Saipan, Guam, and the Battle of the Philippine Sea, with later attacks against the Palaus, Bonins, Yap, Ulithi, Mindanao, the Visayas, the Manila area, Luzon, and Leyte. It then blasted Okinawa and Formosa in October to destroy bases that might launch opposition forces to the Philippines. During the Battle of Leyte Gulf, *Lexington*'s aircraft scored important victories in what would become the climactic American naval victory over Japan. While under constant attack, the ship assisted in sinking *Musashi* and scored hits on three cruisers on October 24. The

Several planes with men around them on the deck of the navy ship USS *Lexington*. Courtesy of UNT Libraries, The Portal to Texas History

following day, it helped sink *Chitose*, the *Zuikaku*, the *Zuiho*, and the *Nachi*.

Lexington closed out the war with strikes on Luzon and Formosa, then entered the South China Sea to strike enemy shipping and air installations against Saipan, Cam Ranh Bay, Hong Kong, the Pescadores, Formosa, and Okinawa. It would hit airfields near Tokyo in February 1945 and help minimize opposition at the Iwo Jima landings, then sail for further strikes against the Japanese home islands and the Nansei Shoto before heading for overhaul at Puget Sound. It made a final return to the Pacific that summer, joining Rear Admiral Thomas Sprague's task force for the final round of airstrikes battering Japanese home islands, with attacks on Honshu and Hokkaido airfields and Yokosuka and Kure naval bases.

Following the Japanese surrender, *Lexington* would continue to fly patrols over Japan. It would provide, under Lieutenant Commander Wall, supply drops to prisoner-of-war camps on Honshu that had been abandoned by the Japanese. Wall would be awarded the Distinguished Flying Cross for this mission. In December the ship was used to ferry home servicemen, arriving in San Francisco on December 16.

Following the war, *Lexington* was decommissioned at Bremerton, Washington, on April 23, 1947, and

Lexington saw extensive service throughout the Pacific War. Following the war, it was decommissioned but modernized and reactivated by the early 1950s. It would be reclassified as an attack carrier, then as an antisubmarine carrier, and finally as a training carrier before being decommissioned and donated as a museum in 1991.

entered the Defense Reserve Fleet, being designated attack carrier CVA-16 in October 1952. Throughout the rest of the ship's life, it would see a refit and recommission and would participate in exercises, maneuvers, and search-and-rescue missions in the Pacific. It was involved in the 1958 Taiwan Strait crisis and served in the Far Eastern tour in late 1960 and into 1961 during tension in Laos. It moved to the Gulf of Mexico during the Cuban Missile Crisis and, into 1969, began operating out of its home port, Pensacola, as well as Corpus Christi, qualifying student aviators and maintaining the high state of training both of active-duty and reserve naval aviators, which became increasingly crucial as the tensions in Vietnam escalated.

Lexington continued as a training carrier for another two decades. It was relieved by *Forrestal* and was decommissioned and struck on November 8, 1991. It became, on August 18, 1980, the first aircraft carrier in US naval history to have women stationed aboard as crew members. *Lexington* was the final Essex-class carrier in commission, after USS *Oriskany* had been decommissioned in 1976. On November 26, 1991, the navy turned *Lexington* over to the City of Corpus Christi.

On June 15, 1992, the ship was donated as a museum and now operates as the USS *Lexington* Museum. The ship is carefully maintained, and restoration work is ongoing. Areas of the ship previously off-limits are being opened to the public every few years. The World War II–era gun battery has undergone partial restoration, using guns that have been salvaged from scrapped ships and mounted in the approximate locations where similar mounts once existed as part of the ship's original fit. Additionally, *Lexington* has shown up in film and television. It served as USS *Enterprise* in the TV miniseries *War and Remembrance* and as USS *Yorktown* for *Midway* and was used for filming in 2001's *Pearl Harbor*, altered to resemble a Japanese carrier and USS *Hornet*. It has also been seen during *Ghost Hunters* and *Ghost Lab* television series and in a 2015 Super Bowl commercial.

Visitor Information

HOURS: 9 a.m.–5 p.m. daily, closed Christmas and Thanksgiving only
Admission and parking fee charged

Hangar Deck and Flight Deck are wheelchair accessible.

As a museum, it operates as "USS *Lexington* Museum on the Bay." The ship is carefully maintained and operated, with a large portion of the ship open to exploration, such as the bridge seen here. Areas of the ship previously off-limits become open every few years.

Battlefields & War   87

USS *Cabot* (CVL-28) (delisted)

Remains/Artifacts of USS *Cabot*
USS *Lexington* Museum on the Bay
2914 North Shoreline Boulevard
Corpus Christi, TX 78402
800-523-9539
https://usslexington.com

Important Dates

Built: **1942**
Added to National Register of Historic Places:
 June 21, 1990
Designated a National Historic Landmark:
 June 21, 1990
Designation withdrawn: **August 7, 2001**
 (both NRHP and NHL)

Following World War II, USS *Cabot* would operate as a training carrier. Here it is seen in 1949 passing Fort Barrancas, Florida. *Courtesy of the United States Navy*

Serving in Spain as the *Dédalo*, the ship is shown in the Mediterranean Sea in June 1988 as a Hawker Siddeley AV-8S Matador flies over it. *Courtesy of the National Archives*

Site Description

Like other Independence-class light aircraft carries, USS *Cabot* was put into service as a light cruiser. Named in honor of John Cabot, navigator and discoverer of what is now North America, it is the second US naval ship to carry this name, the other being from the Revolutionary War era. Following Pearl Harbor, the navy realized it needed more aircraft carriers and light cruisers. *Cabot*, which was still under construction, was converted for use as an aircraft carrier. It was launched in April 1943 in Camden, New Jersey, and commissioned in July with Captain M. F. Schoeffel at the helm. *Cabot,* with more than 1,500 officers and soldiers on board, would participate in numerous World War II operations, beginning with the invasion of the Marshall Islands.

After returning to Hawaii for some repairs, it would participate in the raids on Palau, Ulithi, and Woleai and assist in providing air cover for the Jayapura operation, Trusk, Satawan, Ponape, Iwo Jima, Pagan Rota, Guam, Yap, Ulithi, Formosa, and Okinawa, as well as airstrikes in the Marianas, Mindanao, Visayas, and Luzon. It participated in the Marianas Turkey shoot and the Battle of Leyte Gulf, patrolled Luzon, and fought off kamikaze attacks. During one of these latter attacks, the flight deck sustained serious damage, and sixty-two men were killed or wounded. Following repairs in Ulithi, the ship returned to battle before returning to the States for a complete overhaul and training in Pearl Harbor. Following this, it returned to the Pacific theater, carrying out strikes on Wake Island and participated in training. Its service during the war earned it nine battle stars and the Presidential Unit Citation.

Cabot would return east following the war, earning its decommission in Philadelphia. It was put back into service in 1948 for several training missions before being decommissioned again in 1952. After a dozen years of

USS *Cabot* is on its way from Pearl Harbor in Hawaii to Eniwetok in late July 1945. The carrier launched three strikes on Wake Island in a few days, while the battleship USS *Pennsylvania*, along with destroyers, bombarded the island. *Courtesy of the United States Navy*

sitting dormant, the US Navy loaned the ship to Spain for its naval operations, and it was renamed *Dédalo*.

It would remain in the Spanish service until 1989, earning its retirement to become a museum ship and receiving designations on the NRHP and as a landmark in 1990. The ship made its new home in New Orleans, but fundraisers were unable to pay for the upkeep, and plans to memorialize the ship met with no success. In 1999, the heavily deteriorating ship was auctioned off by the US Marshals Service to Sabe Marine Salvage in Brownsville, Texas. Beginning in November 2000, *Cabot* was cut up. In 2001, *Cabot* was sold for scrap, and its designations were withdrawn; scrapping of the hulk was completed in 2002.

The ship's flight deck and island structure, along with the island structure of USS *Iwo Jima*, were

Under air attack in 1944. USS *Cabot* would suffer during the war but would inflict much more damage on its enemies. *Courtesy of the United States Navy*

obtained for preservation by the Texas Air Museum at Rio Hondo. That museum has since been closed, and *Cabot*'s island has been demolished. The National Museum of Naval Aviation at NAS Pensacola has constructed a replica of *Cabot*'s island, using the original plans, along with a reconstructed section of the flight deck. A large collection of items salvaged from *Cabot* are located at the USS *Lexington* aircraft museum in Corpus Christi, including all the guns and the anchor. A museum room contains information, artifacts, and photographs of *Cabot*.

Visitor Information

This property has been delisted and scrapped. The information below is for items on display at the USS *Lexington* Museum in Corpus Christi.

HOURS: 9 a.m.–5 p.m. daily, closed Christmas and Thanksgiving only
Admission and parking fee charged

A museum in New Orleans was considered for USS *Cabot*. Here, *Cabot* is seen in 1995 at New Orleans, while the buildings on Press Street can be seen beyond the wharves, and Bywater's St. Vincent de Paul Church's red steeple is visible on the horizon.

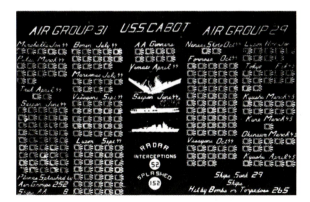

While *Cabot* would suffer hits during World War II, it managed to inflict much damage, sinking twenty-nine ships by 1945 and hitting 265 ships with bombs or torpedoes. *Courtesy of the United States Navy*

Battlefields & War   91

SITES

1. Woodland (1848)
2. Governor's Mansion (1854)
3. Texas State Capitol (1885)
4. Lyndon Baines Johnson Boyhood Home (1901)
5. Samuel T. Rayburn House (1916)
6. John Nance Garner House (1920)
7. Dealey Plaza Historic District (1963)

By the time Texas was annexed by the United States in 1845, the land had been governed as a part of six other nations (including its own) since colonization. Government had roughly been shaped within the Anglo-American tradition through both the 1833 proposed constitution drafted to create a separate state within the Mexican Federal Republic and the 1836 Constitution of the Republic of Texas. Because of its history and a strong population within its borders, Spanish and Mexican influences were readily apparent as well. Entering the United States caused Texas to base its own state constitution on the constitutional principles already common in the United States.

This section will talk more about the ties to history that governmental buildings, individuals, theories, and events have, rather than the mere existence of institutional government. Here are homes of governmental leaders and halls of justice and law, as well as the beginning and end of two overlapping presidencies.

Woodland

Sam Houston State University
1836 Sam Houston Avenue
Huntsville, TX 77340
936-294-1832
https://samhoustonmemorial
museum.com

Important Dates

Built: **1848**
Designated Recorded Texas Historic Landmark:
  1962
Added to National Register of Historic Places:
  May 30, 1974
Designated a National Historic Landmark:
  May 30, 1974
Designated Texas State Antiquities Landmark:
  January 1, 1981

Today, the original Woodland home and Houston's law office remain on 18 acres of Sam Houston's homestead. Students at the Sam Houston Normal Institute purchased the home in 1906 and the grounds as a permanent monument to the father of Texas.

A side view of Woodland, the Houston family home. It has been called the Mount Vernon of Texas. Nearby is his Houston's law office and the Steamboat House, where Houston died of pneumonia in 1863. *Courtesy of UNT Libraries, The Portal to Texas History*

Site Description

Located in Huntsville, the Sam Houston Memorial Museum occupies 18 acres of Sam Houston's original 200-acre farm. The Houston family occupied the home from 1847 to 1858 and, at the instigation of history students from Sam Houston Normal Institute (now Sam Houston State University), began a movement to preserve the homestead in 1905.

Born in 1793, near Lexington, Virginia, Sam Houston would spend much of his youth near the wilderness of the then-western United States in Virginia and later Tennessee. This led to a lifelong observance and sympathy for American Indians and a stint in the military service during the War of 1812. Following his service, he studied and practiced law in Tennessee, where he would rise quickly as attorney, state attorney general, and two-term congressman, culminating with his election as governor of Tennessee in 1827. Sam was plagued as an alcoholic, and as a result his wife left him two years after his election. He resigned his office and moved to Indian Country (present-day Oklahoma) to establish a trading post. Like other traders, he served as an adviser to the Indians, making yearly trips to Washington, DC, to plead their cause. However, seeing opportunities to the south, Houston made his way to Texas.

While he had little influence on the early beginnings of the Texas Revolution, Houston would become influential in the formation of the republic and later the state. He was a member of the convention that

Sam Houston served as the republic's first and third president, was one of the first two to represent Texas in the US Senate, and served as the sixth governor of Tennessee and the seventh governor of Texas. *Courtesy of the Library of Congress*

established a provisional government in Texas and sent Stephen F. Austin to Mexico to secure statehood. With the signing of the declaration of Texas's independence on March 2, 1836, Texas chose to become its own nation. Houston became commander of the local volunteers, then of the Texas regular army. Following

Government 95

In addition to the Woodland home, historic properties on the grounds nearby include the Steamboat House, a kitchen, Sam's law office, a family cabin, a blacksmith forge, a pottery and glassblowing shop, a bar, and demonstration cabins.

the fall of the Alamo, his forces retreated from Santa Anna before redeeming any criticism a few weeks later by surprising the larger Mexican army at San Jacinto, defeating them, taking Santa Anna prisoner, and bringing the revolution to an end.

Following this, Houston was elected president of the new republic. His two-year term resulted in obtaining the republic's recognition from Great Britain, France, and the United States, but his goal was obtaining annexation into the United States. When he was re-elected to office in 1841, he had married the devoutly religious Margaret Lea of Alabama, Texas's national debt sat at nearly $7 million, Native American tribes were in a combative state, and Mexico was showing signs of renewed aggression. When he retired from office three years later, he had brought Texas around to being relatively prosperous and had all but achieved annexation to the United States.

Statehood came in 1849, and, with it, Houston was selected as senator to represent the new state. However, he was alone among his southern colleagues in many ways: he was a strong believer in the Union, he supported Indian rights, and he was the only southern senator to vote for all the compromise measures of 1850. In 1859, Houston was elected governor of Texas on the platform of preserving the Union, but his attempts to avoid secession were unsuccessful. When it was accepted, Houston refused, considering Texas to become an independent republic again and refusing to take an oath to the Confederacy. As a result, Houston was deposed and retired quietly to Huntsville, where he died on July 26, 1863.

Sam Houston Memorial Museum & Grounds

The structures most influential to Sam Houston's later life stand on the grounds of the Sam Houston Memorial Museum in Huntsville. The site contains three historic structures (Woodland, the Sam Houston home; his log cabin law office; and the Steamboat House), three museum/interpretive facilities, and two service buildings. The primary purpose of the complex is for the interpretation of the life of Sam Houston. This is most evident at the Rotunda Museum—where the collection and exhibits focus on Houston's life and early Texas history, using personal articles, family photos, memorabilia, and artifacts—and the War and Peace House, which hosts many non-Houston-related artifacts the university has accumulated. The Log Kitchen is adjacent to his home and is a present-day construction, as are the blacksmith shop and greenhouse.

Upon his move to Woodland, Houston had exchanged part of his property at Raven Hill but would add acreage by purchasing additional tracts over the years. On the land in Huntsville, he received a small log cabin with a chimney, made of mud and sticks, later improved upon with the addition of an open hallway and a second room at the end, creating a "dogtrot." He added a porch across the front, above the two front rooms he added a loft (built for house servants until their quarters were finished), and he would finish off the house with plank doors and flat nails before later adding siding. The following spring, Houston converted the loft into two bedrooms separated by a grilled breezeway; a steep, enclosed staircase was added from the lower to upper hallway, and he moved the front of the house to the back, embellishing the hall with the addition of a pediment and portico of four-square columns. While modest, it would serve his needs; it resembles his childhood home, showed his desire for simplicity rather than opulence (especially helpful when running a campaign), and was of sufficient size for the family (Sam; Margaret; her mother, Nancy Lea; two children; their nurses; and approximately six slaves, who lived in separate outbuildings).

In 1853, Margaret's mother had relocated to Independence, and Margaret expressed a desire for the family to move. With Houston planning to return to senatorial duties in DC, he consented, eventually selling the Huntsville property in 1857 to retire his campaign debt. Following his gubernatorial election and subsequent forced retirement, Houston returned to Huntsville in an attempt to purchase back his property, but he was unsuccessful. As a result, he decided to rent a home on a semi-secluded hill northeast of town, the uniquely designed Steamboat House. It was here that Houston died in 1863.

The Houston homesite passed through a variety of hands over the next fifty-plus years and eventually was moved about 300 yards, was stripped of its additions, and fell into disrepair. Students at the nearby college started a movement to restore the house and its grounds, eventually purchasing the house and part of the land with the intent to convert it into a museum. They also added the law office, the spring site (doubling as a baptizing pool), and additional acreage to help flesh out the grounds. Minor improvements were made, but it took state appropriations to finalize the improvements of the land and buildings to finally realize the site's use as a historic site and museum. The Steamboat House, which had also fallen into disrepair, saw a restoration and was moved to the grounds in 1936.

Visitor Information

HOURS: Tuesday–Saturday, 9 a.m.–4:30 p.m.; Sunday, noon–4:30 p.m.; closed Mondays
Admission fee charged

Located close to Woodland is a 67-foot-tall statue of Sam Houston, created by sculptor David Adickes and named *A Tribute to Courage*. It stands along I-45, between Dallas and Houston.

Governor's Mansion

1010 Colorado Street
Austin, TX 78602
512-305-8524
https://gov.texas.gov/first-lady/governors-mansion

Important Dates

Built: **1854**
Added to National Register of Historic Places: **August 25, 1970**
Designated a National Historic Landmark: **December 2, 1974**
Designated a Texas State Antiquities Landmark: **May 28, 1981**
Designated a Recorded Texas Historic Landmark: **1962**

The 1854 Governor's Mansion has been the home of every Texas governor since 1856. It is the oldest continuously inhabited house in Texas and the fourth oldest governor's mansion in the United States that has been continuously occupied by its chief executive, ca. 1980. *Courtesy of Texas State Preservation Board*

The original mansion, built by Abner Cook in a Greek Revival style, was 6,000 square feet. A 1914 remodel increased its size to 8,920 square feet and brought bathrooms to the house for the first time. *Courtesy of the Office of the Governor*

Site Description

The early history of Texas capitol buildings is a hodgepodge of locations: Washington-on-the-Brazos, Harrisburg, Velasco, Columbia, Houston. This constant relocation made it difficult to provide permanent housing for Texas's chief executive. The first attempt to build a permanent "President's House" came in the early 1840s. The wooden structure was short lived; it quickly fell into ruin and was torn down. In 1848, a stipend was provided for the leasing of quarters; the first four governors chose hotels or boardinghouses during legislative sessions. In 1854, $17,500 was appropriated for a permanent structure and furnishings, enough to build a residence and outbuildings.

A commission oversaw the selection of the architect, design, and construction of the new residence. They selected master builder Abner Cook, a North Carolina native who found his way to Austin via Georgia and Tennessee. Cook was a former construction apprentice and general contractor who became a self-taught architect. Upon moving to Austin in 1839, he supported himself through private commissions of houses and furniture and would eventually supervise the construction of the Texas State Penitentiary and three large Greek Revival homes in Austin—all three of which still stand: Woodlawn (1853), the Neill-Cochran House (1855), and the Governor's Mansion (1855).

Cook began construction on the latter home in 1854, adapting the popular Greek Revival style of architecture to the Texas frontier. An enterprising and diversified businessman, Cook owned a clay pit on the Colorado River, producing the buff-colored bricks for the mansion himself. Additionally, shortly after moving to the area, he partnered with Jacob Higgins in ownership of the Higgins Mill in Bastrop and used the mill to supply the home's lumber. The home was completed in 1856, and Governor Pease, who had been living in a rented home, became the first governor to occupy the mansion, spending his first night there on June 10.

The new 6,000-square-foot, two-story mansion included eleven rooms but no bathrooms and occupied

The mansion was partially destroyed by a four-alarm fire in 2008, when a Molotov cocktail was hurled at the structure. Then governor Rick Perry and his family were in Europe but had also relocated the previous October for a deferred maintenance project, one that included a new fire suppression system. *Photo by Larry D. Moore, 2008, courtesy of Texas State Preservation Board*

The family of Governor James Stephen Hogg, the first Texas governor to have been born in Texas. Following his service as the state's attorney general, he was elected to the office of governor in 1891, serving one term until 1895, the same year his wife died. *Courtesy of the Dolph Briscoe Center for American History, University of Texas at Austin*

the center of a block located a block southwest of the capitol grounds (bounded by Colorado, Lavaca, West Tenth, and West Eleventh Streets). Surrounded by trees and gardens, the home displayed distinctive features that Cook had used in other Austin homes. There were floor-length windows, wide hallways, and a deep veranda, all features designed to provide cooling ventilation in the hot Austin summers, while the "X-and-Stick" balustrades on the porch were a Cook trademark. A broad central hall divided the square layout, placing four main rooms on each floor, two on either side. A rear wing held a kitchen and servants' quarters, while 29-foot Ionic columns spanned across the front of the home.

Inside, the home was sparsely furnished, but each governor brought something new to the home. Sam Houston ordered the massive mahogany four-poster bed now found in the southeast bedroom. His eighth child, Temple Lea Houston, was the first baby born in that bed and in the mansion. James Stephen Hogg, the first native-born Texas governor, took office in 1891, and his four children used the mansion as their playground and home for wayward animals, sliding down the sweeping stair rail and collecting dogs, cats, squirrels, raccoons, and exotic birds. After his youngest son fell off the rail, Governor Hogg hammered tacks down the banister to stop the practice, evidence of which can still be found.

The mansion has undergone several major improvements and renovations, including a wide variety of routine maintenance just to stay modern. Gas lighting was added in the 1870s, telephones and indoor plumbing were added in the 1880s, and electricity was introduced in the 1890s. Governor Oscar B. Colquitt, in 1914, expanded the home's size to 8,920 square feet, adding living space upstairs and a family dining area and replacing the original kitchen facilities. This completed the basic floor plan that remains today, with a total of twenty-five rooms and seven bathrooms. During Allan Shivers's administration in the 1950s, a new roof was built and an HVAC system was installed for the first time. In the 1960s, First Lady Nellie Connally guided the landscaping of the formal gardens, which are still in use today.

The most extensive renovation was a complete refurbishment of the home between 1979 and 1982, with Governor Williams Clements. The Friends of the Governor's Mansion was established to help finance and oversee the efforts. Redecorations happened frequently, but when the 1989–90 legislature officially transferred supervision to the Texas Historical Commission, a new stipulation was enacted forbidding the change of any rooms open to the public or any alteration to the physical layout of the mansion. Governors and their families could, however, still decorate any private room to their own taste.

In January 2008, a deferred maintenance project began, displacing Governor Rick Perry's family and nearly emptying the home of all its contents. During the early morning of June 8, 2008, a four-alarm fire broke out, with evidence pointing toward targeting by an arsonist. In the summer of 2012, four years and millions of dollars later, the collections were returned and the First Family moved back in.

Inside, the Mansion Collection includes fine and decorative arts such as ceramics and glass and silver objects decorating the ten historic rooms in the oldest areas of the mansion. Developed in the 1960s by First Lady Jean Houston Daniel, the Governor's Memento Collection honors the occupants of the home since 1856, with an object representing every governor to live in the mansion. The furniture was primarily American-made during the first half of the nineteenth century, while the paintings and works on paper relate to Texas.

The Texas Governor's Mansion, now having served for over 160 years, is the oldest continuously occupied executive residence west of the Mississippi River and the fourth oldest in the United States. Free guided tours take visitors to ten curated rooms in the mansion.

> **Visitor Information**
>
> HOURS: Guided tours of the Texas Governor's Mansion are available Wednesdays, Thursdays, and Fridays from 2 to 4 p.m.
> *Entrance fees: Admission is only through free guided tours by reservation.*

The Sam Houston Bedroom is one of two official state bedrooms in the Governor's Mansion. Temple Lea Houston was born in the bed and was the first child born in the mansion. Sam Houston Allred, son to Governor and Mrs. James V. Allred, was born in the same bed in 1937. *Courtesy of the Office of the Governor*

First Lady Merle O'Daniel, wife to Pappy O'Daniel, is seen in the State Dining Room. She was very active in gardening, redecorating, and hosting large events, overseeing her husband's second inauguration celebration in 1941. More than 20,000 Texans attended the massive barbecue, which included 19,000 pounds of beef. *Courtesy of the Austin History Center, Austin Public Library*

Government 101

Texas State Capitol

1100 Congress Avenue
Austin, TX 78701

Visitor Center
112 East Eleventh Street
Austin, TX 78701
512-305-8400
https://tspb.texas.gov/prop/tc/tc/capitol.html

Important Dates

Built: **1885**
Designated a Registered Texas Historic Landmark: **1964**
Added to National Register of Historic Places: **June 22, 1970**
Designated a Texas State Antiquity Landmark: **May 28, 1981**
Designated a National Historic Landmark: **June 23, 1986**

Designed in 1881 by Elijah E. Myers, the Texas State Capitol was constructed from 1882 to 1888. At 302.64 feet tall, it is the sixth tallest state capitol. The cornerstone was laid on March 2, Texas Independence Day, and it opened on April 21, San Jacinto Day (although before its completion).

Site Description

The current Texas State Capitol is the third building to serve that purpose. The first was a simple wooden structure that had previously served as the national capital of the Texas Republic and continued as the seat of government upon Texas's admission to the Union. The second was built in 1853, on the site as the current capitol in downtown Austin. It was destroyed in 1881; however, plans had already been made to replace it with a new, much larger structure.

Construction of the Italian Renaissance Revival–style capitol was funded in 1876, authorizing the sale of public lands for the purpose. The builders, known as the Capitol Syndicate, were paid with over 3 million acres of public land in the Texas Panhandle, one of the largest barter transactions in recorded history. This tract would later become the largest cattle ranch in the world, the XIT Ranch.

The designer originally planned for the building to be clad entirely with Hill Country limestone quarried in Oatmanville (present-day Oak Hill), about 16 miles southwest. The high iron content of the limestone led to rapid discoloration. When owners of Granite Mountain, near Marble Falls, learned of the issue, they offered the necessary amount of sunset red granite as an alternative—free of charge. In order to accommodate the transport of the granite, the Austin and Northwestern Railroad was extended 2.3 miles. The project would include over nine hundred workers, including eighty-six granite cutters brought in from Scotland. While the building is built primarily of Oak Hill limestone, most of it is hidden behind the walls and on the foundation. Red granite was later used for many state government buildings in the Austin area. The cornerstone was laid on Texas Independence Day, March 2, 1885, and the building opened to the public on San Jacinto Day, April 21, 1888, not yet fully completed. Its official dedication in May of that year was marked by a weeklong celebration that attracted nearly 20,000 visitors to the dedication and surrounding events. The capitol is a four-story, central-block rectangular building and has symmetrical three-story wings extending west and east with a dome rising

THE SECOND CAPITOL OF TEXAS, BURNED IN 1881.

Above: The current capitol is the third of its kind, replacing the initial wooden structure and this one, built on the current capitol site in 1853 but destroyed by fire in 1881. Luckily, plans were already in place for a larger replacement. *Courtesy of the* Illustrated American

Left: The Goddess of Liberty is shown on the Texas State Capitol grounds, prior to installation on top of the rotunda, in this photograph taken in February 1888. *Courtesy of the Texas State Library and Archives Commission*

Government   103

Built in the Italian Renaissance Revival style, the capitol is modeled on the design of the US Capitol. The interior of the central portion forms an open rotunda beneath a dome, the ceiling of which is featured here.

from the center. It is modeled on the design of the US Capitol and contains 360,000 square feet of floor space, more than any other state capitol building. The capitol contains nearly four hundred rooms, and the interior of the central portion forms an open rotunda beneath its dome. Massive cast-iron staircases flanking the rotunda connect the various levels of the building (the two chambers of the Texas legislature meet in large, double-height spaces in the center of the two wings on the second floor, overlooked by public galleries), while the remainder of the building is filled with office space, courts, and archives.

The capitol building is surrounded by 22 acres of grounds scattered with statues and monuments. The four oldest monuments are the Heroes of the Alamo (1891), the Volunteer Firemen's Monument (1896), the Confederate Soldiers Monument (1903), and Terry's Texas Rangers (1907). The Texas Capitol Vietnam Veterans Monument was dedicated in 2014. Inside the building are portraits of all the past presidents of the Republic of Texas and the state governors. The south foyer features a large portrait of David Crockett, a painting of the surrender of General Santa Anna at the Battle of San Jacinto, and sculptures of Sam Houston and Stephen F. Austin. The Texas Confederate Museum was held here until 1920, when it was moved into the General Land Office Building, which today serves as the Capitol Visitors Center.

Seeing the capitol building as an apex along the horizon, the City of Austin enacted a local ordinance in 1931 that limited the height of new buildings to a maximum of 200 feet, aiming to preserve that visual preeminence. From that time until the early 1960s, only the University of Texas Main Building Tower was built higher than that limit. Despite opposition to future—and taller—projects, subsequent buildings defied that ordinance, culminating in the 395-foot-tall One American Center in 1982. A new bill was proposed that would protect "Capitol View Corridors" where construction would not be permitted. It was signed into law, and thirty state-protected viewing corridors are now in place.

Following a destructive fire in 1983 that killed one and injured four firefighters and a police officer, the capitol was in dire need of attention. The fire caused severe damage to the east wing and compromised much of the framing, which was composed largely of exposed cast-iron posts and beams.

A new Goddess of Liberty statue was placed on the dome (the original eventually made its way to

Visitor Information

HOURS: Standard hours are Monday through Friday, 7 a.m.–10 p.m., and Saturday and Sunday, 9 a.m.–5 p.m. Information and tours are conducted Monday through Friday, 8:30 a.m.–4:30 p.m.; Saturday, 9:30 a.m.–3:30 p.m.; and Sunday, noon–3:30 p.m.

Regular legislative session is held January through May in odd-numbered years. *Admission by donation. Fees charged for additional/special programs and exhibitions.*

Art abounds in the rotunda of the capitol; a mosaic representing the six nations of Texas's history is seen here. The central rotunda is hung with portraits of past Republic of Texas presidents and state governors. It is also a whispering gallery. Multiple portraits, paintings, and sculptures can be found throughout.

The two chambers of the Texas legislature meet in large, double-height spaces in the center of the two wings on the second floor and are overlooked by public galleries on the third floor. The Texas House of Representatives Chamber is seen here.

the Bullock Texas State History Museum), and the Old Texas Land Office was rebuilt and updated, with the Capitol Visitors Center moved inside. In order to minimize any effect of appearance to the building, an expansion to the capitol was built beneath the north plaza, connecting to the existing capitol underground. The extension was completed in 1993 and nearly doubled the square footage available to capitol occupants. The entire project was completed in 1995, and in 1997 the park-like grounds received an additional renovation and restoration.

Lyndon Baines Johnson Boyhood Home

100 Ladybird Lane
Johnson City, TX 78636
830-868-7128
https://www.nps.gov/lyjo/planyourvisit/visitboyhoodhome.htm

Important Dates

Built: **1901**
Added to National Register of Historic Places:
   December 2, 1969
Designated a National Historic Landmark:
   May 23, 1966
Designated Recorded Texas Historic Landmark:
   1965 *(boyhood home)*, **1967** *(birthplace)*

The president's boyhood home was built in 1901 by Blanco County sheriff W. C. Russell. The president's father, Samuel Ealy Johnson Jr., paid $2,925 for the house, which is built in the Folk Victorian style, and the surrounding 1.75 acres. Johnson lived here from age five until his 1924 high school graduation.

The LBJ ranch is located on the north side of US Route 290, with its main access through the state park and historic site. Among the sites preserved are the president's first school, his reconstructed birthplace, the Texas White House (*seen here*), and the Johnson Family Cemetery.

Site Description

While the boyhood home of President Lyndon Baines Johnson is the property listed as a National Historic Landmark, it is part of the larger Lyndon Baines Johnson National Historical Park. The park, located about 50 miles west of Austin, protects the birthplace, home, ranch, and final resting place of the thirty-sixth president of the United States. The park was authorized in 1969 as Lyndon B. Johnson National Historic Site and redesignated as a National Historical Park in 1980. The site covers approximately 1,570 acres, and the Johnson family has continued to donate land to the property, the most recent addition coming in 1995.

The park consists of two discontinuous areas, the Johnson City District and the LBJ Ranch District, which are separated by the Pedernales River. The Johnson City District, located in Johnson City, contains the boyhood home and President Johnson's paternal grandparents' log cabin settlement. It is also the location

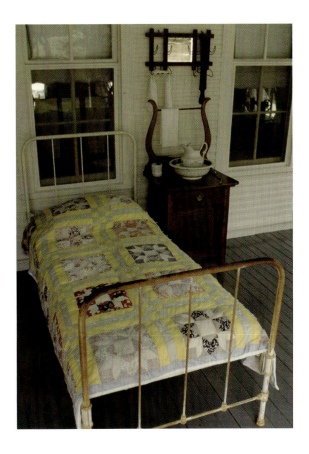

Photograph of the LBJ Boyhood Home's bedroom in Johnson City, Texas. The boyhood home is an 1880s Victorian house where the future president lived with his parents from age five. *Courtesy of UNT Libraries, The Portal to Texas History*

Government 107

Lyndon Johnson was very proud of his roots in Hill Country, Texas. In 1964, he hired architect J. Roy White to reconstruct his birthplace home, which was built in 1889 and torn down in the 1940s. It is the only presidential birthplace reconstructed, refurbished, and interpreted by an incumbent president.

of the national park visitor center. Located about 14 miles west of Johnson City is the LBJ Ranch District, sitting along the north side of the Pedernales River. The ranch was the Johnson family retreat during his period of greatest influence and was commonly referred to as the "Texas White House" because the president spent roughly 20 percent of his time there while in office. It is also the site of the family cemetery and gives visitors a perspective of LBJ's life during his time in office.

The Johnson City Unit is located on the south side of Johnson City. Visitors are welcomed to the visitor center, located in a former hospital, which provides an introduction to the park, exhibits, and films about President Johnson and his wife, Claudia Alta Taylor, more affectionately known as "Lady Bird." Just north of the center is the Johnson Boyhood Home, designated a National Historic Landmark in 1965. This 1880s Victorian home is where Johnson lived with his parents from the age of five. It was restored by Johnson during his tenure as president. West of the visitor center is the Johnson Settlement. This restored prairie contains the dogtrot house of President Johnson's grandfather, as well as a handful of other nineteenth-century agricultural buildings.

The LBJ Ranch, located about 14 miles west of Johnson City, has its main access through the Lyndon B. Johnson State Park and Historic Site, lying on the south bank of the Pedernales River. This location offers a bevy of preserved sites, including the president's first school—the old Junction School—as well as his reconstructed birthplace, the Texas White House, and

Lyndon Johnson, seen here in 1915 at the family home, lived in the boyhood home until his graduation in 1924. *Courtesy of the Library of Congress*

the Johnson Family Cemetery, which is the final resting place of both the president and Lady Bird Johnson. Visitors are provided a permit and take a self-guided auto driving tour from the state park visitor center to see the sites. Due to structural issues, the Texas White House and Pool House were temporarily closed to visitors in August 2018.

The birthplace home is adjacent to the LBJ Ranch. It was constructed in the 1880s by Samuel Ealy Johnson Sr., the president's grandfather. It was here that the president's father, Samuel Ealy Johnson Jr., brought Rebekah Baines Johnson, his new bride, in 1907. On August 27 the following year, Lyndon Baines Johnson was born in the home. The Johnsons would live at the home until 1913, when they moved to Johnson City. The Johnsons sold the house in 1923, and it was demolished after it had deteriorated, although some material was salvaged and used in the construction of a smaller house on the same site in 1935. The Johnson City Foundation acquired that latter building in 1964 and reconstructed it to its 1907 size and appearance. It is now open to the public, filled with authentic pieces and family mementos.

The boyhood home in Johnson City was built in 1901. While modest, it reflects the Victorian style of the period. Following the family's move there in 1913, the house remained the official residence of LBJ until he married Lady Bird in 1934. On the east porch of this house, LBJ made his first political speech as he ran for Congress in 1937. This home was dedicated as a museum in May 1965. Much like the birthplace residence, the home contains authentic period items and furnishings.

The LBJ Ranch is in the heart of the Hill Country and remained the home of Lady Bird Johnson until the early 1990s. The history of the ranch dates back to the Republic of Texas, when Rachael Means, a young widow from Georgia, was granted a tract that included this property. In 1872, the Means family sold the land, and it changed hands several times until 1894. A German family by the name of Meyer constructed a one-room stone house on the property, which became the nucleus of the current home. In 1909, the property was purchased by Clarence White Martin, a relative of the Johnsons, who acquired the property in 1951.

Across the Pedernales, at the state park historical site, sits a handful of buildings and attractions. The area was home to numerous prehistoric peoples, and over 25,000 artifacts have been located on the property, indicating the usage of a stone quarry and midden. Besides the visitor center, which houses an exhibit of Johnson memorabilia alongside an auditorium, the park includes the 1870s Behrens Cabin and the Sauer-Beckmann Farmstead, a historical farm operated as it was in 1918, in addition to a nature trail through wildlife enclosures, an outdoor amphitheater, a swimming pool, tennis courts, a baseball diamond, and picnic areas.

Visitor Information

HOURS: 9 a.m.–5 p.m. daily
No entrance fees

Located in the former Pedernales Hospital, the building became the Lyndon B. Johnson National Historic Park Visitor Center in 1994. Exhibits feature the life and accomplishments of LBJ and Lady Bird's commitment to the environment, and each is accompanied by a thirty-minute movie.

LBJ State Park and Historic Site Visitor Center

HOURS: 8:30 a.m.–4:30 p.m. daily
PARK HOURS: 8 a.m.–5 p.m. daily

This site is located on Highway 290, approximately 14 miles west of Johnson City, and you can begin a self-guided driving tour of the LBJ Ranch with a required free permit. An audio CD is available for purchase. Exhibits, movies, and a gift store are available, as are restrooms and water fountains.

Hangar Visitor Center

HOURS: 9 a.m.–5 p.m. daily

This visitor center serves as the information station for the LBJ Ranch District and features exhibits on life and work at the ranch, Lady Bird Johnson, and the Space Race. A fourteen-minute film is available, and a bookstore is located on-site.

The one-room Junction School served Gillespie County for over thirty-seven years. A four-year-old Lyndon Baines Johnson attended school here briefly before a whooping-cough epidemic closed the school early. The family moved to Johnson City by the start of the next school year.

Samuel T. Rayburn House

Samuel T. Rayburn House State Historic Site
890 West State Highway 56
Bonham, TX 75418
903-583-5558
https://thc.texas.gov/historic-sites/sam-rayburn-house

Important Dates

Built: **1916**
Designated a Recorded Texas Historical Landmark: **1965**
Added to National Register of Historic Places: **June 5, 1972**
Designated a National Historic Landmark: **May 11, 1976**
Designated a Texas State Historic Site: **1975**
Designated a Texas State Antiquities Landmark: **January 1, 2000**

After having served as a US congressman for a few years, Rayburn had saved enough money to build a home for himself and his family. In 1914, he purchased 121 acres of land, and construction of their new two-story clapboard home was completed by 1916.

110   TREASURES OF TEXAS

Site Description

Samuel Taliaferro Rayburn (January 6, 1882–November 16, 1961) served as the forty-third Speaker of the United States House of Representatives. He would serve in that role three times as well as House majority leader and two-time House minority leader during his twenty-four terms as a Democratic congressman (1913–61). He holds the record for the longest tenure as Speaker of the US House of Representatives, having served for over seventeen years in one single run. He was a protégé of John Nance Garner and would become a mentor to Lyndon Baines Johnson.

Born in Tennessee, Rayburn moved early in life to Windom, Texas, in 1887. Following a brief period as a schoolteacher, Rayburn ran and narrowly won his first public election to the Texas House of Representatives in 1906. He would graduate from the University of Texas School of Law, gaining admission to the bar in 1908. On January 10, 1911, at the age of twenty-nine and with only four years as an elected official under his belt, Rayburn became the youngest Speaker of the Texas House of Representatives. The position was viewed and used as mostly ceremonial; however, by law the position was very powerful. Under Rayburn's leadership, he helped codify the Speaker's power, passing numerous pieces of legislation, such as shorter working hours for women, child labor laws, and appropriations for a Confederate widows' home and a tuberculosis sanatorium.

In 1912, he won election to the US House of Representatives, sparking a stint of continually winning reelections until his death in 1961. During his tenure in Congress, he would be involved in helping pass numerous antitrust and railroad-related pieces of legislation, legislation that established the United States Highway System, and New Deal bills that resulted in the formation of the Securities and Exchange Commission, the Federal Communications Commission, the Public Utilities Holding Company Act, the Emergency Railroad Transportation Act, and the Rural Electrification Act. He supported projects that would make life easier for farmers and rural Americans, such as dams and farm-to-market roads; helped create the Flood Control Act of 1936; and established the Southwestern Power Administration, the Soil Conservation Service, and the Civilian Conservation Corps. During World War II,

Photograph of twenty-nine-year-old Sam Rayburn, taken in 1911. At the time, he was serving as the Speaker in the Texas House of Representatives. *Courtesy of UNT Libraries, The Portal to Texas History*

This photograph of the Sam Rayburn House in Bonham, Texas, shows the home prior to its renovation and the removal of the second-story balcony. *Courtesy of UNT Libraries, The Portal to Texas History*

Up the road in downtown Bonham sits a museum and library dedicated to the career of one of Texas's best-known statesmen. However, at the state historic site, one will find extensive exhibits in the visitor center, as seen here, and throughout the property.

he supported the Lend-Lease Act and helped garner funding for the Manhattan Project. Only Rayburn and five other congressmen were aware of this operation; not even most of the president's cabinet or the vice president knew of its existence.

Following the war, Rayburn—as either House minority leader or Speaker—helped pass the Marshall Plan, deal with the Dixiecrats, form and push through civil rights legislation and Truman's Fair Deal, and combat McCarthyism. When Senator Johnson became majority leader, he worked with Eisenhower to pass numerous landmark bills such as the National Interstate and Defense Highways Act, bills that established NASA and the FAA, the National Defense Education Act, the Colorado River Storage Project Act, and the Civil Rights Acts of 1957 and 1960. Additionally, he helped usher Alaska and Hawaii into the United States as the forty-ninth and fiftieth states.

Following his election as House majority leader in 1937 and after the death of William B. Bankhead, Rayburn was elevated to the position of Speaker of the House. He would lead House Democrats from 1940 to 1961, serving as Speaker from 1940 to 1947, 1949

Multiple Rayburn vehicles can be found at the state historic site: a 1951 Dodge Express truck, a 1953 Chevrolet four-door sedan, a 1955 Plymouth Savoy, Rayburn's 1948 International Harvester, a Farmall Model H tractor used on the farm, and Rayburn's 1947 Cadillac Fleetwood.

to 1953, and again from 1955 to 1961. During periods of Republican House control, Rayburn continued his leadership of the Democrats, serving twice as House minority leader, from 1947 to 1949 and 1953 to 1955.

Rayburn's Home

On a 125-acre farmstead on the western outskirts of Bonham sits the home of Sam Rayburn, now a state historic site. Located on the property, along with the main house, are a storage barn, shed, garage, wellhouse, and barn. The main house is a two-and-a-half-story wood-frame structure, with a gabled roof and clapboard exterior. A shed-roof portico protects the main facade and is supported with two-story Tuscan columns.

The home was built in 1916. When originally constructed, the home was smaller than its current iteration but was still a twelve-room farmhouse that cost $2,800. The current configuration came during a major 1934 expansion designed by Dallas architect W. B. Yarborough. A new kitchen was added a few years later. Rayburn occupied the house until his death in 1961. Since he died divorced and childless, his sister lived in the house until her death in 1969, after which it was taken over by the Sam Rayburn Foundation.

In 1972, the foundation turned most of the property (except the barn) over to the state for historic preservation. Three years later, the home opened as a museum under the operation of the Texas Historical Commission. All the furnishings seen are original and remain as they were when the Rayburns lived there, including Rayburn's 1947 Cadillac. Out of the three residences known to be associated with Rayburn, this one is the best preserved and considered to be the most evocative of his life. Throughout his congressional tenure, Rayburn traveled from DC to the Fannin County home to relax with family and tend to farm and ranch work.

Visitor Information

HOURS: Tuesday–Saturday, 10 a.m.–4 p.m.

Self-guided tours at 10:00, 10:40, and 11:20 a.m. and 1:00, 1:40, 2:20, and 3:00 p.m.
Admission fee charged

The Sam Rayburn House State Historic Site preserves the real stories of Sam Rayburn's life. Remaining as they were when he lived in the home, the house and grounds are flush—as seen here in Sam's bedroom and office—with original furnishings, photographs, and personal family belongings.

Government 113

John Nance Garner House

Briscoe-Garner Museum
333 North Park Street
Uvalde, TX 78801
830-278-5018
https://briscoecenter.org/briscoe-garner-museum/

Important Dates

Built: **1920**
Added to National Register of Historic Places:
　December 8, 1976
Designated a National Historic Landmark:
　December 8, 1976
Designated a Texas State Antiquities Landmark:
　May 28, 1981
Designated a Recorded Texas Historical
　Landmark: **1962**

This was the home of Vice President Garner and his wife, Ettie, from 1920 until Ettie's death in 1948. Garner continued living in the house until 1952, when he moved to a small cottage on the property and donated this house to the City of Uvalde as a memorial to Ettie.

Site Description

The John Nance Garner House, located in Uvalde, was the home of US vice president John Nance Garner and his wife, Ettie, from 1920 until Ettie's death in 1948. Garner, a native of Uvalde, lived in the home until 1952, when he moved to a small cottage on the property and donated the main house to the city as a memorial to his late wife. The house is known as the Briscoe-Garner Museum and also as the Ettie R. Garner Memorial Building.

Designed by the most prominent architect in San Antonio (if not all of Texas), Atlee B. Ayers, the two-story Garner home is an H-shaped tan brick home with dark wood shingles highlighted by a row of red clay

Seen here in a photograph taken some time during the 1930s, John Garner was nicknamed "Cactus Jack." He was a Democratic politician and lawyer who served as President Roosevelt's vice president from 1933 to 1941—one of only two individuals, along with Schuyler Colfax, to have served as both vice president and Speaker of the House. *Courtesy of the Library of Congress*

The home, the front of which is seen in this blueprint, is a two-story, H-shaped, hip-roofed brick house. It was built to plans by Atlee B. Ayers, the most prominent architect in San Antonio, and possibly the entire state. *Courtesy of the Library of Congress*

Government 115

In 2011, the Garner Museum was renamed the Briscoe-Garner Museum. Dolph Briscoe served as governor of Texas from 1973 to 1979. He is seen here in 1973. *Courtesy of the Library of Congress*

Briscoe exhibit at the Garner House. The second floor of the home was converted in 2011 for commemoration of Briscoe's life and career as Texas governor in the 1970s. *Courtesy of the Briscoe-Garner Museum, Briscoe Center Archives*

tiles. Ayers has designed multiple historic buildings for a variety of universities, governmental and private businesses, and five Texas county courthouse projects, and he served as the state architect of Texas from 1914 and 1917 and designed the Administration Building at Randolph Air Force Base, also listed as a National Historic Landmark, in 1931. After Garner moved out, the building housed the community library until 1973, when it became a museum, with the first-floor displays documenting Garner's life and career.

John Nance Garner III (November 22, 1868–November 7, 1967) was known among his contemporaries as "Cactus Jack." He began his career as the county judge of Uvalde County, before serving in the Texas House of Representatives from 1898 to 1902 and then winning the election to represent Texas in the US House of Representatives in 1902. Garner served as the House minority leader from 1929 to 1931 before being elevated as the thirty-ninth Speaker of the United States House of Representatives from 1931 to 1933. Garner sought the Democratic presidential nomination in the 1932 election but agreed to serve as FDR's running mate. They won in 1932 and were reelected in 1936. A conservative southerner, Garner opposed Roosevelt in a handful of New Deal legislature and finally broke with him in 1937 over the topic of Supreme Court enlargement. Garner would seek the presidency in 1940, only to lose out to a third term for Roosevelt, who would choose Henry Wallace as his running mate. He and Schuyler Colfax (Ulysses S. Grant's vice president) are the only two politicians to serve as both vice president and Speaker of the House.

Garner's main house and the cottage he retired to are located on the property, with the home transferred from Uvalde to the University of Texas at Austin in 1999, becoming a division of the Dolph Briscoe Center for American History. Extensive renovations in 2011 are now complete; the first floor of the home is still devoted to Garner, while the second floor features new exhibits dedicated to Dolph Briscoe, the forty-first governor of Texas and a Uvalde native.

Visitor Information

HOURS: Tuesday to Saturday, 9 a.m.–4 p.m.; closed Sunday and Monday
Admission: Free

Dealey Plaza Historic District

Covering 15 acres, it is roughly bounded by Pacific Avenue, Market Street, Jackson Street, and right-of-way of Dallas.
Dallas, TX 75202

Important Dates

Built: **1890**
Period of Importance: **November 22, 1963**
Added to National Register of Historic Places:
   April 19, 1993
Designated a National Historic Landmark:
   October 12, 1993

Modern view of Dealey Plaza looking toward the Texas School Book Depository. The historic colonnade can be seen to the left, and next to that is the edge of the wood fence at the top of the infamous "Grassy Knoll."

Photograph of Dealey Plaza and the surrounding area by Squire Haskins in May 1972. The plaza, which is split down the middle by Main Street, sits above a group of railroads and a freeway. *Courtesy of UNT Libraries, The Portal to Texas History*

Site Description

Located in the West End district of downtown Dallas, Dealey Plaza had long been known as the birthplace of Dallas. However, on November 22, 1963, the city park became the site of the most famous assassination of a national leader since President Abraham Lincoln was murdered at Ford's Theater nearly a century earlier.

The city of Dallas grew out of the failed efforts of John Neely Bryan to start a trading post in Texas. He chose a spot at the three-forks area of the Trinity River in 1839, but when a treaty removed all tribes from northern Texas and removed half of his customer base in the process, Bryan pivoted toward establishing a permanent settlement. That little town became Dallas, with Bryan proving influential in its growth as the city gained a foothold and turned into the county seat prior to the Civil War.

Dallas, like many southern towns, suffered during the war. However, this would give way to comparative prosperousness in the Reconstruction South. Dallas would annex East Dallas and Oak Cliff, growing away from its downtown core. As Dallas moved into the twentieth century, a new figure rose to supplant Bryan's influence. George Bannerman Dealey, publisher of the *Dallas Morning News* and leader of efforts to clean up Dallas and push reform, pushed the City Beautiful movement toward Dallas. After Dallas suffered through

Government 119

a massive 1908 flood, Dealey saw an opportunity when he witnessed city-planning engineer George Kessler's layout of the 1904 World's Fair in St. Louis. Dealey recruited him to redesign the state fairgrounds in Dallas and then pushed for his hiring to design a plan for the entire city.

The capstone of Kessler's beautification plan for Dallas was public park space on land donated by Dealey, where today the Stemmons Freeway crosses Commerce, Main, and Elm, just west of the Triple Underpass. While Dealey typically let his actions speak for themselves, his son Ted convinced him to allow the city to name the park space after him. It would become a focal point in civic pride. However, a new interstate system and city growth would move the business center away from the plaza to the east and north. By 1963, if you asked a Dallas resident, the most distinctive feature of Dealey Plaza was a Hertz billboard situated on top of the Texas School Book Depository Building.

On November 22, 1863, President John F. Kennedy was riding in a presidential motorcade through Dealey Plaza. In the vehicle with him were his wife, Jacqueline, and Texas governor John Connally, and his wife, Nellie. As they drove past the School Book Depository toward the railroad underpass, shots rang out, striking both the governor and president, the latter of whom would succumb to his wounds. The morning following the assassination, Dealey Plaza was the central focus of the world. Crowds of mourners and the curious swarmed the plaza to place flowers, cards, letters, and impromptu memorials along Elm Street. Crowds filled the plaza for months, and—while the area would continue to garner attention over the years—the focus had been drawn away from the city's founding and growth. Many residents favored leveling the School Book Depository Building, in the hopes it would drown out the attention paid to the site. However, others wanted to capitalize on it.

Dallas County commissioners optioned the building for purchase in 1976, saving it from the wrecking ball. A campaign began the following year to convert the sixth floor of the building, where Lee Harvey Oswald's perch had been determined to be located, into a historical exhibit. The group expanded and raised funds throughout the 1980s to get the doors open for the new exhibit. Eventually, the exhibit became a museum, which opened in 1989. The museum, coupled with the 1991 Oliver Stone film *JFK*, brought new awareness to the assassination and gave a boost to Dealey Plaza. Fundraising efforts tied to the fiftieth anniversary of the assassination led to another phase of beautification to the park, as it upgraded the plaza's landscaping, fountains, and pergolas as close to its original state as possible.

Important Buildings in the District

Much of what you see in the Dealey Plaza National Historic District is similar to what was there in November 1963, with the addition of the Sixth Floor Visitor Center, the Kennedy Memorial, and its adjacent plaza. Here, we will work our way around the plaza in a clockwise direction, starting with the obvious focal point of the School Book Depository.

Texas School Book Depository
(411 Elm Street)

The seven-story red brick building served as a warehouse and showroom for the Rock Island Plow Company of Illinois. By 1939, space was leased to a variety of tenants, including the Texas School Book Depository Company, which used floors 4 through 6 for storage and corporate office space. On the sixth floor, on November 22, 1963, workers were laying new flooring. By 12:30 p.m., they had gone to lunch, and Lee Harvey Oswald set up his sniper's nest.

Sixth Floor Visitor Center
(Houston Street near Pacific Avenue)

The visitor center, dedicated to President Kennedy's legacy, was constructed in 1989 and is connected to the warehouse/museum building by a 65-foot freestanding brick elevator. The museum's two evidential areas, the sniper's perch in the southeast corner and the area where the rifle was found, are protected by clear glass walls, with no evidence on display.

Dallas Textile ("Dal-Tex") Building
(501 Elm Street)

Constructed in 1902, this seven-story brick building was one of the earliest West End warehouses and was rehabilitated and remodeled in 1986. In 1963, it was occupied by Dallas Textile manufacturers and sales personnel, but some theorists believe that another sniper was set up on the fourth floor. Also, the office of Abraham Zapruder, who filmed the "home movie" footage of the assassination, was here.

Dallas County Records Building and Annex / Hall of Records and Annex
(500–505 Elm Street)

The Dallas County Records Building, sitting across the street from the reflecting pools, was constructed in 1928, and its annex in 1955. Both have seen some modifications but have been carefully restored to retain their original look.

Dallas County Criminal Courts Building
(500 Main Street)

Primarily the county jail, the first couple of floors of this 1915 building were devoted to the courtrooms and administration offices of Dallas's criminal courts system. It has hosted its fair share of celebrity outlaws, such as Clyde Barrow and Benny Binion, and it is where Jack Ruby was tried for the murder of Lee Harvey Oswald and served time.

Old Dallas County Courthouse/ "Old Red"
(Houston and Commerce Streets)

The Old Dallas County Courthouse is best known as "Old Red." Built in 1892, the courthouse building was intricately restored to serve as the Old Red Museum of Dallas County History & Culture. It is now home both to exhibits and the Texas Fifth Circuit Court of Appeals. It is open 9 a.m.–5 p.m. daily and charges admission.

Original black-and-white photographic negative taken by *Dallas Times Herald* staff photographer William Allen on November 22, 1963, showing the view looking onto Elm Street and toward the Triple Underpass from the re-creation of the sniper's perch. *Courtesy of UNT Libraries, The Portal to Texas History*

The Dallas County Criminal Courts Building dates back as far as 1915, with additions coming in 1928 and 1955. Here, Jack Ruby was tried, Clyde Barrow and Pretty Boy Floyd spent time, and inside the old jail are the old hanging gallows.

The 1892 Dallas County Courthouse served as the Old Red Museum of Dallas County History and Culture for years. In 2022, renovations returned it to its original civic use as the new home to the Texas Fifth Circuit Court of Appeals, with exhibits displayed here and in multiple county structures.

United States Post Office Terminal Annex / Federal Building
(southwest corner of Commerce and Houston Streets)

This five-story white-colored building houses the US Post Office's bulk mail facility, with a main facade and entrance on Houston Street and a secondary delivery entrance on Commerce Street.

Missouri-Kansas-Texas (MKT) Railroad Yards
(south of Pacific Avenue, west of Houston Street, and north of Elm Street)

Site of a very active railyard for many years, this area was the old "West End" warehouse district. Many of these warehouses have been renovated into restaurants, stores, and offices.

Kennedy Memorial and Plaza
(east half of double block shared with Old Red)

This 50-by-50-foot open-space memorial to JFK is surrounded by 30-foot-high vertically scored concrete walls. It was designed by architect Philip Johnson, and narrow entries to the cenotaph are open the entire height at midpoints on the north and south sides, with an 8-foot-square gray-black granite slab with Kennedy's name engraved in gold in the center.

Bryan's Original Settlement Site
(west of Houston Street, north of depository building)

The plaza area was part of the original land grant to Bryan in 1843. There is evidence of the first Anglo- and African American settlement of Dallas, but also prehistoric Native American settlements and prehistoric animal deposits.

Visitor Information

While there is no central Dealey Plaza headquarters, the obvious place to visit for further information or assistance is the Sixth Floor Museum, located in the former Texas School Book Depository, which is now known as the Dallas County Administration Building.

Sixth Floor Museum

411 Elm Street
Dallas, TX 75202
214-747-6660
https://www.jfk.org
HOURS: Wednesday–Sunday, 10 a.m.–5 p.m.
Admission fee charged. There are additional charges for public programs and educational programs.

Entertainment

SITES
1. Majestic Theatre (1929)
2. Highland Park Shopping Village (1931)
3. Bastrop State Park (1933)
4. Fair Park Texas Centennial Buildings (1936)

They say everything in Texas is bigger . . . grander. If you work hard, you better play hard. There is no shortage of ways to be entertained in the Lone Star State. Countless museums and art galleries, dance halls and concert venues, nature offerings and the outdoors, theater, the movies, and music for kids, adults, and families—there have been multitudes of ways to relax. Nearly every site I come across brags about being the first—or one of the first—to get air-conditioning into their operation. A/C in Texas is definitely a recreational need when trying to beat the heat and humidity.

Majestic Theatre

224 East Houston Street
San Antonio, TX 78205
210-226-5700
https://www.majesticempire.com

Important Dates

Opened: **June 14, 1929**
Reopened: **1989**
Added to National Register of Historic Places:
    October 1, 1975
Designated a Registered Texas Historic
    Landmark: **1991**
Designated a National Historic Landmark:
    April 19, 1993

Looking toward the stage from the back of the theater. The elaborate setting was designed by theater architect John Eberson, famous for his "atmospheric" theaters. Here the stage is closed off with the Majestic's historic fire curtain.

126   TREASURES OF TEXAS

Site Description

If not for the 76-foot marquee and ticket office along the front of the first floor and the neon sign cascading down the edge of the building, the structure that is home to the Majestic Theatre might be mistaken for just another San Antonio office building. However, inside, one is greeted with one of the most opulent show palaces in America.

Under the direction of architect John Eberson, construction on the eighteen-story office building began in 1927. When theater owner Karl Hoblitzelle leased the land from J. M. Nix, there was a stipulation: no building, or any improvement, could be occupied for theatrical, motion picture, or amusement purposes at any time until April 5, 1928. When the theater opened on June 14, 1929, that date had well passed. Eberson's design had taken nearly two years and stood as the largest—and also one of the last—of his famed "atmospheric" theaters.

Hoblitzelle, a native of St. Louis, Missouri, first worked in real estate for his uncle after high school. Jobs at a soap factory and selling vegetables from the family farm as a market trader followed before he took a job as an event manager at the Louisiana Purchase Exposition of 1904 in St. Louis. During the expo, Hoblitzelle became motivated by the performers and concession operators who indicated that the South, particularly Texas, lacked the venues needed to showcase their work and talent. In 1905, Karl and his brother George cofounded the Interstate Theatres Company in St. Louis, operating vaudeville theaters in Texas and eventually turning it into a chain of 160 movie theaters throughout Texas and the Southeast.

Eberson, a native of Austria-Hungary, immigrated to the United States in 1901 and settled in St. Louis. There, he worked with an electrical contracting company before affiliating himself with Johnson Realty and Construction Company, a theater architecture and construction company. Eberson and Johnson traveled the eastern US, promoting opera houses in small towns, which Eberson would design and Johnson would build.

In 1904, Eberson moved his family to Hamilton, Ohio, where he designed local buildings while continuing his pursuit of designing opera houses. His first, the 350-seat Hamilton Jewel, was constructed in an existing, pre–Civil War building. Following a move to Chicago in

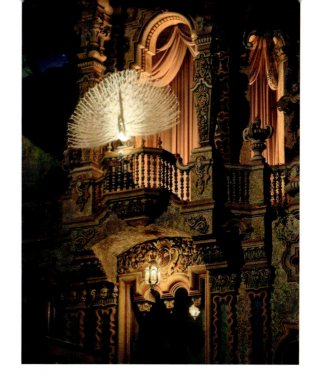

The theater's design was inspired by Spanish mission, baroque, and Mediterranean styles. At its opening, it was hailed as "Mexican Cloister" architecture.

Located throughout the lobby are intricate works of art, designed to transport moviegoers to a more exotic place and meant to create an illusion from the moment you arrived to the moment you left.

1910, he increased his theater architectural commissions, with Hoblitzelle's Interstate Amusement Company as an early client. Through his work with Hoblitzelle, Eberson enhanced his work as he began experimenting

Entertainment 127

with atmospheric design, beginning primarily with the Dallas Majestic (1921), Terre Haute's Indiana Theatre (1922), and Wichita's Orpheum Theatre (1922). When he took on the Houston Majestic in 1923, he had created his first full atmospheric theater. This new style evoked the feeling of a particular time and place for patrons, generally through the use of technology, ornamentation, and architectural elements providing a sense of being outdoors.

This new theater design carried over to nearly one hundred movie palaces in dozens of states and internationally. Considered to be the grandest was the Majestic in San Antonio. Located inside an eighteen-story office building, the theater alone covers 1.8 million cubic feet, occupies most of the block on which it stands, rises six stories, and was the first in the state to be totally air-conditioned. The double-balconied auditorium features four thousand seats facing a 150-by-100-foot stage equipped for a wide variety of productions. Originally, the theater was segregated, with the upper balcony reserved for people of color. It was reached by a separate stairway and elevator, with its own lobby entrance and ticket booth at the east side of the building.

The Majestic's auditorium lived up to its name. The basic design is asymmetrical and elaborately decorated. From the rear walls to the proscenium arch are niches, alcoves, grottos, pergolas, recesses, and campaniles. An ancient castle scene of elaborate baroque ornamentation dominated the east, while the west featured a Spanish-Moorish hillside village. Filling out the scene were an abundance of sculptured foliage, statuary, and banners and a flock of twenty-eight birds—including pigeons, parrots, doves, and more—led by a white peacock, perched high on a balcony at stage right (a newer version of which has since replaced the tattered original). Indirect lighting and a special-effect "cloud machine" produced a realistic sky effect. The technology could manipulate the twinkle rate of the stars as clouds passed overhead.

Above: Taken during the Southwest's May 1943 premiere of *The Bombardier* in San Antonio, this image shows moviegoers waiting under the theater marquee and large advertisements for the celebrities appearing at the premiere. *Courtesy of UNT Libraries, The Portal to Texas History*

Right: Segregation was commonplace in 1920s Texas, and the theater's upper balcony, seen in this photo, was reserved for African American patrons. It was reached by a separate stairway and elevator through a separate lobby entrance. *Courtesy of UNT Libraries, The Portal to Texas History*

On the production side, a stage fly grid system, complete with hydraulic lifts, was in place to move tons of equipment. The main electric switchboard was so powerful it could supply the electrical needs for a town with 15,000 residents. An auxiliary electrical control system operated from the upper balcony, while beneath the stage lay lavish dressing rooms. Outside, a portico at street level is supported by Tuscan columns of polished granite, with a massive brick edifice rising above them, accentuated in symmetrical fashion with small windows. Rising above the office spaces, the building terminates at eighteen stories with twin pavilions with rounded arches, separated by a projecting mission-style parapet.

The last days of regular stage performances at the Majestic came as World War II wound to a close. San Antonio, home to five major military installations all operating at full strength, attracted some of the most glamorous stars to its stage, and while the theater continued to operate, it saw a general decline in attendance. Newer, more streamlined, and space age–style designs began to pop up in surrounding suburbs. By 1974, the only films being shown at the Majestic were blaxploitation films and Spanish-language movies. The doors closed on December 31, 1974, with only the upper office floors remaining occupied.

The theater was listed on the National Register of Historic Places in 1975, and the following year was donated by the Hoblitzelle Interests to the newly formed Majestic Foundation. For the next decade, a wide variety of concerts, performing arts events, and touring Broadway productions graced the stage. The Las Casas Foundation, dedicated to the preservation and restoration of San Antonio's historic buildings for cultural use, ensured that the Majestic would continue to flourish. They raised $4.5 million to restore the theater's original artwork and design, new sound systems and acoustical enhancements were installed, and even the carpet and upholstery were woven to re-create the original design.

The Majestic reopened in 1989 as home to the San Antonio Symphony and a venue for touring productions and concerts. An expansion, which included the acquisition and assimilation of the Little Brady Building (208 East Houston Street) took place in 1995–96, allowing the venue to continue to meet the changing needs of symphonic and theatrical productions. Countless movies have rolled across the screen, entertainers from George Burns to Chris Rock have entertained audiences, and productions from concerts to special events to Broadway productions have graced the stage. The theater remains one of the most magnificent show palaces in Texas and still ranks as one of the most luxurious in the United States.

> **Visitor Information**
>
> HOURS: Majestic Theatre is open primarily to those who are attending performances. Occasionally, the theater is open for tours and by appointment. Refer to the website for up-to-date information and availability.
> *Admission fee charged*

The marquee was originally designed to house an outdoor café that never came to fruition on a balcony above. Atop the eighteen-story "Majestic Building" was a penthouse apartment for Karl Hoblitzelle, the head of the Interstate chain of theaters. The penthouse included a rooftop garden. *Courtesy of UNT Libraries, The Portal to Texas History*

Highland Park Shopping Village

47 Highland Park Village
Dallas, TX 75205
214-443-9898
https://hpvillage.com

Important Dates

Opened: **1931**
Added to National Register of Historic Places:
November 17, 1997
Designated a National Historic Landmark:
February 16, 2000

The Highland Park Shopping Village commands one of the priciest square-foot retail costs in the nation. It is located near the wealthiest neighborhoods in the region and sits next door to Texas's first country club, but it still pales in comparison to luxury retail markets such as New York City, Los Angeles, and Chicago.

Site Description

One of America's earliest suburban shopping centers, Highland Park Village, located in Dallas County's Highland Park, was built in 1931 to serve as both a shopping center and a town square. The center was financed and built by Hugh Prather Sr. and Edgar Flippen, and the sponsors traveled to Spain, California, and Mexico in search of a suitable design. Eventually, they selected a Mediterranean Spanish plan designed by architects Marion F. Fooshee and James B. Cheek. With an innovative idea of arranging a cluster of one-owner stores around a parking area, they had created a model that would serve as a prototype for centers across the country.

The Shopping Village's exit and entrance. *Courtesy of UNT Libraries, The Portal to Texas History*

The development plans for the Shopping Village actually began much earlier. In 1906, entrepreneur John S. Armstrong purchased 1,326 acres of land bisected by Preston Road, an old Indian trace later used as a cattle trail. Armstrong envisioned a new, exclusive planned community just north of Dallas. With this foresight, he and his two sons-in-law, Hugh Prather and Edgar Flippen, hired architect Wilbur David Cook, the designer of Beverly Hills, to lay out this new town, which was named Highland Park and opened in 1907. In 1912, Flippen and Prather lured a country club to the new town, in the hopes of drawing wealthy citizens of Dallas. The Dallas Country Club is the oldest of its kind in the state. In looking toward the future, Flippen and Prather decided that Highland Park needed a shopping center that could function as a town square. However, bankers and merchants were skeptical to lend money for the development, since the long-term thought was an expectation of business remaining in the downtown district. The two men would remain undeterred, traveling to Barcelona and Seville in Spain as well as Mexico, California, and elsewhere to study the architecture of similar projects in order to plan a retail center for Highland Park and push the project forward.

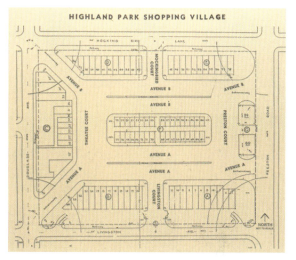

An early map of Highland Park Shopping Village. *Courtesy of UNT Libraries, The Portal to Texas History*

The 1931 grand opening became a huge draw, complete with booths, games, a Ferris wheel, and a raffle for a pony. The original building contained two grocery stores (including Hunt Grocery Co., an upscale store well known for delivering groceries to wealthy customers), the S&S Tea Room, and a handful of other businesses (including Volk Brothers

An aerial photo of Highland Park Shopping Village center before its finishing touches were put in place and it opened to the public. *Courtesy of UNT Libraries, The Portal to Texas History*

Entertainment 131

The Village Theatre, which opened in 1935, cost more than $100,000 to build. AM Theaters purchased it in 1987 and completely demolished the entire art deco interior. It was renovated in 2010.

Clothing and Sammy's Restaurant, among others). By World War II, enough buildings had been added to make a complete square around the parking lot. While the buildings were typically full, the names of the merchants were constantly changing. Following the death of Hugh Prather Sr. in 1959, management of the Shopping Village was taken over by his sons, Hugh Prather Jr. and John.

Another grand opening came in 1951, when hometown football hero and Heisman Trophy winner Doak Walker opened his sporting goods store, but by 1966 the shopping center had lost its luster. When the Howard Corporation bought the village, it no longer was synonymous with the high quality it had been before; they had given little attention to what the proper tenant mix was, landscaping was left to the elements, inappropriate signage popped up, and tenants were allowed to make alterations to the facade that were not in keeping with the historical view of the complex. Spanish arches were covered, and newer materials that did not blend in with the basic stone and stucco began to cover the original facade. However, in 1976, Henry S. Miller purchased the center for $5 million, thoroughly renovated the center, and upgraded the stores. Miller had a deeper emotional attachment to the project, since his father had been an associate of the Flippen-Prather Realty Company from 1917 to 1919 and had become close friends with Hugh Prather and Edward Flippen.

When Highland Park Village celebrated "Fiesta Fifty" in honor of its golden anniversary in the early 1980s, Miller had turned the sleepy shopping center into a luxury shopping destination, a home for some of the most premier designer shops in Texas, including Ralph Lauren and the state's first Chanel storefront. The historical importance of the village was recognized when it was placed on the National Register of Historic Places in 1997 and then designated as a National Historic Landmark in 2000.

In 2009, Highland Park Village was purchased for a record $170 million, the highest total for a retail property that year. The shopping center managed to avoid a recession, upgrading some of the labeled stores even more with names such as Christian Louboutin, Diane von Furstenberg, Tom Ford, Alexander McQueen, and more.

The Village Theater, Texas's first luxury theater, built by Karl Hoblitzelle, is also found in Highland Park Village, opening in 1935. Its historical integrity suffered when the theater was renovated in 1979, converting the balcony into an additional screen, and again when AMC Theatres demolished the entire art deco interior in 1987 and converted it into retail space and two brand-new theater screens upstairs.

Visitor Information

HOURS: Highland Park Shopping Village is always accessible during the established hours of the retail and dining contained within the complex.
No entrance fees

Despite the setbacks suffered to the Village Theater, original terrazzo tiles, rooflines with terra-cotta tile shingles and intricate ornamental detailing, arched boutique windows, and wooden balconies with decorative paintings all can be found throughout the center. Currently, Highland Park Village commands about $125 per square foot, placing it among the priciest retail locales in Texas, although it's inexpensive when compared to places such as Chicago, Los Angeles, and New York City.

Developers traveled to Barcelona and Seville in Spain and also to Mexico and California to study architectural styles to adopt for their new venture.

The unique Mediterranean Spanish-style development became the prototype for shopping centers all over the country. Plans for Highland Park started with the development of the residential neighborhood in 1906 and the Dallas Country Club in 1912. The shopping area is often referred to as "Downtown Highland Park."

Bastrop State Park

100 Park Road 1A
Bastrop, TX 78602
512-321-2101
https://tpwd.texas.gov/state-parks/bastrop

Important Dates

Built: **1933**
Added to National Register of Historic Places:
   September 25, 1997
Designated a National Historic Landmark:
   September 25, 1997

Cabin, Bastrop State Park, designed by architect Arthur Fehr. The walls and chimney are hand-tooled sandstone blocks. While massive, they are scaled to the landscape. Heavy timber framing supports the cedar-shingled roof. *Courtesy of Texas Parks and Wildlife*

Civilian Conservation Corps (CCC) men building the refectory in 1933. Using cedar, oak, pine, and walnut native to the park and the red sandstone quarried nearby, the crew completed a large stone structure that features carved mantles, handmade furniture, and heavy durable roof beams. *Courtesy of Texas Parks and Wildlife*

Site Description

Situated along the eighteenth-century El Camino Real de los Tejas, Bastrop State Park rises like a phoenix out of the Texas Hill Country. The park, a model of the 1930s Civilian Conservation Corps (CCC) projects, transformed how Texans use land recreationally and influenced state park projects throughout the United States.

Bastrop, nestled in the Lost Pines Forest, was settled in 1827. The landscape of loblolly pines, the center of the westernmost forested stand of southern pines, brought notoriety to the area. The dry, less wooded Hill Country made the forest an anomaly, since it was less conducive to the same growth more common only 100 miles east. The subsequent lumber industry aided the establishment and growth of Austin, San Antonio, outposts in the western Texas frontier, and parts of Mexico.

Developers viewed the forest as an ideal place to live and purchased a large tract in 1910, advertising it to wealthy home buyers as a new large subdivision complete with a fully stocked lake and country club by 1915. The lake was the only component to take off. A burgeoning interest in the outdoors, coupled with increasing mobility via automobile, brought about a nationwide outdoor recreation movement.

The movement saw a prominent rise in the number of federal parks, led by the creation of the National Park Service in 1916. A nationwide push followed to expand state park systems in order to further preserve and conserve natural tracts of land. When the Great Depression hit, President Franklin Roosevelt aimed to combat the economic hardship with his New Deal. That series of programs and projects included the formation of the CCC, a mobilized "army" of unemployed youths in their late teens and early twenties led by experienced professionals to improve and expand America's infrastructure.

Within two years, the CCC grew to over 300,000 individuals, and it quickly became a well-oiled machine. As the Park Service grew and utilized the services of the CCC, the Park Service became more disciplined and undertook the planning, design, and construction of a network of state parks. Through 475 state park CCC camps, they would transform how Americans interacted with its landscape.

A CCC-built state park was thoughtfully and methodically planned. Certain areas remained undeveloped "conservation" areas, with roads and trails

Entertainment 135

Overlooking the park's lush spring foliage from the CCC-era overlook and shelter

kept to a minimum, developed areas kept separated to minimize traffic and noise, and the creation of at least one lake, which often served as the centerpiece for outdoor activities. Interpretive centers and trailside museums would weave together the local geological and historical parkscape with smaller exhibit panels at roadside overlooks. All of this was tied together in their architecture programmatically, visually, and structurally to encourage visitors to use the outdoors itself as the museum.

Texas, until 1923, had only five state parks—small in acreage, lightly funded, seldom visited, and relegated to battlefields or other historic sites. The Great Depression changed that; Texas had about 30,000 acres in its coffers and a desire to expand its state park program. Hit hard by the Depression and Dust Bowl, Texas received federal assistance in the form of a high concentration of CCC camps. By the end of the program, twenty-seven camps would build thirty-one Texas state parks—creating a system that continues to make up the heart of the state park system. Few states besides Texas have such an extensive system of CCC parks that retain such a high degree of historical integrity. One highlight then, as it is today, is Bastrop State Park.

Bastrop State Park

The Lost Pines region was a potential state park site as early as 1931. With the prospect of bringing in camps and federal funds, the Texas legislature carved out land for the park while the Park Service set up a regional office in Austin, a mere hour away. By the fall of 1933, CCC Company 1805 arrived, joined in January by Company 1811 and park architect Arthur Fehr.

Construction began immediately to establish the camp, followed by a refectory building and entrance gate. Truck and foot trails were cleared; the automotive loop was surveyed, graded, and surfaced; and, eventually, the park boundaries were fenced in. Trees were removed around the Copperas Creek Lake, and the 1915 dam was replaced, enlarging the water feature. In addition to the naturalistic dam, picnic facilities and foot bridges were installed. Landscaping utilized on-site materials and transplanting nearby native shrubs and trees for ornamental enhancements.

Five tourist cabins, located on a bluff on the lake's western shore, were completed by the spring of 1935. The interiors, finished that summer, included furniture designed and built on-site in the furniture and craft shops of the National Youth Administration (NYA), the CCC's female counterpart. Dubbed "Pioneer Village," the first cabins were costly and inspired by regional pioneer architecture and constructed of local sandstone in heavily battered and randomly laid courses. The following group of six cabins were less expensive: wood-framed with a sandstone veneer. Done by the end of the year, the later cabins became a successful prototype for later projects.

The park developed quickly into the pinnacle of Texas projects by the end of 1935. With assistance from the Works Progress Administration (WPA), a swimming pool (now managed by the YMCA) and golf course were under construction. The latter would eventually expand to eighteen holes, with the original nine unchanged to this day.

Bastrop State Park, already open and attracting thousands, held its opening dedication in March 1937. As work completed, Company 1805 left for Wyoming while Company 1811 moved just down the road, with a focus on nearby Buescher State Park until 1939. The NYA and its craft shops remained in Bastrop until 1942, continuing to supply furniture, ironwork, and other craftwork for state parks throughout the nation.

The park became a showcase in the CCC's portfolio, winning "Best Camp" three years in a row and consistently ranked among the best in the nation. Many of its features and its rustic-style architecture served as models for other state parks and remain to be enjoyed by current visitors. Today, Bastrop State Park is one of only a handful of state parks nationally that retain the evidence and integrity of that era's design, planning, and craftsmanship—even as it expanded multiple times (to its current 6,600 acres).

The story of Bastrop State Park almost ended when the September 2011 Bastrop County Complex fire nearly destroyed the area. Burning for over a month, the fire killed two, destroyed nearly 1,700 homes, and left only 100 acres of the park unscathed. Four million burned trees are to be replaced in a rebuilding phase stretching twenty-plus years. Then, in May 2015, heavy rains compromised the lake's dam, flooding the park, highway, and nearby neighborhoods. It destroyed multiple park features, including some of the historic cabins, which had been spared the earlier fires. Despite the damage and ongoing repairs, the park thrives and remains a jewel in the heart of Texas.

Visitor Information

HOURS: March to November:
Saturday–Thursday, 8 a.m.–4:30 p.m., and Friday, 8 a.m.–6:30 p.m.
December to February: 8 a.m.–4:30 p.m. daily.
Admission fee charged

Park Amenities

CAMPING: To make reservations for campsites or to reserve one of the historic cabins, visitors can make reservations online through the park's website or by phone at 512-389-8900.

The rustic cabins of Bastrop, seen here ca. 1934, feature a skillful combination of rough stonework, a lot of wood, and furniture built on-site. *Courtesy of Texas Parks and Wildlife*

The entrance to Bastrop State Park today

Entertainment

Fair Park Texas Centennial Buildings

2809 Grand Avenue
Dallas, TX 75210
214-670-8400
https://www.fairpark.org

Important Dates

Built: **1936**
Added to National Register of Historic Places:
   September 24, 1986
Designated a National Historic Landmark
   District: **September 24, 1986**
Designated a Texas State Antiquities Landmark:
   January 1, 1984

Located east of downtown Dallas, Fair Park covers 2,770 acres. Many of the buildings were constructed for the Texas Centennial Exposition in 1936. The Cotton Bowl and the Texas Star Ferris Wheel are landmarks on the area skyline.

Aerial view of Dallas with Fair Park's buildings dominating the view. *Courtesy of UNT Libraries, The Portal to Texas History*

Site Description

Fair Park, located in east Dallas near the downtown business district, is the site of the State Fair of Texas. Owned by the city, it is jointly operated by the Dallas Park and Recreation Department and the State Fair of Texas Association. Fair Park houses one of the greatest concentrations of early-twentieth-century art deco exposition buildings in the United States.

Growing out of a personal donation of 80 acres to the Dallas State Fair and Exposition Association, Fair Park would become a central focal point in the city of Dallas, if not the state. Merging with a competitor, this site was chosen as a site for all future fairs, choosing the name Texas State Fair in 1899. This organization suffered at the hands of a major fire that consumed all buildings in 1902, and had to overcome the loss of its biggest income source when the Texas legislators outlawed track gambling on horse racing. The organization worked with the City of Dallas to transform the site into a park in 1904, clearing its debt and remaining in control of the annual exposition, while providing the city with a portion of the proceeds.

The Six Ladies of Fair Park stand 20 feet high on 12-foot pedestals and represent the six flags of Texas. Two artists designed the statues; this one, "France," was designed by Raoul Josset, and it sits out front of the Automobile Building.

The Dallas Historical Society, established in 1922, is the steward of the Hall of State, considered the crown jewel of the Centennial. The building is dedicated to four centuries of Texas history, heroism, and achievement and is considered one of the best examples of art deco architecture in the state.

The Automobile Building started as the Varied Industries Building in 1936. It was destroyed by fire in 1942, and a replacement was constructed in 1947. In 1985 and 1986 it was remodeled to resemble the Centennial Building, and its art deco murals were restored.

In 1906, landscape architect and city planner George Kessler was hired to give Dallas an overhaul. Inspired by the City Beautiful movement, Kessler was responsible for the first formal plan for a site such as Fair Park. Using Kessler's plan, the park was chosen as the site of the Texas Centennial Exposition; Fair Park was expanded in 1936, outbidding San Antonio, Austin, and Houston for the celebration. Utilizing the grounds and buildings of the Texas State Fair and by obtaining additional land for expansion to 180 acres, Dallas also assured the Centennial Committee of $5.5 million of public and private money. Local architect George L. Dahl (of Greene, LaRoche, and Dahl) was selected as the chief architect and technical director of the Texas Centennial Exposition, which was set to open on June 6, 1936. Construction began in October 1935, and in eight months the exposition site was completed; twenty-one of the fifty buildings were permanent additions.

All construction plans had to meet Dahl's approval. Dahl's design featured broad, low buildings with smooth expanses of sun-colored walls, brightened with murals in bold colors and accented by massive sculpture. He dubbed his style "Texanic," describing it as "strong and bold, a quality possessed to an unusual degree by the majority of the residents of Texas."

The main entry gate to the fair, which remained in the same location as for earlier fairs, opened onto an esplanade flanked by exhibit buildings. At the esplanade's terminus was the Hall of State, built by the state. Other major exposition buildings still stand, including the Agriculture Complex and the Civic Center, a museum complex built by the city around a man-made lagoon. The Ford Motor Company spent over $2 million on a temporary exhibit building and entertainment, while buildings constructed by Magnolia Oil Company, Lone Star Gas, and Continental Oil remain on the grounds. The United States government contributed by constructing a $1.5 million Federal Building and a Hall of Negro Life.

The Fair Park Esplanade is a 700-foot-long reflecting pool capped with three fountains that present a show set to music every thirty minutes throughout the day. At the end nearest the Hall of State are two human statues named Tenor and Contralto, representing a male and female athlete.

The City of Dallas, in 1985, initiated improvements for Fair Park, following a number of years of neglect, while the Friends of Fair Park was formed to ensure that restoration continued. In the fall of 1986, Fair Park entered the National Register of Historic Places as a National Historic Landmark. In 1993, the African American Museum was built, and renovations were completed on the Cotton Bowl. Today the site has grown to cover 277 acres.

Cultural District

Numerous structures have been added to Fair Park over the years. In more recent years, the park has added the Texas Star (1985), which is the sixth largest Ferris wheel in North America; the Starplex Amphitheater (1988); the art deco–styled gondola ride Texas Skyway (2007); the Top o' Texas Tower (2013) observation tower ride; and the Texas State Vietnam Memorial. Below are some of the primary examples of the art deco structures that led to the park's inclusion as a National Historic Landmark.

Hall of State

Managed by the Dallas Historical Society, the Hall of State hosts exhibits about Dallas history and culture. The building is considered one of the best examples

Fair Park's Hall of State, built specifically for the Texas Centennial in 1936. *Courtesy of UNT Libraries, The Portal to Texas History*

Entertainment 141

of art deco architecture in the state. The G. B. Dealey Library, located in the East Texas room, holds more than ten thousand bound volumes and three million historic documents, including Sam Houston's handwritten account of the Battle of San Jacinto. The American Museum of the Miniature Arts is currently located here. An exterior frieze commemorates sixty prominent Texas historical figures, while inside are six bronze statues serving as a Hall of Heroes.

Old Mill Inn

The Old Mill Inn was one of the few buildings not to incorporate art deco styling. Clad in fieldstone with heavy timber construction, it was the exhibit building for the flour milling industry and now, sporadically, serves as a restaurant.

Magnolia Lounge and Hall of Religion

The European modernism–style design of this project was part of the original project. The design for the hospitality lounge for the Magnolia Petroleum Company did include elements commonly found in art deco architecture; however, this building is radically different from the other structures at the expo. It is immediately adjacent to the lounge is the former Hall of Religion.

African American Museum

The current building occupies the same site as the Centennial's Hall of Negro Life. The museum boasts a permanent collection that consists of works from highly regarded African American artists. This iteration of the museum was founded in 1974; the new building opened in 1993 with one of the largest African American folk art collections in the US.

The Leonhardt Lagoon

South of the midway, Dahl arranged the park's cultural institutions informally around a tranquil lagoon, offering a peaceful and naturalistic counterpoint to the otherwise bustling exposition. It was redesigned and restored in 1981 and reopened in 1986 and has received recognition as a major earth sculpture and one of the earliest examples of art as bioremediation.

Museum of Nature and Science

This museum occupied two buildings around the lagoon and a planetarium next to the WRR (Texas's first radio station) Building, before moving most of its operations to the new Perot campus at Victory Park in 2012. It remains open on weekends as a secondary campus of the Perot Museum. The History Building, once the Museum of Natural History, was designed for the expo as a monolithic, rectangular box and is clad in limestone. In 1988, the northeast corner was excavated, creating a series of landscaped terraces.

Fair Park Band Shell

The plaster arches of the Fair Park Band Shell feature an essentially art deco composition with streamline moderne elements present in the backstage building.

Texas Discovery Gardens

This was the original Horticulture Building for the expo. It has since been altered by exterior renovations and additions. In the gardens behind the main structure is a model home that the Portland Cement Company originally built for the exposition.

Cotton Bowl

The Cotton Bowl stadium, originally known as "Fair Park Stadium," has seen multiple expansions to the stadium since 1930, growing to host just over 92,000 fans. The Cotton Bowl Classic college football game was played there from 1937 to 2009. During the State Fair of Texas, it hosted the Red River Rivalry between the University of Texas and the University of Oklahoma and the Southwest Airlines State Fair Classic between Grambling State University and Prairie View A&M University. It was also the first home of the Dallas Cowboys, from 1960 until they moved to Texas Stadium in Irving in 1971.

Music Hall at Fair Park

Built in the Spanish Colonial Revival style was the General Motors Building during the Centennial Exposition. It underwent extensive remodeling in 1972. It was the home of the Dallas Opera until 2009 and is the current home for Dallas Summer Musicals.

Women's Building

The Women's Building was originally built in 1910 as a park coliseum and remodeled as an art deco structure for the Centennial Exposition, during which it was known as the Hall of Administration. It was operated as the Women's Museum from 2000 to 2011 and is now used only for special events and exhibits.

Visitor Information

HOURS: 6 a.m.–7 p.m. daily
No entrance fees (although special events may have additional costs)

The Women's Building was constructed in 1910 and used for livestock auctions by day and musical theater performances at night. While the museum closed in 2011, the building is opened for special events and exhibitions.

Entertainment 143

Industry & Innovation

SITES
1. King Ranch (1852)
2. *Elissa* (1877)
3. JA Ranch (1879)
4. Lucas Gusher, Spindletop Oil Field (1901)
5. Walter C. Porter Farm (1933)
6. Space Environment Simulation Laboratory, Chambers A & B (1965)
7. Apollo Mission Control Center (1965)

Texas continues to be a leader in industry and innovation.
The ship channel, the discovery at Spindletop and emergence of the oil and gas industry, the Space Race—so much of what has pushed Texas to that pinnacle of national notoriety came through its continued success and adaptation to stay relevant in a quickly evolving technological nation. In less than one hundred years, Texas saw the first biplane to be used by armed forces in battle become NASA landing men on the moon. The discovery of a few barrels of petroleum turned into pumping oil and shipping millions of barrels around the world from one of the busiest ports in the world. Texas consistently stands as a crucial cog in America's past, present, and future. As technology gets more complex, Texas is sure to continue finding ways to innovate and continue to serve as a leader in the United States.

King Ranch

King Ranch Visitor Center
2205 Highway 141 West
Kingsville, TX 78364
361-592-8055
https://king-ranch.com

King Ranch Museum
405 North Sixth Street
Kingsville, TX 78363
361-595-1881
https://king-ranch.com/museum

King Ranch Saddle Shop
201 East Kleberg Avenue
Kingsville, TX 78363
877-282-5777
https://www.krsaddleshop.com

Important Dates

Built: **1852**
Added to National Register of Historic Places:
   October 15, 1966
Designated a National Historic Landmark:
   November 5, 1961

Rancho de Santa Gertrudis (a.k.a. King Ranch) was founded in 1853 with the purchase of the Rincón de Santa Gertrudis land grant. The Santa Gertrudis Ranch building is the original King Ranch headquarters.

146 TREASURES OF TEXAS

Site Description

Located in South Texas between Corpus Christi and McAllen, King Ranch is the largest ranch in the United States. At roughly 825,000 acres, the ranch is larger than the state of Rhode Island. The ranch is not on a contiguous plot of land but rather four large sections called divisions: the Santa Gertrudis, the Laureles, the Encino, and the Norias. With only a relatively short stretch of shared border, only the first two of the four border each other. The ranch includes portions of six Texas counties, encompassing most of Kleberg and much of Kenedy and with portions also stretching into Brooks, Jim Wells, Nueces, and Willacy Counties.

The history of King Ranch stretches back to the Mexican-American War. Richard King was a river pilot, born in New York City to Irish immigrants. He was indentured at age eleven to a jeweler but ran to sea, eventually attaining his pilot's rating. In 1843, King met Mifflin Kenedy, captain of the steamboat *Champion*, who would later become his business partner in King Ranch. Both men served under General Zachary Taylor, supporting the US invitations of Monterrey a Saltillo, by operating steamboats from Brazos Santiago Harbor in Texas to Matamoros, Mexico, and then upriver to Camargo, Tamaulipas. Following the war, King made a good living hauling merchandise on the Rio Grande, as far upriver as Camargo and Rio Grande City. Kenedy made money carrying goods overland into Mexico.

By March 1, 1850, King and Kenedy entered into a business partnership with Charles Stillman, founder of Brownsville, and James O'Donnell to form M. Kenedy & Co. to transport Stillman's goods from Brazos Santiago Harbor and up the Rio Grande. The

Above: The original adobe jacal home was replaced by a frame cottage, which later burned. This iteration was completed in 1915 and is the family home of Captain King's descendants. Garnering access is nearly impossible since it continues to be considered a family home. *Courtesy of UNT Libraries, The Portal to Texas History*

Left: Assault, the Triple Crown winner in 1946, at King Ranch. Assault was the seventh winner of the American Triple Crown and the only Texas-bred horse to accomplish the feat—all despite being plagued with injuries and illnesses. *Courtesy of America's Best Racing*

Industry & Innovation 147

The home of Captain Richard King (*left*) and his wife, Henrietta (*right*), started as a small adobe hut, then became a five-room prairie-style house and later a three-story Victorian home. When he died in 1885, King was America's greatest cattle baron, and he left everything to Henrietta. *Courtesy of UNT Libraries, The Portal to Texas History*

company survived the Civil War, with Stillman selling his share of the enterprise after the war; the new firm operated as King, Kennedy & Co. until 1874.

The land that would become King Ranch was first sighted by King in April 1852. King had traveled north from Brownsville to attend the Lone State Fair in Corpus Christi. This was a four-day trip by horseback, and, after a grueling ride, King came across the Santa Gertrudis Creek, 124 miles from the Rio Grande; it was the first stream he had seen on the Wild Horse Desert. The land, shaded by large mesquite trees, was so impressive that when he arrived at the fair, he and a friend, Captain Gideon "Legs" Lewis, a Texas Ranger, agreed to make that land into a ranch. The King Ranch LK brand, still in use today, stands for the partners Lewis and King.

King and Lewis set up a cattle camp on Santa Gertrudis Creek in South Texas later that year. Formal purchase of the land began in 1853. The partners purchased a Spanish land grant, Rincón de Santa Gertrudis, of 15,500 acres on Santa Gertrudis Creek in Nueces County. Shortly thereafter, they purchased the Mexican land grant, Santa Gertrudis de la Garza grant, of 53,000 acres. They would go on to acquire more landholdings around the area of the creek during the mid-1850s. After Lewis was killed in April 1855, King acquired his half interest in the Rincón grant at a public sale.

Mifflin Kenedy, with whom King had been associated during his steamboating days, bought an interest in the ranch on December 5, 1860. At that time, all titles were put under the business name R. King and Company. The pair dissolved their partnership in 1868, with King retaining Santa Gertrudis. King, that same year, fenced in a tract of his ranch that surrounded the Santa Gertrudis headquarters. Throughout the rest of his life, King would purchase an additional sixty pieces of land and amass vast land holdings throughout South Texas.

In the early days of the King Ranch, King tried a variety of grazing animals, including cattle, horses, sheep, and goats. His first officially recorded brand was the HK, in 1859. The now-famous Running W appeared in the 1860s and was registered on February 9, 1869, as the official brand for King Ranch, a mark still used to this day. To aid in the running of the ranch, King brought in approximately one hundred men, women, and children he encountered on a cattle buying trip in Mexico, to help tend his herds; they have been known since that time as *los Kineños* or "King's men."

When King died on April 14, 1885, his wife, Henrietta, retained the ranch's legal adviser, Robert Justus Kelberg Sr., as manager. He married the Kings' youngest daughter, Alice, the following year. His work in tick eradication would become one of the greatest contributions not only to the management of the ranch but to the Texas cattle industry as a whole. With Kelberg's health failing in the early twentieth century, his son, Robert Justus Kelberg Jr., became ranch manager in 1918. Under the terms of Henrietta's will, the ranch was incorporated with the Kleberg descendants as its stockholders.

King Ranch Industry

The foundation stock of King Ranch was the longhorn, with many heads bought in Mexico. Throughout the 1800s, King bought several Brahman bulls, shorthorns, and Herefords. The Brahmans, which were uniquely adapted to the South Texas climate, were crossbred with the shorthorns to produce the famous Santa Gertrudis cattle, officially recognized as a breed by the US Department of Agriculture in 1940; this breed would become a primary focus at the ranch.

In the early part of the twentieth century, King Ranch began to diversify. While continuing to develop its cattle activities, the ranch also began to breed and race quarter horses and thoroughbreds, developed practices to protect the environment and assist in wildlife conservation and habitat maintenance, began oil and gas production, and entered the timber industry and real estate business.

The thoroughbred operation reached its pinnacle in 1946, when Assault won the Triple Crown—a success nearly matched in 1950 when Middleground won both the Kentucky Derby and Belmont Stakes. During this time, the ranch also expanded its cattle operation for a short time, including property held in Kentucky, Pennsylvania, Florida, Mississippi, Cuba, Australia, Brazil, Venezuela, Argentina, Spain, and Morocco. Oil exploration, through Humble Oil and Refining Company (now ExxonMobil), began as early as 1919 and became a profitable gamble in 1945 with the discovery of the Borregos oil field. Following that, several major oil and gas discoveries were made on the ranch, leading to the construction of a large refinery in Kingsville to handle its South Texas production.

During the latter part of the twentieth century and on into the twenty-first, King Ranch would see the transformation of operations into a professionally managed but family-owned enterprise when Darwin Smith took over in 1988, making him the first head not related to founder Richard King by blood or marriage. While the importance of the King Ranch has been its vast enterprise of agribusiness and land resource assets, it has also become a popular tourist destination. Visitors to the ranch can enjoy agricultural, wildlife, and historical tours at the ranch. It has diversified and grown into a major agribusiness corporation with interests not only in cattle ranching but also in feedlot operations, farming, citrus groves, pecan processing and sales, commodity marketing and processing, recreational hunting, retail operations, and ecotourism. Today, King Ranch has transitioned from a frontier Texas ranch to one of the largest privately held corporations in the United States.

This June 1929 image shows just a small portion of the King Ranch. It started out as a 15,500-acre cow camp in 1853 and today is the largest ranch in the United States. At nearly 825,000 acres, it is larger than the state of Rhode Island. *Courtesy of UNT Libraries, The Portal to Texas History*

Visitor Information

King Ranch Museum
HOURS: Tuesday–Saturday, 10 a.m.–3 p.m.
Admission fee charged

King Ranch Visitor Center
HOURS: Tuesday–Saturday, 10 a.m.–3 p.m.
TOURS: Tuesday–Saturday at 11 a.m. and 1 p.m.

Tours available by reservation: daily ranch tours, nature tours, special interest tours, and motor coach tours

King Ranch Saddle Shop
HOURS: Monday–Saturday, noon–6 p.m.

A King Ranch barn under construction, as seen on November 11, 1948. Improvements and expansions to the ranch continue to this day, since it is an active ranch. *Courtesy of UNT Libraries, The Portal to Texas History*

Industry & Innovation

Elissa

2200 Harborside
Galveston, TX 77550
409-763-1877
https://www.galvestonhistory.org/sites/1877-tall-ship-*Elissa*-at-the-galveston-historic-seaport

Important Dates

Launched: **October 27, 1877**
Added to National Register of Historic Places:
  March 21, 1978
Designated a National Historic Landmark:
  December 14, 1990

The masts of the *Elissa* tower over the docks of its neighbors. Sailing the world for more than a century, the ship delivered good to ports in Mexico, England, Australia, India, and more.

150 TREASURES OF TEXAS

When the tall ship *Elissa* was brought in, this was how the dock area looked. Its home has much improved since. *Courtesy of Galveston Historic Seaport*

Site Description

The tall ship *Elissa*, a three-masted wood barque, is one of the oldest ships still sailing the open waters today. Launched in 1877, it was designated a National Historic Landmark in 1990 and currently serves as a museum ship in Galveston. When it isn't sailing, the ship calls the Texas Seaport Museum at Pier 21 home. Public tours are available year-round, and the ship is sailed and maintained by volunteers.

Elissa was built in Aberdeen, Scotland, and launched on October 27, 1877. It was one of the last of a dying breed: a merchant vessel at a time when steamships were overtaking sailing ships. It also sailed under the Norwegian flag as the *Fjeld of Tonsberg* and in Sweden as *Gustave of Gothenburg*. In 1918, *Elissa* was converted into a two-masted brigantine and received an engine. It was sold to Finland in 1930 and was owned by Gustaf Erikson, who reconverted it into a schooner. It was sold to Greece in 1959, sailing under the names *Christophoros*, *Achaeos* (1967), and the *Pioneer* (1969).

Over the years, *Elissa* actively traded in and out of US ports as an active participant in America's maritime commerce, bringing cargoes to and from Boston, New York, Pensacola, Savannah, and twice at Galveston. Its first trip to its future home came in December 1883, laden with bananas from Tampico. The next month, it arrived with over 700,000 pounds of cotton consigned to Liverpool. The next winter, it was the only vessel known to have put into port at Boston during the great blizzard of 1885.

In 1970, facing destruction in Piraeus, *Elissa* was purchased and rescued for the San Francisco Maritime Museum. Not much came of the purchase, and *Elissa* sat in a Piraeus salvage yard for five years. Galveston Historical Foundation purchased the ship for $40,000. Following a year of repairs to its hull, in 1979 *Elissa* was towed to Gibraltar, where it was prepared for an ocean tow, which commenced on June 7, 1979.

Elissa survived numerous modifications over the

Starting out as "*Gustave*" and seen here in drydock 1918, the *Elissa* was fitted with a propeller and oil engine. As steam began to dominate the shipping trade, sailing ships were either scrapped or converted into auxiliary vessels with engines. This conversion kept the ship from the scrapyard, and it worked cargo through the 1960s. *Courtesy of Galveston Historic Seaport*

years, including the installation of the engine and the incremental removal of all its rigging and masts. It features an iron hull, and the pinrail and brightwork are made of teak. The ship's masts are Douglas fir from Oregon, and its nineteen sails were made in Maine, covering 12,000 square feet. It is painted white with a block topping. The ship has a single deck, with a largely open hold. The hold usually features exhibits and accommodations for additional crew when moored. The ship was restored diligently, preparing it to majestically sail once again.

In 1985, *Elissa* made its first voyage as a restored sailing ship, traveling to Corpus Christi, Texas. The following year, it sailed out of Galveston Bay and along the eastern United States to take part in the Statue of Liberty's centennial. In 2005, the Texas state legislature deemed it Texas's official tall ship, and it escorted USS *Texas* (SSN-775) into Galveston Harbor to be commissioned the following year. All continued well until July 2011, when the US Coast Guard surprised Texas Seaport Museum officials by declaring *Elissa* to be "not seaworthy." During an inspection, an action

Visitors to the *Elissa* are allowed to explore nearly the entirety of the ship, including the captain's quarters, seen here. Today, you'll find it moored along Pier 21 next door to the Seaport Museum.

152 TREASURES OF TEXAS

taken twice every five years, the Coast Guard revealed a corroded hull, uncovering the worst corrosion since it was rebuilt in 1982.

Facing a daunting restoration project, the museum raised $3 million for the project. This paid for hull replacement and a host of other long-overdue maintenance projects. They replaced the 22,000 board feet of Douglas fir decking, including the construction of new quarterdeck furniture out of high-quality teak. The project finished in January 2013, with the ship returning to sailing in March the following year by running a series of daily sails for two weeks out of Galveston.

Elissa remains one of the world's oldest sailing hulls still in operation, behind only the 1871 coasting schooner *Lewis R. French* out of Christmas Cove, Maine. Two other older ships are still afloat but do not sail the waters anymore; Britain's *Cutty Sark* (located in a dry berth) and the 1863 *Star of India* on display in San Diego. *Elissa* is one of nine historic square-rigged vessels preserved in the United States, with only it and the Coast Guard training ship *Eagle* sailing with any regularity. It serves as a symbol of the Gulf coast's historic beginnings as a seaport and active waterfront and as a treasure of a bygone era of technology and maritime trade.

> **Visitor Information**
>
> HOURS: March to November:
> Saturday–Thursday, 8 a.m.–4:30 p.m., and Friday, 8 a.m.–6:30 p.m.
> December to February: 8 a.m.–4:30 p.m. daily.
> *Admission fee charged*
>
> Seaport Package: If you plan to visit *Elissa*, consider purchasing the Seaport Package. You gain admission to *Elissa*, take a harbor tour (on the smaller motorized tour boat *Seagull II*), and gain admission to the Texas Seaport Museum.

At the time the *Elissa* was built by Henry Fowler in Aberdeen, Scotland, steamships had already begun replacing commercial sailboats. Despite this, the *Elissa* would thrive before its life as a freighter came to a close in Piraeus Harbor, Greece, in the 1970s.

Industry & Innovation 153

JA Ranch

JA Ranch Offices
418 South Polk Street
Amarillo, TX 79101
806-944-5212
https://jaranch.org

Important Dates

Built: **1879**
Added to National Register of Historic Places:
   October 15, 1966
Designated a National Historic Landmark:
   December 19, 1960

Seen here is the southeast elevation of the main house at the JA Ranch Headquarters in Paloduro, Texas. *Photo by Guy R. Giersch, courtesy of the Library of Congress, Historic American Buildings Survey*

Veteran Texas cattleman Charles Goodnight entered Palo Duro Canyon in 1876, near Amarillo, by way of an old nearby Comanche trail. The following year, in partnership with John Adair, he moved farther into the canyon to lay out the headquarters of the JA Ranch.

Site Description

Located in the Palo Duro Canyon of Amarillo, the JA Ranch is the oldest cattle ranching operation in the Texas Panhandle. Founded in 1876 by John George Adair and Charles Goodnight, one of the most influential cattle barons of the late nineteenth century, the ranch continues as an ongoing business, operated by Adair's descendants. Its beginning likely is traced to the summer and fall of 1876, when Goodnight drove 1,600 longhorn cattle from Pueblo, Colorado, to the Palo Duro Canyon, where he established his home ranch near the Prairie Dog Town Fork of the Red River.

Charles Goodnight, a native of Illinois, joined the ranks of the Texas Rangers in 1857. Following the Civil War, Goodnight would become involved in cattle herding operations that recovered many thousands of heads of cattle left unsupervised during the war, blazing major herding trails across the expanse of West Texas. After starting a ranching operation in eastern Colorado, Goodnight returned to the Palo Duro Canyon area, the site of a major operation he had led against the Kiowa and Comanche as a Ranger; he established a small ranch there in 1874. John Adair, an Ulster Scots immigrant, met Goodnight in Denver and expressed his interest in getting into the cattle business, and Adair agreed to furnish the capital Goodnight would need to build up the ranch. The two men entered into a partnership, with Goodnight managing the operations and Adair providing resources. Under Goodnight's oversight, the ranch would grow to over 700,000 acres. Goodnight would eventually retire to a smaller ranch nearby in 1889.

Over the years, the land would be expanded, with some of it leased out and some of it sold off. By 1945, the JA's operations were confined to 335,000 acres in Armstrong, Briscoe, Donley, and Hall Counties. Watered by the Prairie Dog Town Fork and its tributaries, plus several hundred natural lakes, dirt tanks, and fifty-eight wells, the ranch had twelve winter branch camps and five farms that raised feed for the livestock. Nearly two-thirds of the extant JA properties were rolling pastureland, while the winter range in Palo Duro Canyon afforded maximum protection and the

Industry & Innovation 155

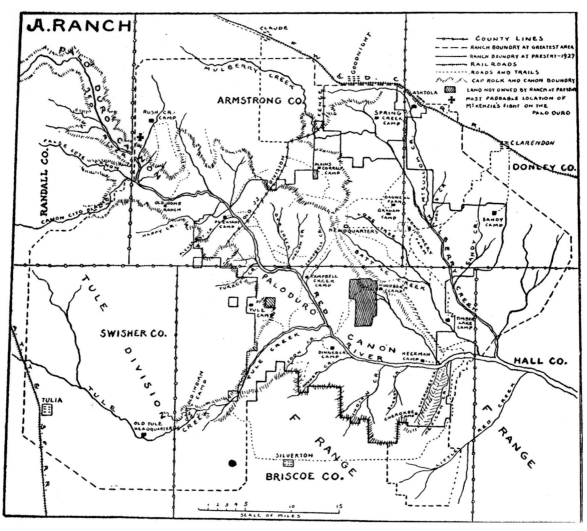

When the Goodnight-Adair partnership dissolved in 1887, Charles Goodnight took the 140,000-acre Quitaque Ranch and 20,000 head of cattle for his interest. *Courtesy of JA Ranch*

Construction on the current ranch house was started in 1879. At the time of construction, it was just a cabin built from cedar logs. Here it can be seen as the left part of the main house in this 1903 photograph. *Courtesy of JA Ranch*

The canyon was an ideal spot for a ranch. It was naturally fenced in by the overhanging caprock, it furnished water and shelter in the winter, and the adjacent plains were ideal for summer grazing.

Visitor Information

JA Ranch is a privately owned ranch and is not open to the public.

summer range was free from land waste. As of 1990, the ranch was mostly fenced and cross-fenced.

The ranch became known for its purebred Herefords and Angus bulls (at one time considered to be one of the finest-quality herds of cattle in the nation). Quarter horses were raised primarily for ranch use, a small buffalo herd was maintained, and tillable land continued to be leased. A herd of longhorns, courtesy of the JA, roamed in Palo Duro Canyon State Scenic Park for years, and in 1960 the house was designated a National Historic Landmark. Two of the ranch's buildings, the old milk house and an oat bin, were given to the Ranching Heritage Center at Lubbock in 1971 and 1988.

The main ranch house now serves as a museum devoted to Charles Goodnight and is located just south of US Route 287. Ranch headquarters were moved here, at the choice site at the foot of the Caprock, 25 miles east of the old Home Ranch. It is a two-story home, with its oldest portion being an antebellum-era log cabin. The main portion of the house, beginning in 1879, has rough stone walls on the ground floor and a wood-framed second story. Nearby outbuildings include the original nineteenth-century stables and corral, a house for bunking ranch hands, and also a bookkeeper's house, wagon boss's house, blacksmith shop, wagon yard, and milk and meat cooler. The old Home Ranch house was used as a line camp until it burned in 1904.

Industry & Innovation 157

Lucas Gusher, Spindletop Oil Field

Spindletop–Gladys City Boomtown Museum
Lamar University
5550 Jimmy Simmons Boulevard
Beaumont, TX 77705
409-880-1750
https://spindletop.org

Important Dates

Oil Struck: **January 10, 1901**
Added to National Register of Historic Places:
  November 13, 1966
Designated a National Historic Landmark:
  November 13, 1966

Spindletop–Gladys City Boomtown Museum is a re-creation of the oil boom town of Gladys City. A nearby "Spindle Gusher" stands to erupt on a semiregular basis—albeit with water, not oil.

Multiple derricks were common in oil fields such as the one where the Lucas gusher was. In the foreground of this 1901 scene are wooden shacks, stacks of wooden boards, and smokestacks with smoke plumes rising out of them. *Courtesy of UNT Libraries, The Portal to Texas History*

Site Description

Located 3 miles south of Beaumont, Texas, the Spindletop dome oil field was derived from the Louann Salt evaporite layer of the Jurassic geologic period. On January 10, 1901, a well struck oil, or "came in," blowing at a height of over 150 feet for nine days at a rate estimated to be at 100,000 barrels of oil per day. It was more powerful than any previously seen in the world. Gulf Oil and Texaco, now part of the Chevron Corporation, were formed to develop production at Spindletop, a discovery that would lead the United States into the oil age.

The Industrial Revolution of the mid-nineteenth century had created a need for a cheaper and more convenient fossil fuel source than coal. This need was filled by petroleum, or oil. Prior to Spindletop, oil was primarily used for lighting and as a lubricant. Edwin Drake had drilled the first well specifically intended to extract oil in 1859 in northwestern Pennsylvania. By the end of the century, Pennsylvania had produced more oil than any other state.

In Texas, Native Americans had known about the sticky black tar seeping from the earth for centuries, using it for medicinal purposes. By the end of the nineteenth century, there had been several discoveries of oil in the southeastern part of the state, with small fields near Nacogdoches and Corsicana. In 1900, the state produced a total of 863,000 barrels, a small fraction of the national pull of sixty-three million

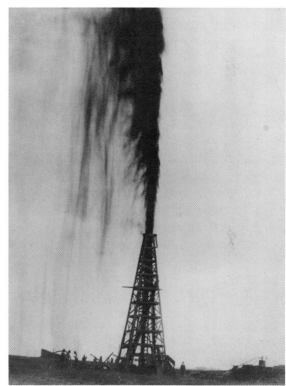

The Lucas gusher, seen here in 1901, is a spindletop that is gushing oil out of the top of it. On the ground surrounding the spindletop are several workers, two holding a large hose. *Courtesy of UNT Libraries, The Portal to Texas History*

barrels. However, with the amount of oil discovered at Spindletop, burning petroleum as a fuel for mass consumption suddenly became not only possible but economically feasible. The discovery would generate a frenzy of oil exploration and economic development throughout the state, known as the Texas Oil Boom, with the United States becoming the world's leading oil producer.

Industry & Innovation   159

The actual site of the Spindletop gusher sits on private property. Visitors are encouraged instead to visit Spindletop Park. Here, the gusher location is visible with the installed binoculars from the viewing platform, which includes informational placards. A fuller interpretation is located at the nearby museum.

Spindletop Hill, just south of Beaumont, was formed by an underground salt dome, pushing the earth above it higher as it grew. Pattillo Higgins suspected there might be oil lurking under the area's salt domes, including the one at Spindletop. It would leak gas, and Pattillo would light it as a parlor trick for his Sunday school classes. In 1892, Higgins organized the Gladys City Oil, Gas and Manufacturing Company to explore that possibility, meeting widespread skepticism from petroleum and geologic experts.

After years of attempting to drill down into the earth, his group would be continually met with a quicksand-like substance, halting their efforts. Higgins backed out from the operation. Eventually he ran a newspaper advertisement for fellow investors, bringing on board engineer Anthony F. Lucas, who agreed with Higgins's view on the salt domes. Lucas would convince Pennsylvania oilmen John Galey and James Guffey to finance a new drilling operation.

Drilling efforts at Spindletop began in October 1900 and by early January 1901 had far surpassed earlier efforts, reaching a depth of 1,020 feet and overcoming the difficulties met in drilling into the sandy ground. On January 10, mud began bubbling out of the hole, causing workers to flee as mud came gushing out at a high speed, followed closely by natural gas, then oil. The Lucas Geyser reached a height of over 150 feet and soon was producing close to 100,000 barrels a day, more than all the other oil wells in America combined.

This Texas pink granite monument was erected in 1941 near the original site of the Lucas gusher. The continued withdrawal of oil, sulfur, and brine caused the Spindletop dome to subside and forced the monument to be moved. It now sits at the museum on the Lamar University campus.

Tens of thousands of people flocked to the Spindletop oil field after the strike, transforming the area into a bustling boomtown within months. In 1901, Spindletop saw the earliest beginnings of the Gulf Oil Corporation (bought by Chevron in 1984) and also spawned the oil giants Texas Fuel Company (now Texaco), Amoco, and the Humble Oil Company (later Exxon). By the end of the year, Spindletop had produced over 3.5 million barrels of oil, rising to 17.4 million the following year. The discovery ushered in a new era of Texas-based industry, becoming enormously influential in the state's future development. The discovery also drove down the price of oil, destroying the monopoly held

160   TREASURES OF TEXAS

by Standard Oil and John D. Rockefeller. Also, thousands of new prospectors arrived in Texas, looking for their own fields.

While the oil boom surrounding Spindletop had largely waned by World War I, its impact would stretch on much longer. Numerous oil companies, along with the refineries and marketing entities to support them, would lead to a massive increase in jobs and income throughout the state. The abundance of oil found would fuel the expansion of the shipping and railroad industries and help propel the development of new innovations such as automobiles and aviation. By the end of the twentieth century, the oil, refining, chemical, and petrochemical industries continued to dominate in Texas, with the impact of electronics, aerospace, and other associated technological fields increasing in importance.

In 1941, a monument commemorating the importance of the Lucas Geyser was erected at Spindletop Hill; it was later moved after the Texas Gulf Sulphur Company began using the site for a salt-brine extraction in the 1950s. This pink granite monument now resides at the Spindletop–Gladys City Boomtown Museum on the Beaumont campus of Lamar University, which is located several miles from the original site of the Lucas Gusher. With the withdrawal of oil, sulfur, and brine from beneath its surface, the Spindletop dome has since subsided; while the monument has been moved, the wellhead is marked at Spindletop Park by a flagpole flying the Texas flag, located about 1.5 miles south of the museum. The museum was dedicated in 1976 and preserves the history of the oil gusher era in Beaumont. It features an oil derrick and multiple reconstructed Gladys City building interiors furnished with authentic artifacts from the period. The gusher is re-created at the museum site by using water and running it for about two minutes.

Visitor Information

Spindletop–Gladys City Boomtown Museum

HOURS: Tuesday–Saturday, 10 a.m.–5 p.m., Sunday, 1–5 p.m.; closed Monday. Last admission time is 4:20 p.m., and the gift shop closes at 4:30 p.m.
Admission fee charged

Tours are available for groups of ten or more; call ahead for prices and tour times.

Lucas Gusher reenactment: Call ahead or check the website for dates of the two-minute reenactments, since they are performed irregularly.

Spindletop was the largest oil gusher the world had seen. Beaumont's population of 10,000 tripled in three months, eventually rising to 50,000. While Gladys City boomed during the early days, it quickly became overrun by roughnecks and wildcatters following the discovery.

Industry & Innovation   161

Walter C. Porter Farm

Poetry Road and FM 986
Terrell, TX 75160

Not open to the public. Historic markers at site location.

Important Dates

Built: **1933**
Designated a National Historic Landmark:
 July 19, 1964
Added to National Register of Historic Places:
 October 15, 1966

A westward view of the Porter Farm tomato barn. This building is located on the south side of the demonstration platform. The total farm property was roughly 500 acres. While not historically significant, the tomato barn stands on the primary demonstration land.

Site Description

The Porter Farm was the site of the first cooperative farm demonstration, organized in 1903 by Dr. Seaman A. Knapp. The project successfully demonstrated methods to expand crop production. Out of this project, the US Department of Agriculture's Agricultural Extension Service developed.

Dr. Knapp had taken up farming late in life and moved to Iowa to raise general crops and livestock. He became active in the Teachers of Agriculture in the 1880s and became so impressed with the organization's teaching method that Dr. Knapp drafted a congressional bill for the establishment of experimental research stations, thus laying the foundation for a nationwide network of agricultural experiment stations. In 1886, he moved to Louisiana and began developing a large tract of agricultural land in the western part of the state.

Knapp was unable to persuade local farmers to adopt his new techniques and was failing at enlisting northern farmers to move to the region to serve collectively as an educational catalyst. However, when he provided incentives for farmers to settle in each township, he found success. The proviso was that each, in turn, would demonstrate to other farmers what could be done by adopting his improved farming methods. Northern farmers began moving into the region, and native farmers began buying into Knapp's methods, leading, by 1902, to Knapp's employment by the government to promote good agricultural practices in the South.

On the basis of his own experience, Knapp was convinced that demonstrations carried out by the farmers themselves were the most effective way to promote these methods. These efforts were aided by the infestation of the boll weevil into the southern cotton industry, causing enough damage to instill fear among merchants and growers that the cotton economy would evaporate. This motivated more people to get involved.

At the urging of these concerned merchants and growers, the Department of Agriculture set up a farm demonstration at Walter G. Porter's farm, the first in a series of steps that eventually led to passage of the legislation to formalize Cooperative Extension work. US Department of Agriculture officials were so impressed with the success of this demonstration that they appropriated $250,000 to combat the weevil, a measure that also involved the hiring of farm demonstration

Dr. Seaman A. Knapp organized the first cooperative farm demonstration at Walter C. Porter's farm in 1903. By 1904, the success was such that some twenty USDA agents were employed in Texas, Louisiana, and Arkansas, with designs to spread into Mississippi and Alabama. *Courtesy of* The Demonstration Work: Dr. Seaman A. Knapp's Contribution to Civilization *(1921) by Oscar Baker Martin*

The boll weevil inflicted immense suffering on southern farmers after it entered the United States in 1892, sparking interest in farm demonstrations on how to deal with the pest. *Courtesy of the USDA, Agricultural Research Service*

Industry & Innovation 163

agents. By 1904, approximately twenty agents were employed in Texas, Louisiana, and Arkansas, with the movement appearing to spread to neighboring Mississippi and Alabama.

To cover potential losses and indemnify Porter from trying Knapp's methods, the area farmers and businessmen set aside $1,000. Dr. Knapp worked with Walter Porter to set aside 70 acres of his farm for the project. The designated land was light sandy loam with a clay subsoil and was planted to grow cotton and corn for twenty-eight years without the use of commercial fertilizers. Together they utilized carefully placed plantings, crop rotation with nitrogen-fixing legumes, and the use of commercial fertilizers, all of which doubled normal yields of cotton. Their success enabled Knapp to persuade the US secretary of agriculture, James Wilson, to visit the farm and see the results. Wilson awarded Knapp a move to open an office for the Farmers' Cooperative Demonstration Work in Houston.

Knapp hired thirty-three agents, who were assigned to counties in 1906. The Texas legislature authorized county commissioners' courts to appropriate money for salaries in 1911. The Agricultural and Mechanical College of Texas (now Texas A&M University) and the Department of Agriculture reached a cooperative agreement soon afterward. From their project, farm demonstration work spread rapidly across the country and became one of the great educational institutions in America. Organizations such as Ladies' Canning Societies and 4-H Clubs intensified county fair activities—all stemming from the extension work began on the Porter Farm. By 1978, there were extension agents in every Texas county, supported by subject-matter specialists and administrators at Texas A&M. The Texas Agricultural Extension Service is supported by a joint effort of county, state, and federal governments.

The boll weevil was an invasive species to the United States, having migrated from central Mexico. It inflicted immense suffering on southern farmers

The Porter Farm was the site of the first cooperative farm demonstration in 1903. It successfully demonstrated methods to expand crop production, the experimental use of fertilizers on some plots, and crop rotation. The success of this project led to the creation of government Extension Service programs.

A 1919 advertisement for learning more about the boll weevil, the scourge of farmers in the South. *Courtesy of the US Food Administration, Educational Division*

> **Visitor Information**
>
> Not open to the public. Historical markers are located at the intersection of FM 986 and Porter Road, on the right when traveling north on Route 986.

after it entered the United States in 1892 and by the 1920s had nearly devastated the cotton industry in the South. Knapp's work led to the creation of government Extension Service programs, which went on to develop methods to combat boll weevil infestation in the area.

The Porter Farm, located about 3 miles north of Terrell in northern Kaufman County on FM 986, is now a historic site covering about 500 acres, although a majority of the agricultural demonstrations occurred on only 70 acres. The property today includes the Porter homestead, a one-and-a-half-story clapboard Cape-style frame house located on the southeast side of FM 986. The demonstration land is primarily on the northwest side of the property. Don't be fooled; that tomato barn also standing on the land is not historically significant.

Industry & Innovation 165

Space Environment Simulation Laboratory, Chambers A & B

Space Center Houston
Building 30
1601 East NASA Parkway
Houston, TX 77058
281-244-2100
https://spacecenter.org

Important Dates

Built: **1965**
Added to National Register of Historic Places:
 October 3, 1985
Designated a National Historic Landmark:
 October 3, 1985

This 2007 view of Test Chamber A's thermal vacuum gives one a comparison of how large the structure is. Inside the open door, two people are standing inside, looking up. *Courtesy of NASA*

Site Description

Located at the Lyndon B. Johnson Space Center in Houston, in Building 32, is NASA's Space Environment Simulation Laboratory (SESL). Designed to test Apollo program spacecraft and equipment, the lab is able to perform simulations on a large scale. The vacuum and thermal environments encountered in space can be simulated inside this facility. Built in 1965, it continues to be used to test equipment to this day.

The SESL features two test chambers: a large and small one. Both are cylindrical and feature the ability to provide a vacuum with configurable lighting that can simulate sunlight beaming from a variety of angles. The size of both chambers allows NASA scientists to replicate operating temperatures, fluid lead rates, and changes in the properties of thermal coatings and other materials on full-scale flight hardware. Testing equipment in these environments is essential to provide a higher safety level that could be used for manned operations and flight hardware. The results of the tests conducted inside the SESL facilities were crucial to the safety of the astronauts and, eventually, the success of the entire manned space program.

The SESL has tested most of the crucial equipment needed for space flight since the lab's construction in 1965. The facility tested all the Apollo command, service, and lunar modules; spacesuits for extravehicular activity; and systems for the Skylab-Apollo and Apollo-Soyuz missions, various space shuttle systems, and additional large-scale satellite systems.

Chamber A is the larger of the two historic chambers. It has a diameter of 45 feet and a circular floor that can be rotated 180 degrees, and test subject equipment gets moved through the use of four overhead cranes. Outside the chamber are 100,000-pound-capacity cranes—double those inside the chamber—that lift equipment in and out. In addition to the solar lighting arrays, the facility has the capability of generating the thermal plasma fields experienced in the outer atmosphere and in low earth orbit. Two man-sized airlocks, one at ground level and another at 31 feet, allows test crew members to move from ambient air pressure to the thermal-vacuum environment and back. When

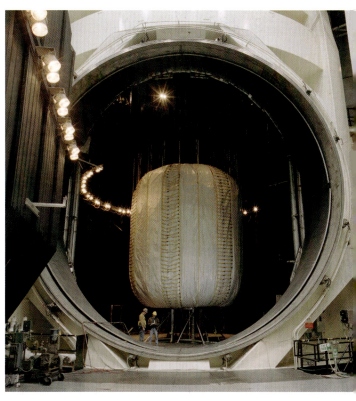

Above: Seen during a 1998 testing is the Inflated TransHab mockup inside Chamber A. The large-volume inflated space vehicle was a proposed design for a habitation element for lengthy space missions. The door to Chamber A has a 40-foot diameter and weighs 40 tons. *Courtesy of NASA*

Right: The installation of a boiler plate on Apollo on April 22, 1966, inside Chamber A. *Courtesy of NASA*

Industry & Innovation 167

Astronaut standing outside the Manned Spacecraft Center at NASA's headquarters in Houston. Here, seen in March 1963, are astronaut Alan Shepard with Robert Gilruth (father of the US manned space program) and other early astronauts Deke Slayton, Gordon Cooper, Scott Carpenter, Wally Schirra, and Gus Grissom. *Courtesy of NASA*

the inner door is bolted, either airlock can be used as an altitude chamber for independent tests.

To test the James Webb Space Telescope, NASA remodeled and upgraded Chamber A. As of 2013, this chamber stood as the largest high-vacuum, cryogenic-optical test chamber in the world. It is 55 feet in diameter and 90 feet tall. It is equipped with a gaseous helium shroud that is capable of lowering temperatures to 11 degrees Kelvin (−439.9 degrees Fahrenheit). Additional test support equipment in Chamber A includes infrared cameras, television cameras to monitor testing, and mass spectrometers.

Chamber B is the smaller of the two chambers, with a diameter of 20 feet. It is served by two 100,000-pound cranes. Like its sister, Chamber B has two airlocks; one of them is configured to a water deluge system and other elements needed to simulate the oxygen-rich environments that would be encountered on a spacecraft. It too has a solar lighting array. This one is much simpler than Chamber A and utilizes mirrors to accomplish certain lighting angles. The smaller size of Chamber B makes it possible to more efficiently perform tests on smaller objects and in a much more rapid turnaround time frame.

Apollo 11 astronaut Neil Armstrong is seen here in May 1969 readying himself for thermal vacuum training in Chamber B in Houston. These simulations help simulate low-gravity environments for the astronauts to practice and work in. *Courtesy of NASA*

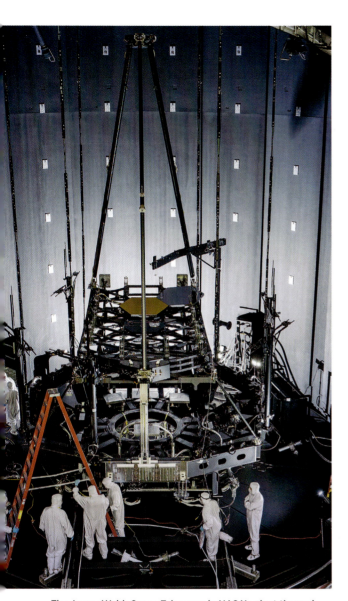

The James Webb Space Telescope in NASA's giant thermal-vacuum chamber, Chamber A, being prepared for its cryogenic tests in December 2017. Originally used for manned spaceflight missions, it gets adapted for crucial spaceflight tests for other projects as well. *Courtesy of NASA*

Visitor Information

Neither of the SESL chambers are open to the public for tours at any level of what Space Center Houston offers for general visitation or via guided tours.
SPACE CENTER HOUSTON HOURS: 10 a.m.–5 p.m. daily, closed Christmas and Thanksgiving. Extended evening hours (generally 6–10 p.m.) are also offered seasonally. Call or check the website prior to visiting.
Admission and parking fee charged

NASA Tram Tour: Free with admission. There is an Astronaut Training Facility Tour and a Mission Control Center Tour. The latter requires a timed ticket, which is available on a first-come, first-served basis, and the MCC is only one stop on the open-air tram tour. Other tram tours do not require a timed ticket. The last tour departs two hours prior to the center closing, and all may be interrupted due to inclement weather.

Space Expert Tour (includes admission): Additional fee charged. This tour is an in-depth exploration of the center's collection.

Industry & Innovation

Apollo Mission Control Center

Space Center Houston
Building 30
1601 East NASA Parkway
Houston, TX 77058
281-244-2100
https://spacecenter.org

Important Dates

Built: **1965**
Added to National Register of Historic Places:
   October 3, 1985
Designated a National Historic Landmark:
   October 3, 1985

Overall view of Mission Operations Control in MCC in 1969, the year of the Apollo 11 moon trip. *Courtesy of NASA*

170   TREASURES OF TEXAS

Front view of Building 30, which houses Mission Control, in 1984. *Courtesy of NASA*

Site Description

NASA's Apollo Mission Control Center is located within the Christopher C. Kraft Jr. Mission Control Center (MCC), better known by its radio call sign, Houston. This is NASA's facility at the Lyndon B. Johnson Space Center, located southeast of downtown Houston, which manages the flight control for America's human space program. Currently, much of the work done involves the astronauts aboard the International Space Station (ISS), with future manned missions to the moon and, later, Mars. The center is located in Building 30 and is named after Christopher C. Kraft Jr., NASA engineer and manager who was instrumental in establishing the agency's Mission Control operation and served as its first flight director.

The center was first used in June 1965 for Gemini 4, the second crewed Project Gemini spaceflight. Housing two rooms, known as Mission Operation Control Rooms (MOCR), this center together controlled

Mission Operations Control Room (MOCR) for the Sts-9, Johnson Space Center, in 1989. *Courtesy of NASA*

Industry & Innovation   171

Outside Space Center Houston, where visitors can tour portions of Johnson Space Center, which contains numerous exhibits, inside and outside, that portray the role of NASA in the exploration of space

nine of the twelve Gemini missions, all the Apollo moon missions, Skylab, and twenty-one space shuttle flights until 1998. Inside each of the two rooms is a four-tier auditorium, which is dominated by a large map screen. With the exception of the Apollo lunar flights, the map screen featured a Mercator projection of Earth, dotted with the locations of tracking stations and a three-orbit "sine wave" track, which denoted the spacecraft in flight.

Each of the tiers in the room was specialized, being staffed by a variety of controllers responsible for specific spacecraft systems. On the second floor of Building 30 was located MOCR. This was used for Apollo missions 5 and 7, Skylab, and the Apollo-Soyuz Test Project. Located on floor 3 was MOCR 2, which was used for all the Gemini flights except Gemini 3, and all other Apollo flights, including Apollo 11, the first crewed moon landing. MOCR 2 was designated a National Historic Landmark in 1985. It was last used in 1992 as the flight control room for STS-53, a space shuttle *Discovery* mission in support of the Department of Defense. Following its final mission, the space was converted back to its Apollo-era configuration in order to preserve it for historical purposes.

The Apollo Mission Control Center consists of three wings: a mission operations wing (MOW), an operations support wing (OSW), and an interconnecting lobby wing. Inside, the technical management of each mission was vast. They would cover a wide spectrum of vehicular systems, including flight dynamics and crew activities, life systems, recovery support, and ground operations. As news media covered the rapidly advancing space flight projects, the activity at Mission Control become a familiar sight to millions of Americans. Spoken back to this location were famous phrases such as "That's one small step for a man, one giant leap for mankind" during Apollo 11 and "Houston, we've had a problem here" from the failed Apollo 13 mission. In addition to Launch Complex 39 at Kennedy Space Center in Cape Canaveral, Florida, the Apollo Mission Control Center is the symbol many identify with the manned space program.

Plans for the restoration of MOCR 2 were conceived in 2013. The project finally came to fruition in January 2018, with the removal of the first set of consoles. These were sent to the Kansas Cosmosphere in Hutchinson. There, they received archival cleaning and restoration to Apollo-era configuration, to be reinstalled on display back in the control room. Following a two-year-long effort to restore the rest of the room to its Apollo-era configuration, on July 1, 2019, the newly restored Mission Control was reopened to the public. The Historic Mission Control Center is replete with period-appropriate accents such as cigarette packs, ashtrays, mission medallions, seats, wallpaper, carpeting, and upholstery. This was accomplished using digitized 16 mm film taken during the missions, which allowed for the correct identification of color schematics, original column markings, and otherwise unknown artifacts.

In 1992, JSC built an extension to Building 30, which houses two new flight control rooms, designated White and Blue, for use for space shuttle and ISS purposes. It also houses the International Space Station Flight Control Room. There are multiple other facilities in operation in this section of JSC.

Today, the Mission Control Center is accessible for viewing via Space Center Houston's tram tour, out of the nearby visitor center. However, tours do not enter the room itself; it is viewable only from behind the glass in the restored viewing room. In July 2010, Space Center Houston utilized resynchronized air-to-ground voice recordings and film footage shot in Mission Control during the Apollo 11 powered descent and landing, the first time this material was released for public viewing.

> **Visitor Information**
>
> **HOURS:** 10 a.m.–5 p.m. daily, closed Christmas and Thanksgiving. Extended evening hours (generally 6–10 p.m.) are also offered seasonally. Call or check the website prior to visiting. *Admission and parking fee charged*
>
> **NASA Tram Tour:** Free with admission. There is an Astronaut Training Facility Tour and a Mission Control Center Tour. The latter requires a timed ticket, which is available on a first-come, first-served basis, and the MCC is only one stop on the open-air tram tour. Other tram tours do not require a timed ticket. The last tour departs two hours prior to the center closing, and all may be interrupted due to inclement weather.
>
> **Space Expert Tour (includes admission):** Additional fee charged. This tour is an in-depth exploration of the center's collection.

The entrance to Johnson Space Center today, where both Mission Control Center and Space Chambers A and B are located

Industry & Innovation 173

Texas Heritage

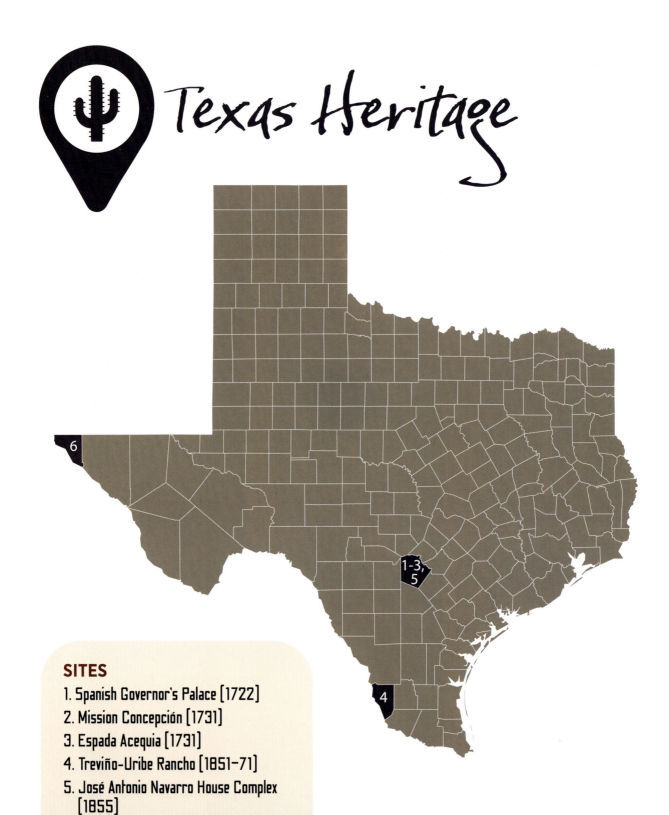

SITES
1. Spanish Governor's Palace (1722)
2. Mission Concepción (1731)
3. Espada Acequia (1731)
4. Treviño-Uribe Rancho (1851–71)
5. José Antonio Navarro House Complex (1855)
6. Rio Vista Bracero Reception Center (1942–64)

Any discussion about Texas heritage is incomplete without mentioning its Spanish, Latino, and Tejano history. Texas has a rich cultural heritage that serves as a reflection of the Lone Star State's diverse and storied population and a remarkable and deep history. Trademarks of a Hispanic influence, from its food to a variety of languages and an array of musical styles, have webbed a distinct influence throughout the state. People from all backgrounds and from lands near and far have called this land home, birthing a tapestry of cultures to make Texas what it is today.

Spanish Governor's Palace

105 Plaza de Armas
San Antonio, TX 78205
210-207-7527
https://www.spanishgovernorspalace.org

Important Dates

Built: **1722**
Added to National Register of Historic Places:
April 15, 1970
Designated a National Historic Landmark:
April 15, 1970

A long line of presidio captains lived in this small home. After the Civil War, a variety of businesses moved as neighborhoods became established. Through the 1920s, this building housed businesses such as a pawn shop, a produce store, a saloon, school classrooms, a tire shop, and more.

Image of the Spanish Governor's Palace at the 1968 World's Fair, known as HemisFair '68, held from April to October 1968 in San Antonio, Texas. *Courtesy of UNT Libraries, The Portal to Texas History*

Site Description

Located in downtown San Antonio, this historic adobe structure from the Spanish colonial era served as the Spanish governor's palace in the early eighteenth century. It is the last visible trace of the colonial Presidio San Antonio de Béxar complex and is the only remaining example in Texas of an aristocratic Spanish colonial in-town residence.

Plans for the palace originated as early as 1722 but were not completed for occupancy until 1749. Set above the front entrance is the keystone, marked with the coat of arms of the Habsburg dynasty, honoring Spanish king Ferdinand VI, and the date 1749. At first, the building served as the residence mission and working offices of the local presidio captain, a company store, and the setting for high society celebrations. Later, it became the home of the Spanish governors who lived in San Antonio. In 1772, the building would become the capitol building of the Texas region of Spanish Texas.

The palace, or Comandancia, is a one-story masonry and stucco building. The building features ten

San Antonio's Military Plaza, showing the former courthouse and city hall known as the Bat Cave at the top right, with the Spanish Governor's Palace to its left. The photograph was taken by Ernst Wilhelm Raba, looking west from the roof of San Fernando Cathedral. *Courtesy of UNT Libraries, The Portal to Texas History*

Texas Heritage 177

The living room at the palace is from 1749. The family would gather here in the evening for dinner and entertaining visitors.

rooms with a large courtyard and fountain. Located on the west side of Plaza de Armas, it has stood sentinel for nearly three hundred years. Since it served as the presidio's captain's residence, it was also known as Casa del Capitán and, more recently, the Spanish Governor's Palace. Throughout its first two hundred years, seven generations of prominent Tejano families owned the home.

Construction commenced sometime in the early 1730s, likely by presidio captain José de Urrutia. The captain built a one-room office out of adobe brick on his property, located on the west side of the presidio between Plaza de Armas and San Pedro Creek. New Spain's military offered their commanders substantial pay through their management of the garrison supply post; however, elaborate quarters were not included. In 1763, the presidio captaincy changed hands, but the home stayed within the family. It was handed over to Luis Antonio Menchaca, Urrutia's grandson and a prosperous landowner and cattle rancher. He would pass the land and building to his own son, José Menchaca. During the father and son's ownership, they

Today, the palace is the only building still standing of the Presidio San Antonio Béxar and is one of the oldest residential buildings still standing in the state. The long one-story stone structure covered in stucco surrounds a traditional Spanish patio and courtyard, seen here.

would expand the residence by at least 50 percent over three decades.

Records listed, by 1804, an inventory of six rooms: the *sala* (parlor), the *recámara* (bedroom), two *zaguáns* (halls), the *cocina* (kitchen), and a room that doubled as the office and company store. By this time, the house was roughly fifty-five years old and had passed through four generations of the Urrutia-Menchaca family. That year, however, was the last, since José Menchaca sold the Comandancia to Juan Ignacio Pérez, the new captain of San Antonio de Béxar. He would serve as interim governor of Texas for nine months in 1816–17. A century later, this brief and temporary post would be the only basis for the palace's most consistent name: Spanish Governor's Palace.

The home would remain in Pérez's family for generations. When Juan Ignacio died in 1823, his son Ignacio inherited the residence. When he died in 1852, his will stipulated that the estate divide the property room by room (a common practice in Béxar at the time) so the house could be transferred to his widow and his three daughters in separate pieces—each receiving one or more rooms by deed. This division eventually fell away, and by the end of the century, Ignacio's granddaughter, Concepción Linn Walsh, and her husband, Frank T. Walsh, acquired full ownership of the house.

Throughout the years, the building watched the neighborhood grow up around it and adapted, taking on the pockmarks of time. An 1819 downpour flooded the San Antonio River and filled the Comandancia with 5 feet of rainwater. Over the next century the building would be inundated another four times. The neighborhood surrounding it would take on an increasingly commercial role. Hardware stores, exchanges, and a schoolhouse were constructed; in 1850, a new city hall and jail went up just 50 feet away. Merchants hawking agricultural goods on the plaza were common daytime occurrences, while at night the Chili Queens, women who offered up chili con carne and other Mexican American dishes, fed passersby. The building itself would serve a variety of purposes, housing a saloon, boardinghouse, pawn shop, and used clothing store . . . decaying slowly into an eyesore along the way.

Remaining above the doorway all those decades, the old royal mark attracted the attention of preservationist Adina De Zavala. Her article in the *San Antonio Express* spoke of the link to the city's Spanish colonial origins

Visitor Information

HOURS: Tuesday–Saturday, 9 a.m.–5 p.m.; Sunday, 10 a.m.–5 p.m.; Monday, closed
Admission fee charged

and renamed the Comandancia the "Spanish Governor's Palace." It took thirteen years for the city council to allocate enough money to purchase the property from the Walshes. When, in 1929, the transaction brought ownership to the City of San Antonio, it was only the second time the title had changed hands outside of inheritance. The reconstruction of the residence became one of the city's earliest preservation projects, opening as San Antonio's first city-owned museum in July 1930. It is now managed by the City of San Antonio's Center City Development and Operations Department.

The passageway, located between the dining room, kitchen, and terrace, includes a staircase that leads to a loft. This area was added to the building during the 1930s and was interpreted as storage areas for garden vegetables and herbs.

Mission Concepción

807 Mission Road
San Antonio, TX 78210
210-533-8955
https://www.missionconcepcion.org

Important Dates

Built: **1731**
Added to the National Register of Historic Places: **April 15, 1970**
Designated a National Historic Landmark: **April 15, 1970**

San Antonio's Mission Concepción, located at 807 Mission Road

180   TREASURES OF TEXAS

Site Description

Franciscan friars established Mission Nuestra Señora de la Purísima Concepción de Acuña (better known as Mission Concepción) in 1711. It started as Nuestra Señora de la Purísima Concepción de los Hainais in East Texas, the second of six Franciscan missions established on both sides of the current Texas-Louisiana border by the Domingo Ramón–St. Denis expedition. It was originally intended to serve as a base for converting the Hasinai to Catholicism, and the friars were to teach the Hasinai what was needed for them to become Spanish citizens. Completed in 1755, it is the oldest unrestored stone church in the United States.

Within days of the founding of the first three missions, three thousand Tejas Indians were reported as candidates at the missions. At Concepción, temporary huts for church and dwellings were built by natives, and baptisms were recorded almost immediately. The mission and presidio had to struggle to receive any supplies from distant Mexico. A severe drought resulted in a poor harvest and hunger; epidemics broke out, killing hundreds; and a war with France caused the evacuation of the missions. While the missionaries would return and reestablish the East Texas outposts, multiple factors resulted in the relocation of the three missions. The friars moved the mission in 1731 to San Antonio, on the east bank of the San Antonio River about halfway between Misión San Antonio de Valero to the north and San José to the south. Later archeological findings suggest that Concepción was

A cabinet card of the Mission Nuestra Señora de la Purísima Concepción de Acuña near San Antonio, Texas. *Courtesy of UNT Libraries, The Portal to Texas History*

In this cabinet card photograph of the Mission Nuestra Señora de la Purísima Concepción de Acuña, grass grows wild from ruined parts of the stone building. A well is visible in the foreground. *Courtesy of UNT Libraries, The Portal to Texas History*

Texas Heritage 181

The Mission Concepción Catholic Church continues to operate, as it has since 1731, in the chapel to this day. It is the oldest unrestored stone church in America.

built on the site of a previous mission—either San Francisco Xavier de Nájera (1722–26) or San José's original location.

Efforts were made to bring various tribes together to the new missions, and one thousand natives are reported to have been willing to join. At first, temporary shelters were built at Concepción, and an acequia was started. It would irrigate the surrounding fields for over a century. Concepción prospered during the early 1730s, despite frequent Apache-led raids and quarrels between the missionaries and the civilians. These tensions, however, would result in policies detrimental to the missions. Following an epidemic of smallpox and measles, the population of Concepción dropped temporarily from 250 to 120 before rebounding in 1740.

Adobe buildings gradually replaced the original huts; farms produced surplus food, several workshops were in operation, and the cattle had multiplied. The mission would become enclosed by a stone wall; inside, it consisted of a sanctuary, nave, *convento*, and granary. When the mission was originally built, brightly painted frescoes decorated both the interior and exterior; however, only traces of this artwork still exist on the weathered facade of the building. Experts were brought in to restore some of this artwork on the interior ceilings and walls of the convento in 1988. The Archdiocese of San Antonio completed another restoration of the mission's interior in 2010, exposing more frescoes in the sanctuary and nave. The western entrance to the church is aligned to the sunset in such a way that an "annual double solar illumination event" occurs every year on or around August 15, the feast day of the Assumption of Mary.

The mission thrived over the next half century, but in 1793, San Antonio de Valero was suppressed as a mission. A census revealed a population of fifty-three, of which only forty-one were Indians—the rest being hired servants and their families. Concepción was later reduced to a sub-mission of San José and would come under the control of the civil authorities of San Antonio. From 1815 on, Concepción merged with San José, and while it was not completely abandoned, by 1819 church services there had been abandoned. Mexican independence finally did it in, and all mission property was sold at auction by the government in 1824.

On October 28, 1835, Mexican troops under Colonel Domingo de Ugartechea and Texian insurgents led by James Bowie and James Fannin fought the Battle of Concepción here. The thirty-minute engagement serves as the first major engagement of the Texas Revolution. Here James Bowie defeated Martín Perfecto de Cos's Mexican troops, with some of the mission's buildings seeing damage during the fight. In 1841, the Republic of Texas conveyed the title of ownership of the church and land to the Catholic Church, but the mission continued to serve primarily as a barn and later as a supply depot by the United States Army.

In 1855, the land was given for use to Marianist brother Andrew Edel, founder of St. Mary's Institute in San Antonio. The Marianists obtained a clear title in 1859 and purchased additional land for farming that would supply and support the school. The church was cleaned, repaired, blessed, and reopened by the end of May 1861. In 1869, the Marianists leased out the mission farmland but continued to use the church. Minor restoration work came in 1887.

When the Marianists transferred the title of Concepción to the bishop in 1911, an orphanage was built on the grounds and staffed by the Sisters of Charity of the Incarnate Word, who also built a convent there in 1926. This was followed by the construction of St. John's Seminary (1919–20), Margil Hall (1935), and St. Mary's Hall (1947). Restoration work, mostly comprising roof repairs and replastering, was undertaken on the mission church during the 1930s by the federal government. Archeological excavations also started around this time but became more serious in the 1970s, when ruins were found of the first friary, the adobe church standing in 1745, the granary and associated workshops, and three rows of Indian quarters.

Standing today are the stone church, the sacristy and the president's office (often called the infirmary), and portions of the second friary and adjacent arched corridor, all built between 1755 and 1760. The modern Mission Road bisects the former mission compound and separates the cluster of buildings from the quarry. Masses are still celebrated on Sundays, on holidays, and during special celebrations. The mission is part of San Antonio Missions National Historical Park. In 2015, the United Nations designated Concepción and four other missions as a World Heritage Site, making it one of only twenty-three such establishments in the United States and the first in Texas.

Visitor Information

The church is open and accessible to all. Please call ahead if you are planning to visit its interior.

While the mission's exterior paint has long since faded or been worn down by time and the elements, geometric designs in blazing colors once covered the church. However, remnants of original frescoes, such as this one, are still visible in several rooms.

Espada Acequia

San Antonio Missions National Historical Park
9405 Espada Road
San Antonio, TX 78214
(210) 932-1001
https://nps.gov/saan/index.htm

Important Dates

Built: **1731–45**
Designated a National Historic Landmark:
  July 19, 1964
Added to National Register of Historic Places:
  October 15, 1966
Designated Contributing Property:
  October 6, 1975

The Espada Aqueduct, seen here at the city's Aqueduct Park, showcases European engineering prowess and masonry work. It has survived for over 275 years, withstanding multiple major floods.

Site Description

Built in 1731 by Franciscan friars in what is now San Antonio, the Espada Acequia, also known as the Piedras Creek Aqueduct, was built to supply irrigation water to the lands near Misión San Francisco de la Espada. The main ditch, or *acequia madre*, continues to carry water to the mission and its former farmlands. This water is still used by residents living on these neighboring lands.

The survival of the new mission depended upon the planting and harvesting of crops. In south-central Texas, intermittent rainfall and the need for a reliable water source made the design and installation of an acequia system a high priority. Managing irrigation was so crucial to the Spanish colonial settlers that they measured cropland in *suertes*—the amount of land that could be watered in one day.

Knowledge of the methodology and use of acequias was originally brought to the arid regions of Spain by the Romans and the Moors. When Franciscan missionaries arrived in the desert Southwest, they found the system worked well in the hot, dry environment. In some areas, such as New Mexico, it blended in easily with the irrigation system already in use by the Puebloan Native Americans. The friars used stone, reinforced with slabs of caliche, to construct their acequia.

In order to distribute water to the various missions along the San Antonio River, the missionaries oversaw the construction using American Indian workers for

Built by Franciscan friars in 1731 in what is now San Antonio, the Espada Acequia was built to supply irrigation water to the lands near Mission San Francisco de la Espada. It is the oldest Spanish aqueduct in the United Sates.

The Espada Aqueduct, seen here in this late 1890s photo, spans a 6-mile creek with two arches and one support pier. Prior to this, the Spanish would have used hollowed-out logs to carry water over the creek. *Courtesy of UNT Libraries, The Portal to Texas History*

When the stone aqueduct was complete, water flowed across the top in a channel until reunited with the earthen ditch on the other side. Once it left the aqueduct, the acequia carried the water southwardly toward Mission Espada and the farm fields.

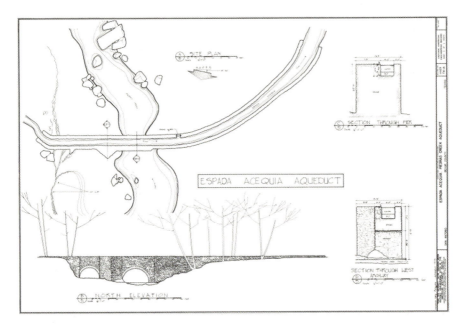

A site plan for the Espada Aqueduct was drawn by Gary Rogers as part of the Historic American Buildings Survey in 1973. This shows how the water for irrigation passes over Piedras Creek to get to Mission San Francisco de la Espada. *Courtesy of the Library of Congress, Prints and Photographs Division*

seven gravity-flow ditches, dams, and one aqueduct. This 15-mile network irrigated approximately 3,500 acres of land. The acequia not only conducted potable water and irrigation but also powered a mill. In an early report, the Mission Espada was able to irrigate fields in which multiple vegetables and cotton grew; that year, 8 bushels of corn were planted, yielding 1,600 bushels.

Eventually, the acequia fell into disuse in the 1880s. A project to restore the aqueduct came together in 1895 and continues to carry water for irrigation to this day. Today, the Espada Aqueduct is located within the confines of the San Antonio Missions National Historical Park. At 4 miles long, this remains one of the best-preserved and best-functioning examples of a Spanish acequia in the United States. It is the only remaining Spanish aqueduct in the United States. It lies just north of the Mission Espada, inside a small park with a parking lot that marks the location and historical significance of the aqueduct. There, you can see a portion of the acequia from the San Antonio River branch of the low-elevation Piedras Creek. This system is in its most complete and original form along the route at the park.

Visitor Information

The above address is for the aqueduct. If more information or assistance is needed, the primary visitor center is located at the Mission San José, which is located at 6701 San José Drive.
PARK HOURS: Sunrise to sunset
MISSION SAN JOSÉ VISITOR CENTER HOURS: 9 a.m.–5 p.m. daily
No entrance fees

Treviño-Uribe Rancho

604 Treviño Street
San Ygnacio, TX 78067
956-765-5784
https://www.nps.gov/places/trevino-uribe-rancho.htm

Important Dates

Built: **ca. 1830**
Expanded: **1851–71**
Designated a Recorded Texas Historical Landmark: **1964**
Designated a National Register of Historic Places: **July 16, 1973**
Designated a National Historic Landmark: **August 6, 1998**

Opportunities were limited by the location of the ranch, the sparse population of the area, and the lack of rail access. Additionally, the frontier's nature, harsh environment, and threatening tribes, along with isolation and limited building materials, all meant that settlers developed specific architectural techniques that would provide function and protection.

Not much has changed since the rancho was erected. Mexican pioneer settlers and ranchers began to cross the Rio Grande into present-day Texas starting in the late 1700s. *Photo by Arthur W. Stewart, courtesy of Library of Congress*

Site Description

The Treviño-Uribe Rancho, a fortified home in the small frontier town of San Ygnacio, is located about 30 miles south of Laredo. The home dates to 1830 and is now one of the oldest surviving buildings from the Spanish-Mexican settlement period. Located on the north bank of the lower Rio Grande River, the fortified home sits atop a bluff overlooking the river. The town of San Ygnacio would eventually become a large center of trade along the Mexican border by the mid-1800s.

This multiroom sandstone building is arranged in an L shape, with thick stone walls forming an enclosed rectangular compound. There are no windows, only loopholes through which defenders might fire at attackers. The main entrance to the compound is a fortified arched gateway with heavy wooden double doors. The six-room chambers, which retain many of the original features, are evidence of multiple building periods that took place throughout the nineteenth century. A river-stone masonry wall surrounds the complex,

Buildings of the Treviño-Uribe Rancho. It is one of the finest surviving examples of domestic borderlands architecture in the United States. It was initially constructed around 1830 as a modest single-room rancho. It expanded through five building campaigns over the next forty years.

enclosing a large interior courtyard. While the original purpose of the building was to provide defense, as it aged there was more craftsmanship afforded to it, and the decorative details highlight that.

During the eighteenth century, the San Ygnacio area was part of a large Spanish colonial land grant, extending to both sides of the Rio Grande River. Early

Texas Heritage 189

By 1871, *rancho* additions—including this dining hall—show that strategic defensive measures were no longer central to design purposes. Proximity to gates and increasing doors and exterior openings lend to that development.

Likely used more as an outpost, Blas María Uribe maintained his primary residence in Guerrero while the rancho served a dual purpose: fortified shelter and ranch. Featuring living spaces, a dining area, and a kitchen, the building also featured high, thick sandstone walls as well as a windowless facade, gunports, and a secured gate entry. *Photo by Arthur W. Stewart, courtesy of the Library of Congress*

ranchos were established on the south bank of the Rio Grande, including Revilla, which sat across the river from San Ygnacio and was later replaced by Guerrero. Jesus Treviño, a wealthy landowner from Revilla, purchased acreage on the north bank of the river and built a single-chamber stone structure in 1830. This is the oldest surviving portion of the rancho.

Due to the ongoing threat of raids from the Comanche and Apache and later due to upheaval over revolutions and massive land grabs, Treviño built a one-room stone building. Standing at 296 square feet, this building would serve as his ranching headquarters for the next twenty years and remain the centerpiece of the complex. With walls 26 inches thick, no windows, and two 5-foot-tall towers with gunports, as well as a flat roof with a lookout perch, the need for defense determined the form of the building. Its 3-inch-thick south door, which is still in place today, was made of mesquite with a cypress panel. Inside, the door was secured by a mesquite crossbar.

The structure was not intended to be a permanent habitation but more likely was intended to be used as shelter from the elements and Native American attacks. Treviño's son-in-law, Blas María Uribe, added to this structure in phases between 1851 and 1871. This transformed the once-small structure into the much larger compound seen today, and it became a more permanent home. Additional rooms and walls were constructed to surround the extant Cuarto Viejo (Old Room) and enclosed a courtyard with livestock corrals. One feature of note is a native stone made into a polished sundial and set into the north wall of the fort. The defensive features were not abolished and, in fact, became better equipped. Protective parapets were added, gunports were installed, and fireproof roofs were made from *chipichil* (a mix of lime, sand, and gravel), turning it into a site of refuge for the entire surrounding community.

This house would become known locally as Fort Treviño. The final construction effort was finished in the 1870s, with the addition of the large sandstone room (*la casa pinta*), or parlor, one designed specifically as a social function. Along with the courtyard, it became a space in which family and members of the community could gather to relax or celebrate.

> **Visitor Information**
>
> HOURS: First Sunday of every month, noon–5 p.m. Private tours are available from River Pierce Foundation on a suggested donation basis.
> *No entrance fees, but donation suggested*

With only a few exceptions, since the 1870s the fort would see very few significant changes. Since 1998, when the compound received its National Historic Landmark designation, the River Pierce Foundation has been working to preserve the building. It took a decade to purchase the entire property from its original owners, and two additional years to complete its restoration. It stands as the founding structure of the border town of less than a thousand people. Its restoration work took it back to 1936, using that date as the best documentation that they could find. This still allowed them to keep all major historical features but take away all the accretions added after 1936. The historic San Ygnacio district had thirty-six stone buildings and is the last South Texas community to exhibit such a large collection of the once-numerous sandstone structures built in the middle and late nineteenth century.

José Antonio Navarro House Complex

228 South Laredo Street
San Antonio, TX 78207
210-226-4801
https://thc.texas.gov/historic-sites/casa-navarro

Important Dates

Built: **1855**
Designated a Recorded Texas Historic Landmark: **1962**
Added to National Register of Historic Places: **March 1972**
Designated a National Historic Landmark: **December 23, 2016**

The Casa Navarro State Historic Site celebrates the life of José Antonio Navarro, whose life and career in Texas spanned four sovereign nations—Spain, Mexico, the Republic of Texas, and the United States—and also saw the emergence of the Confederate States of America.

Site Description

José Antonio Navarro was a Tejano soldier, educator, politician, and revolutionary whose life and work threads itself through the fabric of Texas's early history. Navarro's influence in bringing Texas to independence and then statehood was crucial; the state's narrative would be vastly different without his presence. While names such as Houston, Bowie, Crockett, Austin, and Travis are at the apex of early Texas history, Navarro's name and legacy is often overshadowed, despite his role in the creation of Texas.

Born in February 1795 in present-day San Antonio, to a distinguished noble family, José was the eighth of twelve children. Studious, he eventually taught himself law, but when his father, a former soldier and Spanish *alcalde* (mayor), died, he quit his formal education and stepped in to run the family store.

Early-nineteenth-century San Antonio was rife with chaos; class systems were uneven and harsh, which would lead to increased tensions and, finally, open rebellion. José admired and supported the freedom fighters, which included his uncle Francisco Ruiz, and would himself join the movement in 1813 before fleeing with his uncle and brothers for the United States as the rebellion grew more violent and out of control. They lived in exile for three years before returning.

José Antonio Navarro is seen in this portrait photograph by Ernst Wilhelm Raba. Navarro stands with his left hand resting on the back of a chair in front of a painted backdrop. *Courtesy of UNT Libraries, The Portal to Texas History*

The front/west facade of the two-story stuccoed limestone building originally used as a law office by José Antonio Navarro at 230 Laredo Street. *Courtesy of UNT Libraries, The Portal to Texas History*

Mexico finally secured its independence from Spain in 1821 with Coahuila y Tejas, becoming a state in 1824. Following their return to San Antonio, the Navarros and Ruizes became community leaders. José married Margarita de la Garza, raised seven children, practiced law, and served as a land commissioner for the Green DeWitt Colony, and later the Béxar District. He assisted in colonization projects, becoming an early proponent of Texas's independence from Mexico. Navarro befriended the like-minded Stephen F. Austin, forming a partnership whose connections and influences would push that project to American colonization.

By 1828, Navarro was serving in Congress in Mexico City, representing Coahuila y Tejas. His work opened the door for colonists to settle on land through Austin's 1823 land grant contract, known as the "Old Three Hundred," the first organized and approved influx of Anglo-Americans to Texas. They settled between the Brazos and the Colorado Rivers, from the Gulf coast to the San Antonio Road, with their capital at San Felipe de Austin. Their settlement and their status as educated and wealthy would lead to another revolution for independence in 1835 and 1836.

Tensions rose during the 1830s, with the crescendo coming in San Antonio. While the Alamo was being

Texas Heritage 193

The interior of the buildings at Casa Navarro interprets the life of this important rancher and merchant, who was one of only two native-born Texans to sign the Texas Declaration of Independence.

besieged, Navarro, his uncle, and a group of pro-revolutionary men were drafting the Texas Declaration of Independence at Washington-on-the-Brazos. Navarro struggled over signing away Texas from its homeland and whether he was seeking independence or trying to reimplement the Mexican Constitution of 1824 that Santa Anna usurped. In the end, he helped draft and approve the declaration establishing the Republic of Texas.

Out of the sixty men to sign the document, Navarro and his uncle were the only native Tejanos, while Lorenzo de Zavala and Juan Seguín were Latinos; the rest were Anglos from the United States. The new republic covered a considerable portion of the present-day American Southwest and into the Rocky Mountains, including present-day Texas and what is today the Panhandle of Oklahoma, far southeastern Kansas, about half of New Mexico, and land stretching northward through Colorado and Wyoming.

Throughout the rest of his life, Navarro continued to hold public office positions, continuing his fight to improve the Texans' way of life but also defending the land rights of Tejano families from the immigrants he had helped enter their country, ultimately watching many Tejano families lose generational lands. Defying his own reluctance, he joined the failed Santa Fe Expedition of 1841. The joint commercial and military expedition to secure parts of northern New Mexico and gain control over the lucrative Santa Fe Trail resulted in his capture, a trial, and a death sentence (later commuted to life imprisonment) from the Mexican government. He managed to escape three years later through the help of sympathetic guards.

Navarro quickly returned to his political life. He would become a representative in the Republic of Texas Congress from Béxar County, worked to promote Tejano-friendly legislation, worked to bring academic institutions to San Antonio, and supported the annexation of Texas by the United States. On March 1, 1845, that support became reality, and Navarro became an instrumental figure in drafting the first state Constitution of Texas and its admittance as the twenty-eighth state. He was the only Tejano delegate to the convention, and, in helping to draft the constitution, he persuaded his fellow delegates to strike the word "White" as a requirement for voting rights. Navarro served two terms in the Texas Senate before finally retiring from politics in 1849.

In his retirement, Navarro spent much of his time on his San Geronimo Ranch. Most every spring, summer, and fall was spent on the 6,000-acre ranch near Seguin. The concrete home he built there has since been demolished, but a Texas Historical Marker locates the site. He continued to be influential in politics, writing historical and political essays for a variety of publications, seeking to defend and preserve Tejano legacies from xenophobic and racist Anglo histories being issued at the time. Navarro, always the rebel, supported secession with the rest of the Southern states when the Civil War finally came to pass, and all four of his sons would fight for the Confederacy. Navarro would later sell his ranch and live full time at his home in San Antonio, where he died in January 1871.

The Navarro Complex

Located in the heart of the Laredito ("Little Laredo") neighborhood, near the central business district, lies the José Antonio Navarro House Complex State Historic Site. Originally covering about 1.5 acres, the property was purchased by Navarro in 1832 and today is Texas's only preserved historical Tejano site. Navarro built this complex during the 1850s, a time when San Antonio was a thriving, bustling city. Two-century-old landmarks stood sentinel when Navarro built his complex just a short walk along San Pedro Creek from the Spanish Governor's Palace and San Fernando Cathedral. Another ten-to-fifteen-minute walk leads to the Alamo.

While the complex was constructed in the two decades following the purchase, a portion of the kitchen may date back to the Spanish colonial era. Constructed of limestone, caliche block, and adobe, three buildings, along with a common patio, are enclosed by a low-slung wall. Here, Navarro built a one-story home for his family and a kitchen next to his two-story *despacho*, a merchant and law office building. The site is significant not just because of who lived there but because it is the sole surviving compound in the city and is a prime example of the architecture of San Antonio in the 1850s, including both a residence and a place of business.

Located on the southwest corner of the complex, Navarro's *despacho* is a stuccoed limestone office building that he used as a law office. Nearly square in its plan, there is a single room on each of the building's two stories. Two doors located on the first story feature transom windows to help move air through the building. Placed directly above the doors, on the second floor are two more windows. A single door on the rear of the building opens to the patio at the east.

Just a few feet north is the family home, fronting on South Laredo Street. Made from limestone and adobe, the single-story home with an attic showcases deep porches on the front and rear. The architecture style is typical of early one-story Texas homes and contains a wide front gallery and a rear L branch with a gallery extending from an inset rear porch. Three rooms open onto the rear gallery.

The three-room adobe and caliche *cocina*, or family kitchen, sits detached at the rear of the property, forming the south boundary of the complex. It too features front and rear porches with a hipped roof that continues as an overshoot roof for both porches. Three rooms make up the floorplan: two that open to the porches, both with a fireplace, and an end room at the north. The end room is the oldest portion of the building and has massive stone lintels and six-over-six-light windows. At the buildings' convergence sits the gravel and flagstone patio. Landscaped, the common space was likely where the Navarro family would gather to eat and converse.

The entire complex is enclosed by a low wall. The wall's south-facing facade, bordering Nueva Street, now displays a 50-by-8-foot tile mural designed by San Antonio artists Jesse Treviño and his wife, Elizabeth Rodríguez, in 2012 depicting the Laredito neighborhood. During the 1960s, the complex was in danger of demolition as blocks of Laredito were flattened during an urban renewal effort. Following extensive conservation work with Navarro's descendants, the San Antonio Conservation Society saved the property and deeded the property to the Texas Parks and Wildlife Department in 1975; it would open as a state historic site in October 1997.

Today, the complex offers a glimpse of homelife in 1850s San Antonio. The main dwelling is filled with period-appropriate antiques of Texas, Louisiana, and Mexico. The *despacho* contains an exhibit of pictures and documents telling the Navarro story and includes copies of the Declaration of Independence of Texas and copies of the equivalent documents from both the United States and Mexico. The *cocina* continues to be used as a kitchen, with the San Antonio Conservation Society preparing special food for social functions and programs.

Visitor Information

HOURS: Tuesday–Saturday, 10 a.m.–5 p.m.; Sunday, noon–5 p.m. Closed Mondays, Thanksgiving, Christmas Eve and Day, New Year's Eve and Day
Admission fee charged

Rio Vista Bracero Reception Center

Rio Vista Farm
800–860 and 901 North Rio Vista Road
Socorro, TX 77927

Important Dates

Built: **1915**
Period of Significance: **1942–64**
Designated a National Historic Landmark:
  December 13, 2023
Added to National Register of Historic Places:
  February 22, 1996 *(as Rio Vista Farm Historic District)*

Plans call for the restoration and interpretation of the Rio Vista Farm site. In addition to its historic role, the site also served as a shooting location for the 2000 movie *Traffic*. *Courtesy of the City of Socorro*

The deteriorating adobe buildings, seen here at Rio Vista Farm, sheltered the poor during the Great Depression. It then served as a processing center for the Bracero Program. *Courtesy of the City of Socorro*

Site Description

Throughout its century-long history, the Rio Vista Farm has shaped the borderland region, helping to establish a foundation for modern Mexican American communities. Rio Vista was started as El Paso County's second "poor farm" for public welfare programs, and it eventually sheltered children during the Great Depression and served as a point of entry for the Bracero Program. The farm was used as one of five processing centers for migrant workers during this program; at the height of the program, there were roughly three million men on-site at one time. This significant but often-overlooked side of the American experience is emblematic of the arrival of many skilled Mexican guest workers brought into the United States to aid with the farm labor shortages across America during and after World War II.

Running from 1942 to 1964, the *bracero* (laborer) movement consisted of workers who came to the United States from Mexico to work on farms and railroads. These men would leave their communities and families with the hope of finding economic opportunity, sometimes in incredibly difficult conditions. The process for registering in the program was similar for all migrants. They would be transported from a part of Mexico to various processing centers throughout the United States, such as Rio Vista, before being allowed to work. After processing and relocation to the facility, thousands of braceros would wait for a job offer to work the fields in other parts of the country. Additional reception centers for this program were located in El Centro, California; Nogales, Arizona; Eagle Pass, Texas; and Hidalgo, Texas—with shorter stints located in El Paso and Harlingen, Texas.

The Rio Vista Bracero Center embraced more than 4.2 million contracts for the millions of unique individuals coming through processing. The peak came in 1956, with nearly 500,000 contracts being issued, deploying braceros to thirty-eight states, with a heavy concentration along the Mexican border. This pattern of Mexican migration contributed to a postwar

Built in 1915, this site originally served the area as the El Paso Poor Farm, the city's second. It has since hosted an array of public welfare programs, served as a temporary base for a Civilian Conservation Corps unit, and served as the reception and processing center for the Bracero Program. *Courtesy of the City of Socorro*

increase in the US Latino population, especially in Texas and states to the west. They composed nearly a quarter of US agricultural workers by 1959, enhancing the profitability in America's agribusiness sector. The highly skilled workers worked at relatively low wages, thus permitting the expansion of certain crop sectors.

While at the Rio Vista Farm facility, one of five such processing sites, the braceros would go through a registration process. Included in this process was having to strip naked and get fumigated with DDT, a pesticide meant to kill lice. The United States would eventually ban the use of DDT in 1972 due to adverse environmental effects and potential human health risks. Running from 1942 to 1964, this program served as the United States' largest guest worker program, with an estimated 4.6 million short-term labor contracts issued to Mexican workers, some coming through multiple times. While it did not provide a pathway to citizenship, many braceros would go on to become citizens.

Of the remaining eighteen white adobe buildings at Rio Vista, only five have received maintenance and are currently in use. The remaining structures sit empty and are in a state of severe deterioration. The main building, built in 1915, is the most dilapidated, but it does retain much of its primary character-defining features and is one of two extant properties dating to the initial operation of the county poor farm. Other buildings include the administrative offices, dormitories, mess hall, school, recreation hall, Quonset, and quadrangle. Multiple buildings are also on-site that are listed as noncontributing to the site's listing as a National Register of Historic Places district.

With the designation of the site as a National Historic Landmark, preservation of the complex by the City of Socorro will continue to include the stabilization of the site's multiple adobe structures for its reuse and interpretation. The National Trust for Historic Preservation named the complex a National Treasure in 2016, leading to increased visibility on the site and its eventual application for the National Historic Landmark Program. A historical marker, placed in 2000, sits south of the Rio Vista mess hall.

Visitor Information

The Rio Vista Bracero Reception Center is not currently open to the public. With a projected 2027 opening, the site will be the nation's first Bracero History Museum.

Temporary clerks, seen here at Rio Vista in El Paso, needed to be proficient in both English and Spanish. The clerks typed and filled in the necessary forms, such as these fingerprint cards, after obtaining all necessary information from the applicant. *Courtesy of USCIS*

Once forms I-100 (A) and (B) (micas) were typed for the applicant, the applicants moved to the next station. Here, these Rio Vista clerks stapled photographs to the cards. Following the appropriate inspections and receiving Bracero Program documentation, workers would then board transportation to the farm of their new employer. *Courtesy of USCIS*

Mexican braceros are seen having boarded the train and saying goodbye to their families. They are leaving a recruitment center in Mexico, heading to a reception center such as Rio Vista in the United States. *Photo courtesy of USCIS*

Upon arrival, immigrant inspectors would greet the braceros in lines such as these. This process is gone through to approve the arrival of the braceros in Hidalgo, Texas, in 1957. *Photo courtesy of USCIS*

Texas Heritage 199

Residential Life

SITES
1. Roma Historic District (1821)
2. Strand Historic District (1850)
3. East End Historic District (ca. 1886)

With such a rich and cultural heritage within the state of Texas, it can sometimes become muddled how things once were. Throughout Texas, the National Park Service has designated a handful of historic districts as National Historic Landmarks. These sites give visitors a chance to see the structures and locales that became indicative of how life once was in these areas.

There are both residential and commercial locales listed here. Some of these districts, such as Roma, are little changed and provide an excellent slice of life from the city's yesteryear. Others, such as the Strand in Galveston, have seen considerable changes. While the buildings themselves are little changed in appearance, many have undergone transformations, some multiple times. They've changed from warehouses to tourist shops, groceries to cafés. However, they do provide visitors with a chance to see what visitors and residents would have seen decades ago.

Roma Historic District

Properties along Estrella and Hidalgo Streets, between Garfield Street and Bravo Alley
Roma Historic District Visitor Station
77 Convent Avenue
Roma, TX 78584
210-849-0099
https://www.cityofroma.net/residents/historic-district

Important Dates

Established: **1821**
Added to National Register of Historic Places: **July 31, 1972**
Designated a National Historic Landmark District: **November 4, 1993**
Designated a Recorded Texas Historic Landmark: **1973**

Designed by Pierre Yves Kéralum, the Church of Our Lady of Refuge of Sinners was constructed in 1853. The church, of which only the tower remains, was a brick Gothic Revival structure and the first of several designed by Kéralum along the lower Rio Grande.

202   TREASURES OF TEXAS

The Roma Historic District provides an intact example of a lower Rio Grande valley border town. It served as an important port and shipping center on the Rio Grande from 1829 until the 1880s. The architecture mirrors its sister city Ciudad Mier on the Mexican side of the river. *Courtesy of UNT Libraries, The Portal to Texas History*

Site Description

The Roma Historic District preserves an intact example of a border town in the lower Rio Grande valley. Roma was an important port and transshipment point on the Rio Grande from 1829 to the 1880s. The architecture in Roma mirrors its sister city of Ciudad Mier on the Mexican side of the river, as well as Guerrero Viejo upriver.

The site was first settled as early as 1760, was established in 1821 in what was then the Spanish province of Nuevo Santander, and was named "Roma" in 1848 in honor of the Italian city. The site offered a convenient crossing on the Rio Grande, also known as El Paso de la Mula (Pass of the Mules), and was notable for a salt trade from Roma to Monterrey.

The area later became the Mexican province of Tamaulipas with Mexican independence but then became part of Texas with the establishment of the republic in 1838. Although there was a battle at Mier during the Mexican-American War in 1848, the region remained part of Texas. During the Civil War, the

These stone house ruins rest next to the Vale/Cox House on the northwest corner of Convent and Water Streets and date back to at least the 1840s. Originally, this was a one-story, sandstone structure facing the Rio Grande and could have been used as secondary structure for John Vale.

Residential Life   203

The Manuel Guerra House and Store was designed and constructed by Heinrich Portscheller in 1878. The building has commercial retail space on the first floor and residential space above. To the rear is a long one-story building, which likely served as a warehouse for the store.

region became wealthy on the cotton trade, which was transshipped via Mexico to Europe. While steamboats were able to access Roma through the mid-nineteenth century, lowering water levels as a result of development upstream ended river shipments by the 1880s. Bypassed by railroads, Roma stagnated and, inadvertently, preserved itself from development.

The city is known for its buildings of river sandstone, caliche limestone, and molded brick, using *rejoneado* (patterned large and small stones) and *sillar* (stone laid in an ashlar pattern) masonry techniques. Both employ an outer finish of rough lime plaster detailed with bands of smooth colored plaster, characteristic of northern Mexico. Additionally, Roma features molded brick, a German innovation, as a technique in flat brick roofing and as decorative brick use in this region. German builder Enrique (Heinrich) Portscheller designed multiple buildings with this product and employed the use of wrought-iron balconies, similar to those seen in both New Orleans and Monterrey. Roma preserves the bulk of his work.

The historic district comprises thirty-eight contributing buildings, of which sixteen are stone buildings from the 1829–70 period and nineteen are brick buildings from the 1880–1900 period, with the rest from post-1900. The district is divided up into four areas: the Plaza, the Wharf, the Customs House, and the Northwestern Zone.

The Plaza area is a rectangular public square that runs northeast perpendicular from the Rio Grande out to the Our Lady of Refuge Catholic Church, which was constructed in 1853 and has only the tower left from that era. Roma features an open-ended plaza facing the Rio Grande and Mexico on the far bank, while Estrella and Portscheller Streets intersect the Plaza. The lower plaza is defined by walled compounds, which included commercial uses, most notably in the Guerra store, which dominated the town's commerce.

The earliest historic building is the Mission Church, which Catholic priests founded in 1829.

The Wharf area, along Hidalgo Street and upward to Juarez and Estrella Streets, dealt with river commerce and consisted of warehouses and stores, as well as the Roma–Ciudad Miguel Aleman Bridge, the wharf, and seven other historic buildings. Located on the riverbank south of the Plaza area and west of Juarez Avenue, the wharf property is where the Rio Grande travelers docked their keelboats and steamboats in the mid-nineteenth century. This was the city's center of trade, and many warehouses and stores are included here, including the Rodriguez House/Warehouse and the Portscheller-built Nester Saenz Store. The bridge, built in 1929, is the last surviving international suspension bridge on the Rio Grande. It is 700 feet long and 16 feet wide, with twin steel towers grounded in concrete piers at each end. It still connects Roma to Ciudad Miguel Aleman, Tamaulipas, Mexico. Since it is unable to carry any heavy loads, a modern bridge runs parallel to accommodate the demands of border traffic.

The Customs House area includes Lincoln and Water Streets, comprising a mixture of commercial and residential structures, chiefly of stone construction and dominated by a brick family compound at Zaragoza and Estrella. There is a concentration of ten stone and brick buildings at Estrella and Water Streets, and it derives its name from the historic 1883 US Customs House / City Hall / Jail. The one-story customhouse was placed on the highest point on the bluff, overlooking the river. Nine additional domestic and commercial historic buildings built between the 1840s and 1890s define this area.

The Northwestern Zone is associated with the Arroyo de los Negros, the location of a secondary ferry crossing on the Rio Grande. However, no buildings or features in this part of the historic district relate to the city of Rome's historic core.

The Roma Historic District's nineteenth-century brick-and-stone craftsmanship makes the town a significant stop on any tour of Hispanic architecture in the lower Rio Grande valley. The town's walled family compound recalls Roma's Spanish heritage, and the stone and brick techniques are native to the region. Visitors can take a self-guided driving or walking tour around the district to see thirty-eight historic properties. The plaza has a parking lot, and both the Roma Historical Museum in the old Mission Church and the Roma Historic District Visitor Station in the Plaza provide opportunities to learn more about the area's history.

> **Visitor Information**
>
> Certain buildings and locations may have restricted access hours.

Roma, even with its buildings in various states of repair, stands as a rare surviving intact community and represents the evolution of a key nineteenth-century border town. Its preservation allows visitors to see the different building technologies used along the lower Rio Grande in the nineteenth century.

Residential Life   205

Strand Historic District

Roughly bounded by Avenue A, Twentieth Street, the railroad depot, and the alley between Avenues C and D
Galveston, TX 77550
409-797-5000
www.downtowngalveston.org/index.html

Important Dates

Built: **1839, 1850**
Designated a National Historic District: **January 26, 1970**
Added to National Register of Landmarks: **May 11, 1976**

The Grand 1894 Opera House has survived major storms in 1900 and 1915 and then Hurricanes Carla and Alicia, as well as neglect. It is one of the few remaining theaters of its era in Texas, it was restored in 1974 and again in 1990, and today it continues to serve Galveston as a performance hall.

206 TREASURES OF TEXAS

The Hendley Building, located at Strand and Twentieth, is thought to be the island's oldest surviving commercial structure. Erected in the late 1850s by shipping magnates William and Joseph Hendley, it was the city's most expensive pre–Civil War commercial building and still bears scars from the 1863 Battle of Galveston. *Courtesy of the Rosenberg Library, Galveston, Texas*

Site Description

Today, the stretch of Avenues A, B, and C in Galveston—more popularly known as "the Strand"—is a district of Victorian-era buildings now housing restaurants, antique stores, and curio shops. It is a major tourist attraction for the island city of Galveston and plays host to two very popular seasonal festivals. However, throughout the nineteenth century, the port city of Galveston boomed, rivaling its inland neighbor of Houston as the largest and most important city along the Texas coast. The Strand, which runs parallel to the bay and is located very close to the harbor, grew into the region's main business center, becoming known as the "Wall Street of the South."

Drawn up in the late 1830s, the original plat of Galveston shows Avenue B. However, when German immigrant Michael William Shaw opened his jewelry store on the corner of 23rd and Avenue B, he did not like the name "Ave. B." Using the name of a street in London taken from the Old English word for "shore" or "riverbank"—and meaning "beach" in his native German—Shaw changed the name of the street to "Strand" on his stationery. He felt that such a name would have higher-class connotations for a jewelry store. Shaw went on to convince other business owners along the stretch of street to change the name, and it stuck.

The earliest buildings along the Strand were usually wooden. These types of structures were extremely vulnerable to fires as well as to the storms that hit the island frequently throughout the nineteenth century. Eventually, they were replaced with iron-fronted brick buildings. The oldest still standing are in Hendley Row and date to 1855 and 1858. The Berlocker Building, located at Strand and Mechanic Street, was built in 1858, while most others date to the 1870s and 1880s.

The Strand would become a popular place for major businesses to locate, mostly because of the Port of Galveston's enormous vessel traffic. With between 700 and 1,400 vessels annually, it became a hotspot

Virtually nothing on the island was left untouched following the 1900 hurricane. The storm landed at nightfall and raged throughout the night, bringing a tidal surge of 15 feet. Corpses and debris were strewn everywhere by daybreak. Galveston was essentially destroyed. *Courtesy of the Rosenberg Library, Galveston, Texas*

Residential Life   207

Located just off the Strand on Postoffice Street, the 1861 United States Customs House was an important fixture symbolizing Galveston's status as a leading seaport and commercial city in the nineteenth century. It survived the 1885 Galveston fire due to its revolutionary use of fireproof cast iron in its construction.

for industry and would feature the state's five largest banks, along with wholesalers, commission merchants, attorneys, cotton brokers, and slave auctioneers. In 1881 alone, businesses in the district sold roughly $38 million worth of services and merchandise. Between 1838 and 1842, eighteen newspapers began operation; only the *Galveston News*, founded in 1842, remains.

With the Strand located so close to the harbor, the area suffered somewhat during the Civil War, especially when Union forces barricaded the city during the Battle of Galveston. Confederate forces fought throughout the district, primarily on and around Kuhn's Wharf at 21st Street, with several buildings, including the Hendley buildings, suffering damage from shots and shells. The war forced many businesses to close and relocate to nearby Houston until the end of the war. Most of the businesses moved back to the Strand, enjoying growth and prosperity until the end of the century.

The city of Galveston had weathered numerous storms by 1900, all of which the city survived easily, leading to a sense of complacency. Galveston had grown to be the fourth largest Texas city in population, had among the highest per capita income rates in the United States, and was serving as the state's center of trade and one of the busiest ports in the nation—much of it centered within the Strand. Even two storms in 1875 and 1886 that essentially wiped the Matagorda Bay city of Indianola off the map did little to move efforts for the creation of a protective seawall in Galveston.

The massive hurricane that hit Galveston in early September 1900 became the deadliest natural disaster in US history and the fifth deadliest Atlantic hurricane overall, leaving between 6,000 and 12,000 dead in its wake, many in or near Galveston. The storm surge flooded the coastline with 8 to 12 feet of water, destroyed about 7,000 buildings on the island, including 3,636 homes, and causing some form of damage to every dwelling. Over a quarter of the islanders were left

While the 1900 Galveston hurricane was the most destructive storm in the nation's history, handfuls of buildings survived its wrath. Today, markers abound throughout the Strand interpreting the history of the buildings. One such marker includes a badge, such as this, denoting the building's survivability during the storm.

homeless. The disaster ended Galveston's golden era, turning investors inland toward Houston. In response, engineers designed and oversaw plans to raise the Gulf of Mexico shoreline along the island by 17 feet and erect a 10-mile seawall.

Along the Strand, many of the buildings suffered catastrophic damage in the 1900 hurricane. Some buildings, such as the W. L. Moody Building, lost entire floors; others lost their elaborate cornices and flourishes. Many businesses now saw the Strand's location close to the wharf as a detractor and elected to move away from the Strand, transforming it into a warehouse district. It wasn't until the 1960s when the Junior League of Galveston County began a revitalization in the district by restoring two historic buildings. That effort sparked a project that continues to this day. In 1973, the Galveston Historical Foundation joined the Junior League, creating a trust fund for restorations in the Strand District, which brought in significant private investments to the area.

Almost 108 years to the day of the deadly 1900 storm, on September 13, 2008, Hurricane Ike made landfall near Galveston, and the storm and its surge caused significant and catastrophic damage to the Strand. The seawall helped to somewhat buffer the damage, but it was so significant it prompted the National Trust for Historic Preservation to add the district to the 2009 list of Most Endangered Places.

While not back to its splendor of the Wall Street of the South, the Strand has once again become a source of civic pride and a huge attractor for visitors and residents alike. While it extends throughout Galveston, the Strand usually refers to a five-block business district between 20th and 25th Streets. Today, the Strand features historical exhibits, museums (such as *Elissa*, another National Historic Landmark), art galleries, restaurants, nightclubs, and hotels. It's the location of one of the larger Mardi Gras celebrations outside New Orleans and a Christmas festival known as Dickens on the Strand, which celebrates the city's Victorian heritage.

Also known as the Gresham House, the 1892 Bishop's Palace is a defining home in the East End Historic District. Architectural historians have listed this home, seen here in an early postcard, as one of the most significant Victorian residences in the country. *Courtesy of the author's collection*

Visitor Information

HOURS: The district is open to the public day and night throughout the year. Check with individual businesses for their hours of operation. Multiple historical markers and signs will provide historical information.

This is the island's shopping and entertainment center. The only entrance fees charged are for individual attractions.

The Strand Historic District covers roughly thirteen blocks, encompassing Galveston's primary commercial area from the 1850s through the early 1900s. The area was often referred to as the "Wall Street of the South" and was the economic lifeblood of the port city. *Courtesy of the Rosenberg Library, Galveston, Texas*

Residential Life   209

East End Historic District

Irregular pattern including both sides of Broadway and Market Streets
Galveston, TX 77550
Covering 150 acres, it is roughly bounded by Eleventh Street, Broadway, 19th and 16th Streets, and Market and Postoffice Streets.

Important Dates

Built: **beginning 1840**
Period of Importance: **late nineteenth century**
Added to National Register of Historic Places:
   May 30, 1975
Designated a National Historic Landmark:
   May 11, 1976

Located along Broadway, Sacred Heart Church was the fourth church established on Galveston Island, dating to 1884 and designed by noted architect Nicholas Clayton. After its destruction in the 1900 storm, this iteration, constructed in 1903 and 1904, has become a prominent landmark on the island.

210   TREASURES OF TEXAS

Site Description

Much like its more commercial neighbor, the Strand, Galveston's residential-oriented East End Historic District has one the best-preserved and largest concentrations of nineteenth-century architecture in Texas. The district was developed primarily during Galveston's reign as the state's preeminent port; it is bounded, roughly, by Broadway to the south, Market Street to the north, 19th Street to the west, and 9th Street to the east.

The city's history as a port dates back to 1830, when Mexico established a customhouse on Galveston Island. After the Texas Republic formed in 1836, the island was developed as the republic's principal port. Galveston's street network was platted in 1838, and by 1850 it had become the second largest port on the Gulf coast, behind only New Orleans. The early growth on the island included the construction of many Greek Revival houses on the eastern end of the island, some of which still stand. Following the Civil War, Galveston experienced significant growth. The densely populated East End suffered significant damage in 1885 due to a large fire, destroying homes from 16th to 20th Streets and from the Strand past Broadway. The tight grid pattern of lots and the existence of multiple alley residences made fighting the fire extremely difficult.

The rebuild, however, was swift, with entire blocks already rebuilt in 1886, providing opportunities for local architects such as Alfred Muller, George Stowe, and Nicholas Clayton.

No area of Galveston was particularly spared from the 1900 hurricane that killed at least six thousand people on the island alone. More than 3,600 homes were destroyed on Galveston Island. *Courtesy of Library of Congress*

A survivor of the 1900 storm, the Edward T. Austin House, known commercially as the George Manor, is located on Market Street and was built in 1851. In 1867, a Greek Revival wing was constructed.

Residential Life 211

The East End consists of several historic neighborhoods. Among the palaces—such as Bishop's Palace, the Moody Mansion, and Ashton Villa—structures with a bevy of architectural styles, such as these shotgun houses, can be found.

The East End District became Galveston's preeminent residential district. It was here that the city's civic and business leaders built their houses, curtailed only by the growth of Houston as a competing port; the building boom was finally ended by the 1900 Galveston hurricane. One of the oldest homes in the district was built by Wilbur Cherry, an early newspaper publisher, on Cherry Street in 1852. The most opulent would be Bishop's Palace, completed in 1893 for politician and lawyer Walter Gresham. This all-stone four-story Victorian-style home, located on Broadway and 14th Street, was designed by Nicholas J. Clayton, withstood the 1900 hurricane, and welcomed hundreds of survivors of the hurricane afterward. After spending time as the residence for the bishop of the Roman Catholic Diocese of Galveston, it was opened to the public in 1963, and tours are given to this day.

The district is home to over 550 buildings covering over fifty city blocks, growing from the original forty blocks to the east and north in 1994; many of these

Two civil engineering projects were pursued with the goal of mitigating the impact should another destructive event like the 1900 hurricane occur: building a seawall and raising the island's elevation. The projects took years and involved pumping sand and dirt below the island, raising the elevation of some five hundred city blocks from between 8 and 17 feet.

212 TREASURES OF TEXAS

residences are indicative of the Victorian architectural styles. A number of relatively unaltered examples of the Greek Revival survive from the island's earlier days, as do other Queen Anne–style homes. Numerous properties in the district are listed on the National Register of Historic Places or as Recorded Texas Historic Landmarks, including Bishop's Palace, the George Washington Grover House (1520 Market Street), and the Isaac Heffron House (1509 Postoffice Street).

Visitors to the East End Historic District will find homes ranging from small, simple cottages to large, elaborate homes with pillars, ornate carvings, stained glass, huge porches, wrought-iron fencing, and many other features that make each home unique. The island, at its widest, is only about 2.5 miles. You can easily walk blocks of the district with ease. With the district still primarily residential, visitors are only a quick trip away from the seawall area, which is loaded with restaurants, shops, and the beach. Some of the homes even offer up short-term rentals for vacationers if you would like to stay in the heart of the district itself.

Visitor Information

The East End Historic District does not have a headquarters or visitor center, so feel free to drive the district or, better yet, walk—many of the homes are adorned with historical markers. While the churches are open during services, the only East End building open to the public for tours is Bishop's Palace.

Bishop's Palace
1402 Broadway Street
Galveston, TX 77550
409-762-2475
https://www.galvestonhistory.org/sites/1892-bishops-palace

HOURS: Wednesday–Monday, 10 a.m.–5 p.m.
Admission fee charged

A lithograph of a bird's-eye view of Galveston in 1871. The East End neighborhood is in the center to left center of the map.
Courtesy of the Center for American History, University of Texas at Austin

SITES
1. Harrell Site
2. Hueco Tanks State Park & Historic Site
3. Landergin Mesa
4. Lower Pecos Canyonlands Archeological District
5. Lubbock Lake Landmark
6. Plainview Site

In much the same way as the Latin and Spanish influence on Texas is apparent, the Lone Star State has much thanks to give to its ancestral residents. Looking at the history of Texas through an archeological lens uncovers layers of history just now being identified and understood.

Native tribes, nomadic tribes, and emerging tribes (some becoming established, and others assimilated) have led to a tapestry of cultural riches that will be providing new details for generations to become. However, because of the fragile nature of nearly all of these archeological sites, many have been deemed off-limits to the casual visitor and therefore have had their more exact identifying locale markers removed from the official list of National Historic Landmarks and this book. A few offer limited, restricted opportunities, and others require you to learn more online or at a nearby community museum. While you may not be able to physically visit these sites, learning about their history will give you an interesting, and important, understanding of Texas's full spectrum of history.

Harrell Site

Located near South Bend, southern Young County

Important Dates

Period of Importance: **ca. 1200 to 1600 CE**
Added to National Register of Historic Places:
October 15, 1996
Designated a National Historic Landmark:
July 19, 1964

Possum Kingdom Lake, also known as "Hell's Lake," in 2010. *Photo by Mark Quadling and Henry Quadling; courtesy of the TARL Archives*

216 TREASURES OF TEXAS

Site Description

Located in southern Young County, the junction of the Salt Fork (the main branch of the Brazos River) and the Clear Fork tributary has been a favored place to settle for at least five thousand years. The layout of the river, with its wide, curving river terraces, offered ideal camping spots with easily accessible water, woods, plants, and animals inhabiting either the wooded edges of the river or the surrounding grasslands.

The junction of the rivers is one of many places in Texas where permanent water and the favorable landscape have attracted generations of settlers. The rivers teemed with fish and waterfowl, the woodlands provided pecans and lumber as well as shelter for multiple kinds of game, the river floodplain was fertile enough for agriculture, and the adjacent grasslands attracted bison and antelope, while the limestone caprock along the hills flanking the valley provided materials for hearths and ovens.

For thousands of years, it served primarily as a stopping place for hunter-gatherers, used primarily for a few days or weeks as a camp-over site. However, around one thousand years ago, people set up camp longer, establishing villages, a pattern that intensified after 1200 CE, when villagers began raising crops and hunting buffalo. In the early 1850s, a remnant group of Kickapoo Indians chose the spot to establish a small village, just upstream from the Brazos Indian Reservation—the last refuge for the Caddo, Tonkawa, Kichai, and Waco tribes. Following their removal to Oklahoma in 1859 and the Kickapoo fleeing to Mexico, white settlers moved in to claim the choice

Wielding picks and long-handled shovels, WPA workers dig through sandy Brazos River deposits at the Harrell Farm. *Courtesy of the TARL Archives*

Example of a shell midden, Argentina, 2007. *Courtesy of the TARL Archives*

A distinctive array of tools, weapons, and pottery have been uncovered at the Harrell site. *Courtesy of the TARL Archives*

An archeologist examines a feature on the southwestern edge of the "Great Midden." *Courtesy of the TARL Archives*

Workers at the Harrell site, during an investigation at Excavation Area 3, 1937. *Courtesy of the TARL Archives*

land parcels along the Brazos and its feeders. Since that time, the Brazos River junction has been home to several generations of farmers, including the Matt D. Harrell family for whom the site is named.

Archeological excavations at the site began in 1937–38, uncovering evidence of prehistoric villages that had existed there about five hundred to one thousand years ago, as well as traces of earlier campsites—some buried under 25 feet of mud and sand. Remains such as bison-bone hoes, corncob fragments, pottery, flint knives, and more were left behind by the villagers, representing the southernmost example of Plains Villager culture. Odd bits of Caddoan- and Puebloan-type pottery, shell ornaments, and tools made from materials from a more distant source show that these villagers were part of a more extensive network of late-prehistoric groups linked by kinship, language, trade, and shared cultural traditions. Additionally, a small prehistoric cemetery—thought to be from roughly 1200–1500 CE—with the remains of thirty-two individuals was uncovered. The skeletons in a mass grave section show that the site was once the scene of violent events, perhaps from raids, and several skulls show evidence that may indicate scalping, rare in prehistoric human remains in Texas.

These earliest excavations were conducted under the auspices of the Works Progress Administration and one minimally trained archeologist leading dozens of unskilled laborers. Despite this, the artifacts found and notes collected (although never a formal report) resulted in revisits to the site. In 1946, famed archeologist Alex D. Krieger reexamined the site collection, concluding that the site lay at a crossroads between the more technically advanced Mound Builders of East Texas and the Puebloan cultures to the Southwest, representing the southernmost expression of the Plains Village tradition. This was prior to carbon dating, and his determination came from a belief that all the items located were from the same time period, as opposed to a layered, multicomponent find.

The site remains a bit of a mystery and is still one of the few intensively excavated sites in the west-central part of North Texas. However, it has never been critically reevaluated. Only educated guesses can be formulated about the site's history unless more research and excavation work are performed in the future. Collections from the WPA investigations at the Harrell site are housed at the Texas Archeological Research Laboratory at the University of Texas at Austin. The Harrell site is closed to the public, and the location is restricted.

Visitor Information

The Harrell site is closed to the public, and the location is restricted.

Workers uncover more burned-rock features at the bottom of a deep excavation unit. More than 90,000 cubic feet of dirt was removed at the site. *Courtesy of the TARL Archives*

Archeological Sites 219

Hueco Tanks State Park & Historic Site

Located 32 miles northeast of central El Paso on US Highway 62/180, then turn north on Ranch Road 2775.

Park mailing address:
6900 Hueco Tanks Road No. 1
El Paso, TX 79938
915-857-1135
https://texasstateparks.reserve america.com

Important Dates

Period of Importance: **1000–1824**
Designated a National Historic Landmark: **January 13, 2021**
Added to National Register of Historic Places: **July 14, 1971**

La Cueva del León in Hueco Tanks State Park. Light can be seen filtering through the rocks from above and from the right.
Courtesy of UNT Libraries, The Portal to Texas History

Photograph of the Hueco Tanks in El Paso County, Texas. *Courtesy of UNT Libraries, The Portal to Texas History*

Site Description

The unique geology and abundance of water at this location made the Hueco Tanks site a refuge for both nature and humans for over ten thousand years. Hueco Tanks is an area of low mountains in El Paso County, Texas, and is located in a high-altitude desert basin between the Franklin Mountains to the west and the Hueco Mountains to the east. Formed thirty-four million years ago from magma and limestone, the Hueco geology emerged through erosion where weather carved odd sculptures into the landscape. These hollows, known as *huecos* ("whey-coes"), pockmark the rock surfaces, catching rainfall where microhabitats developed, supporting a diversity of plants and animals and becoming an oasis in the Chihuahuan Desert.

This presence of water here drew humans to the area following the end of the last ice age. Hunter-gatherers crossed the region, finding the huecos to be a reliable source of water and leaving designs, or pictographs, painted on the rocks as they passed through. Many of these designs survive, and this well-preserved and protected collection of pictographs is part of the park and historic site and can be seen on guided and self-guided tours.

The desert landscape at Hueco Tanks State Park in El Paso, Texas, consists of a variety of flora and fauna. Here, prickly pear and ocotillo sit at the bottom of a cluster of rocks in a 2002 photo by Randy Mallory. *Courtesy of UNT Libraries, The Portal to Texas History*

Some of the most compelling pieces are those left by members of a group called the Jornada Mogollon, who did not just pass through; they stayed and occupied the site starting around 1150 CE. They built pit-house structures, planted simple crops, fashioned stone tools, and painted animals, birds, and large-eyed

Archeological Sites **221**

The cave painting found at Site 17 in Hueco Tanks State Historical Park. The image depicts a winged animal. *Courtesy of UNT Libraries, The Portal to Texas History*

storm deities across the rock surfaces. Additionally, the Jornada painted over two hundred face designs, or masks. This is considered the largest known assemblage of pictographic "masks" in the US. They can be found beneath rock overhangs, within boulder shelters, and at randomly odd and hidden places throughout, while the more "modern" graffiti dates back to the 1840s.

Later the area was occupied by Mescalero and Lipan Apache and Jumano people. While Spanish and Mexican travelers were rare visitors, the Comanche, Kiowa, and Tiguas used the area frequently. The Kiowa called the area Tso-doi-gyata-de-dee, or "Rock cave where they were surrounded." The Kiowa signed a treaty with the US in 1837. However, shortly after, Mexican soldiers forced them into a six-day siege in Hueco Tanks, during which most of them died.

The Tanks later became a stopping point on a western trail for several decades in the mid-nineteenth century. Following that, they were the center of an active cattle ranch for over sixty years and a popular recreation spot for over one hundred years. The composition of the landscape made the archeological record both highly visible and easily damaged by both natural and human impact. By the mid-twentieth century, a number of artifacts had been carried away by visitors prior to the location being conveyed to the State of Texas in 1969.

Hueco Tanks is the only place in the region where every prehistoric and historic time period is represented. The landscape contributed greatly to this phenomenon. Water was the main resource that spurred repeated visitations and use of the area. Beginning in prehistoric times, the water was retained by simple dams, allowing great numbers of people to gather. The rock hills provided settlement: shelter, a canvas for rock imagery, a base for food processing, and supplies for heating elements and plant roasting pits. Folsom points left by Paleoindian hunters have been found, and evidence of later homes and fields were

Cave graffiti, seen here at Site 17, is almost as historic. "M. F. Wayland, Jul. 25th, 1884" is written into the wall inside of a drawn frame of geometric shapes. Other words and initials can be seen on the wall. *Courtesy of UNT Libraries, The Portal to Texas History*

also found, evidencing more intensive occupations between 1000 and 1300 CE. Found pottery suggests an interregional trade network involving groups to the north, to the northwest, and into Mexico.

Native groups established a trail running through the Tanks toward water and salt sources in the east. Their descendants guided later military scouts and travelers along it, beginning in 1692. Later, gold seekers, cattle drovers, military and railroad surveyors, and adventurers would mark their names on the rocks, and a stage station was briefly established by the Butterfield Overland Mail at the Tanks in the late 1850s. The first permanent historic occupation was Silverio Escontrias's ranch, operating from 1898 until 1956. Starting in the 1940s and 1950s, military training took place at the Tanks, while recreational activities that began before the turn of the century helped lead to the establishment of the area as a state park in 1970. This designation allows the park to be open to the public for recreational use while allowing authorities the opportunity to protect the archeological deposits under the auspices of the Antiquities Code of Texas.

The Escontrias Ranch House serves as the park's interpretive center for Hueco Tanks State Park and Historic Site. Campers, hikers, rock climbers, and nature lovers are drawn to the unique landscape within the park, while the Mescalero Apache, Kiowa, Comanche, Ysleta del Sur Pueblo, Pueblo of Isleta Indians, and others find spiritual connections to the oasis.

Visitor Information

Open to the public. Guided tours and self-guided tours are available. The historic site also offers camping and hiking and is a popular spot for bouldering and rock climbing.
Admission fee charged
HOURS: Open daily. October–April: 8 a.m.–6 p.m.; May–September: Friday–Sunday, 7 a.m.–7 p.m., Monday–Thursday, 8 a.m.–6 p.m.

Hueco Tanks is mainly a day-use park but also manages twenty campsites. Access to the park is restricted in order to protect the fragile archeological resources. Guided tours must be booked a minimum of one week in advance by calling 915-849-6684. The park issues permits to seventy people each day to access the North Mountain area for self-guided visits. You can attempt to reserve permits up to ninety days prior to your visit by calling the customer service center at 512-389-8911. The site often reaches capacity, so reservations are required for each person seeking a permit (you can reserve permits for up to four people—including yourself and only those people in your household). You can check availability online.

All visitors to the park are required to watch an orientation video prior to camping or visiting the self-guided area. Return visitors must watch the video once per year. Pets must be leashed and are allowed only in the campground and on the paved picnic area trail; they are not allowed on any gravel trails or mountains. Campers are required to arrive at least one hour before the park closes for check-in and orientation; no late check-ins are allowed. There are no campfires allowed, since fires that produce ash can damage the rock images, so no charcoal or firewood is allowed inside the park (only gas grills and camp stoves). Also not allowed are drones and unmanned aerial vehicles (UAVs).

You can access West Mountain, East Mountain, and East Spur only with a tour guide. Due to staff constraints, tours are conducted Wednesdays through Sundays throughout the year, but only if requested early enough to confirm a guide.

Archeological Sites   223

Landergin Mesa

Address restricted
Near Vega, Texas

Important Dates

Built: **ca. 1300**
Added to National Register of Historic Places:
October 15, 1966
Designated a National Historic Landmark:
July 19, 1964

Archeologists perched atop Landergin during the 1984 excavations sponsored by the Texas Historical Commission (THC). *Photo by Christ Lintz, courtesy of the Texas Historical Commission*

The Antelope Creek people lived mostly on terraces like these overlooking the river or inside canyons with springs. *Courtesy of National Park Service*

Site Description

Located near Vega, Texas, the Landergin Mesa archeological site preserves some of the most significant Texas Panhandle cultural ruins. This large site contains numerous isolated structures with unique artifacts that date back to the Antelope Creek phase. This period of prehistoric sites in the upper Texas and Oklahoma Panhandles found humans as semi-sedentary, hunting bison and becoming horticulturalists between 1200 and 1500 CE. This is evidenced by the uncovered unique architecture of the Antelope Creek phase. There were also well-preserved examples of Borger cord-marked ceramic vessels from that period. The most impressive location on the mesa is a rectangular stone structure comprising numerous rooms.

The mesa is located in Oldham County, Texas, in the watershed of the Canadian River. Relatively modest in size, it rises about 180 feet above the valley floor and has relatively steep sides—features that would have afforded residents a highly defensible position with views spanning the surrounding countryside. The mesa's top layer is thick sandstone, with a sheer drop around much of the mesa's circumference. Its usable surface is covered by a large building remnant containing multiple chambers. An area outside the structure was found littered with evidence of domestic occupation, including manos (a groundstone tool used with a metate to process or grind food by hand) and pottery remains.

In the areas in the valley below, as well as at other nearby landforms, evidence has been found of prehistoric human habitation. Radiocarbon dating places the period of occupation around 1300 CE. Climatic conditions in the central plains around 1200 CE had caused Upper Republican peoples to move south from Nebraska to the Oklahoma and Texas Panhandles. The mesa itself most likely would have been utilized almost solely for its defensive value. There is no source of water and no room for gardening atop the mesa.

This example of cord-marked pottery is from the Landergin Mesa site. Radiocarbon dating places the period of occupation here around 1300 CE. *Courtesy of Fernbank Museum of Natural History*

Mesa Alamosa, a smaller version of Landergin, some 5 miles east. This landmark was likely used as a defensive retreat position by Antelope Creek villagers. *Photo by Christ Lintz, courtesy of the Texas Historical Commission*

Main houses and fields would have been located down in the valleys, with the mesa used as a site of retreat during times of conflict. It is presumed through eco-archeological research that sometime between 1300 and 1450 CE, the successive generations that continued to occupy the site, growing from small hamlets to homesteads and subhomesteads, began to struggle to acquire food. The documentation of remains from a swath of animals shows a trend of long-term resource depletion. Once the work of acquiring food became too difficult in the increasingly drier conditions, and the immediate area could no longer be effectively farmed, families were forced to move elsewhere for survival.

As the climate of the Canadian Breaks grew drier in the sixteenth century, a tribe of buffalo hunters, the nomadic Jumanos, infiltrated the abandoned farms. They survived by trading dried meats and hides to settlers to the west and then later encountered the Spanish conquistadors on their quest to find gold.

Since the 1960s, archeologists studying the Plains village sites of the Texas Panhandle and adjacent regions of the southern plains have struggled to make sense of what they have encountered. The Antelope Creek culture was less uniform than previously thought. Sites such as Landergin Mesa drew archeologists because of the larger villages arranged into pueblo-like blocks of houses. However, they now appear to be the exception to the rule and pale in comparison to the truly large and fortified villages in the central and northern plains. At Landergin Mesa, maybe a few dozen people resided—living in small family groups of hamlets or smaller farmsteads—whereas in the larger communities, hundreds of people lived in large villages.

In 1981, Robert Mallouf, the state archeologist for Texas, directed excavations at Landergin Mesa for the Texas Historical Commission in order to determine the site's merits as a continued listing as a National Historic Landmark. THC sponsored additional excavations in 1984. It was a unique site because it did not have an immediate water source or agricultural land and, seemingly, was used primarily for defensive measures. Unfortunately, the site has been regularly subjected to archeological vandalism by pothunters and relic hunters. Investigations eventually found that despite extensive looting, the architecture and primary deposits remained intact in some areas of the site.

The mesa was found to have had a long history of intermittent occupation beginning in Late Archaic and Woodland times. Most of the structural remains dated to the Antelope Creek phase, during which the half-acre mesa top saw intense use. During the 1984 excavation, ten structures were identified from seven different occupations, all within a relatively small excavation area covering just 452 square feet. Most of the houses were found to have been built as isolated structures, rather than the more common contiguous rooms one might expect due to the limited amount of space. This led to the belief that the site was a refuge during threatening times rather than a permanent village.

Partly due to long-term relic hunters pilfering the site and in order to retain the site's historical integrity for future archeological purposes, the site is closed to the public, and the address is restricted. Additional hazards include long-term drought and overgrazing, both of which have caused massive erosion during the last century plus. These drought cycles are not limited to modern society; they plagued the Plains villagers as well. Then, however, overgrazing was not the issue it is today. In dry periods, the bison either moved elsewhere to find water, or they died.

Visitor Information

This archeological site has restricted access and is not open to the public.

A fragment of a charred basket found on the floor of a burned Antelope Creek house; very few of these baskets survived.
Photo by Steve Black, courtesy of PPHM collections

Lower Pecos Canyonlands Archeological District

Discontinuous areas within Val Verde County, Texas
Del Rio, Comstock, and Pecos, Texas, environs
Closed/restricted to public access
Guided tours of the White Shaman Preserve are available by reservation through the Witte Museum in San Antonio.

Witte Museum
3801 Broadway Street
San Antonio, TX 78209
210-357-1910
https://www.wittemuseum.org/white-shaman-preserve

Important Dates

Period of Significance: **2250 BCE–950 CE**
Added to National Register of Historic Places:
   March 31, 1971
Designated a National Historic Landmark:
   January 13, 2021

Hanging Cave, inside which are several pictographs, is so named because it seems to hang over this narrow channel.
Courtesy of ANRA-NPS Archives at TARL

Rock-shelters form in limestone cliffs and vertical faces where softer or fractured layers of rock occur. Since these layers erode faster than the surrounding harder rock, over time they become prominent shelters. *Courtesy of ANRA-NPS Archives at TARL*

Site Description

The Lower Pecos Canyonlands serves as one of the most distinctive and significant archeological regions in North America. The Native Americans who once lived here were primarily normal, just like any other tribe of the prehistoric era. However, the site has become exceptional due to a combination of ecological and geological factors. The jagged canyonlands that served as their home contain a rich cultural legacy of ordinary—and some extraordinary—items that are now rarely found in other areas of North America. Covering over 1,500 acres, there are at least thirty-five heavily important sites with extant deposits or collections and twenty-seven with Pecos River–style rock imagery. Canyonlands was added, with Hueco Tanks, in January 2021 as a National Historic Landmark, the first in Texas since 2016. Archeologists have found perfectly preserved food remains, vivid rock art over four thousand years old, grass-lined beds, painted deer bones, and more. Using these factors, and accompanying finds, scientists across the humanities spectrum are piecing together a detailed understanding of both the human and natural past. Due to the unusual collection of finds, and the opportunities for vandalism, the site is now protected with restricted access to protect this unique resource.

The Canyonlands covers the areas surrounding the junctions of the Pecos and Devils Rivers with the Rio Grande just upstream from Del Rio. The majority

Close-up of European man, likely a Spaniard, at Vaquero Alcove. Style shares strong personalities with the Plains Bibliographic style. *Courtesy of SHUMLA*

Archeological Sites 229

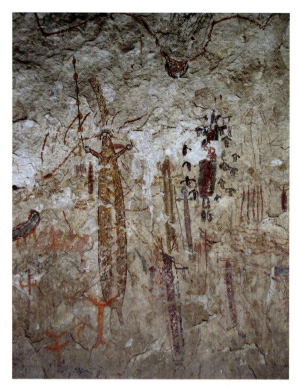

The Pecos River style, believed to be the oldest identified rock art in the region, as seen here in a 2011 photograph, consists of multicolored, humanlike figures and animals. *Photo courtesy of SHUMLA*

Archeological assistant at Fate Bell Shelter, 1932, holding modern whisk broom above prehistoric fibers. *Courtesy of ANRA-NPS Archives at TAR*

of the best-known part of the area lies within Texas, but the region extends southward into northern Coahuila, Mexico. These rivers, and their tributaries, have formed deeply carved canyons within which are located a number of rock-shelters. For over 13,000 years, prehistoric hunter-gatherers lived in the regions, occasionally occupying these rock-shelters as refuge from harsh weather, but primarily living throughout the canyons and high above in the uplands, where grasslands were plentiful.

The region is fairly arid, and these dry conditions, coupled with the protected rock-shelters, resulted in the preservation of oftentimes fragile materials, such as wooden artifacts, woven sandals, musical instruments, tools fashioned from animal bones, and plant food refuse that would decay quickly elsewhere in Texas.

One of the defining finds in the Canyonlands is the rock art adorning the walls of a number of the rock-shelters. These vivid images, in red, black, white, and yellow, were created by hunter-gatherers as early as 5,500 years ago and are considered among the best-preserved examples of rock art in the world. While generally considered primitive, these paintings and carvings are anything but. Hundreds of different symbols and motifs occur, representing at least four major styles, the earliest and best known being the Pecos River style from five thousand to six thousand years ago. Found here are pictographs (painted images), petroglyphs (carved, pecked, or incised images), and various kinds of mobile art such as painted pebbles.

There are other crucial sites in the Canyonlands, though few have undergone as rigorous a study. Researchers have found terrace sites along the floodplains, flint quarries and resulting refuse scattered throughout, and evidence left behind from the practice of using heated or hot-rock cooking techniques (hearth fields, ring middens, and burned-rock middens) on stream terraces, hillslope terraces, or the shallow rocky soils in the uplands. While these peoples probably leaned heavily on plant resources, they were omnivores and are considered hunter-gatherers, as evidenced by the only known example in the region of a bison kill site. Located at the Bonfire Shelter, it is the oldest and southernmost such site in North America.

Due to the extraordinary preservation conditions, from both the art and archeological aspects, the hunting-and-gathering life and economy of these prehistoric peoples can be studied in great detail. However, much of this research is relatively new. The first expeditions in the 1930s were mounted by museums intent to gather items for displays. It wasn't until the late 1950s and early 1960s that serious research began, much of it prompted by the construction of a large dam on the Rio Grande to create the Amistad Reservoir. This project flooded out the lower Devils and Pecos River canyons, irrevocably damaging untold hundreds of rock-shelters and their pictograph-adorned walls. The rest of the area retains its integrity of location and setting and has not been subjected to much modern development; population remains low, and infrastructure impacts are largely limited to rights-of-way for highways and pipelines. Of more danger is exfoliation, fading, wasp nest construction, and, at least in three low-lying overhangs, flooding.

The items recovered from the sites prior to the dam's construction, as well as the supporting documentation, are now curated at the Texas Archeological Research Laboratory on behalf of the National Park Service. While the site is closed to the general public and has restricted access, back in 1931, San Antonio's Witte Museum began leading expeditions and teams to pictograph sites in the lower Pecos, including the White Shaman Preserve near the Seminole Canyon State Historical Park. The museum houses over 20,000 artifacts from the ancient site, offering some of them on display, and allows for limited registration of guided tours to this site, a National Historic Landmark.

Visitor Information

Closed/restricted access to the public

Tours to White Shaman, through the Witte Museum, are offered every Saturday. Additionally, the museum offers seasonal guided tours to numerous additional prehistoric and historic sites throughout the lower Pecos region of West Texas.
TOURS: September through May, every Saturday at 12:30 p.m. (generally completed by 3 p.m.). Reservations are required and limited. Participants must be age twelve and up; all minors are required to be accompanied by a parent or legal guardian. The tour is 1 mile, round trip, and requires climbing numerous stairs and steep slopes with loose rocks.

Excavation crew working in suffocating dust of Fate Bell Shelter in 1932, a problem faced by all excavators. *Courtesy of ANRA-NPS Archives at TARL*

Archeological Sites 231

Lubbock Lake Landmark

Museum of Texas Tech University
2500 Broadway
Lubbock, TX 79409
806-742-2011
https://www.depts.ttu.edu/museumttu

Important Dates

Built: **ca. 13,000–11,000 BCE**
Added to National Register of Historic Places:
June 21, 1971
Designated a National Historic Landmark:
December 22, 1977

Though small, the visitor center at Lubbock Lake portrays the history of the National Historic Landmark, considered one of the premier archeological and natural history sites in North America.

The relatively nondescript landscape of Lubbock Lake Landmark site. In 1936, a Folsom point was found by accident on the land here. By 1939, the West Texas Museum, now the Museum of Texas Tech University, had secured funding from the WPA for their first excavation.

Site Description

The Lubbock Lake National Historic and State Archeological Landmark (a.k.a. Lubbock Lake site) is an archeological preserve covering about 300 acres on the southern High Plains of Texas in Yellowhouse Draw. The draw is an intermittent tributary of the Brazos River and sits on the northern edge of Lubbock. Museums have carried out most of the excavations done at this site. The first investigation of Lubbock Lake was funded by the Work Projects Administration and

Demetrio Leon, Lazaro Oliva, Jesus Mininez, and Manual Vargas composed the crew that helped excavate Area 8 during 1959–61 under the direction of F. Earl Green and W. Curry Holden. They located protohistoric and historic camping sites and correlated the stratigraphic records unearthed in two previous excavations. *Courtesy of UNT Libraries, The Portal to Texas History*

Archeological Sites   **233**

Near the Lubbock Lake Visitor Center is a large bison sculpture. Hunter-gatherers from the Clovis to Protohistoric people, the Apache and Comanche nations, and the founding settlers of Lubbock all have relied on this animal. Evidence covering nearly 12,000 years of occupation on the southern High Plains can be found here.

was carried out by the West Texas Museum (now the Museum of Texas Tech University) in 1939 and 1941. Excavations in 1948, 1949, and 1951 were conducted by the Texas Memorial Museum, with the West Texas Museum returning for additional work in 1959 and 1961. A later project, begun in 1972, was carried out under the auspices of the Museum of Texas Tech University, with excavations under a Texas Antiquities Committee permit.

The site was excavated in 1950, uncovering burned bone from the first Paleoindian period. Originally thought to date from the Folsom occupation, it has actually been shown to have a later occupation. The lake is a deep, well-stratified site with a virtually complete cultural, faunal, and floral record dating back over 11,500 years and defining five major stratigraphic units that include evidence from the following: Clovis; Plainview; Firstview; Early, Middle, and Late Archaic periods; Ceramic period with Puebloan trade evidence; Protohistoric-period materials of possible early Apache occupation; the historical record; and other aboriginal materials reflecting late Apache and Comanche occupation.

The Historic period begins when contact with Europeans was established; such deposits indicate the presence of the modern horse, metal, and glass. Evidence of Anglo-American habitation has been found in the most recent archeological deposits, some reflecting the use of the area by buffalo hunters in the 1870s. Later artifacts, such as rifle cartridges, metal hardware, square nails, buttons, and a beer bottle, are more indicative of settlement. What is now the city of Lubbock was founded at Lubbock Lake with the establishment of the Singer Store in 1881, the likely source of such found materials. The store was the first commercial enterprise in the area and served early ranchers, the military, and occasional Indian groups before burning down in 1886 and relocating farther downstream.

The site is a protected state and federal landmark, with evidence of ancient people and extinct animals dating back over 12,000 years of use by ancient cultures on the Llano Estacado, and is now part of the Museum of Texas Tech University. The documentation and specimens collected from Lubbock Lake excavations are housed in the Archeological Division of the Museum of Texas Tech University, and the Texas Memorial Museum and Texas Archeological Research Laboratory, University of Texas at Austin. Visitors to the Museum of Texas Tech University can watch active archeological digs. Volunteers help with the ongoing excavations each summer, making the site accessible for nonscientists to get involved. There are also guided and self-guided tours of the site offered throughout the year.

Visitor Information

HOURS: Tuesday through Saturday, 10 a.m.–5 p.m., Sunday, 1–5 p.m.
No entrance fees

The first explorations of the site began in 1939. By the late 1940s, several Folsom-period bison kills were discovered. The landmark currently serves as a field laboratory for geology, soils, and radiocarbon-dating studies and continues to be an active archeological and natural history preserve. *Courtesy of UNT Libraries, The Portal to Texas History*

In a location of an ancient bison kill from a then-unidentified Paleoindian group, charred bison bones produced the first-ever radiocarbon date for Paleoindian material, dating back 9,800 years. Excavations continue today and are conducted on an annual basis. *Courtesy of UNT Libraries, The Portal to Texas History*

Plainview Site

Address restricted
Near Plainview, Texas

Important Dates

Period of Importance: **ca. 7800–5100 BCE**
Added to National Register of Historic Places:
October 15, 1966
Designated a National Historic Landmark:
January 20, 1961

Materials collected at this site not only have suggested its repeated use as a kill site but also have shed light on the hunting and butchering techniques of that time period. *Courtesy of UNT Libraries, The Portal to Texas History*

Site Description

The 1-acre Plainview site is located in Hale County, on the banks of Running Water Draw. It is a prehistoric kill site, a location where hunters either drove the animals off a cliff or trapped them in a river bend. Fossil remnants uncovered here number over one hundred animals, including a prehistoric version of the American bison. Also found were more than twenty projectile points and other stone artifacts. Due to ongoing issues with vandalism and illegal digging, the site is closed to the general public.

The location had long been known in local circles as a source of prehistoric artifacts. However, it was not formally investigated until the 1940s, after a gravel mining operation began in the area. In 1944, E. A. Sellards (director of the Bureau of Economic Geology and the Texas Memorial Museum of the University of Texas), geoarcheologist Glen L. Evans (Sellards's chief assistant and close collaborator), and vertebrate paleontologist Grayson Meade (Texas Technological

Plainview point spear tips, commonly found in the central plains, were first described at this site, dating back to 7800–5100 BCE. Over one hundred animals have been found here, as were more than twenty projectile points and other stone artifacts. *Courtesy of UNT Libraries, The Portal to Texas History*

The Plainview site is located on the banks of Running Water Draw in Hale County. It is a kill site, meaning that this is where hunters would drive animals off a cliff or trap them in a river bend. *Courtesy of UNT Libraries, The Portal to Texas History*

Archeological Sites

The site had a reputation as a source of prehistoric artifacts for a long time but was not formally investigated until the 1940s. The excavation site was enlarged over the next several decades and has since uncovered that the site was repeatedly used as a kill site. *Courtesy of UNT Libraries, The Portal to Texas History*

While excavation sites are off-limits, visitors can visit the nearby site. Located in the Lloyd C. Woods Park is an improved visitor site, including a gazebo, a Texas Historical Marker, a bison statue, and a 22-foot Quanah Parker Tail Arrow.

College) led the first systematic investigation of the stie. Plainview point spear tips, commonly found in the central plains, were first described here and date to 7800–5100 BCE. While the remains of numerous animals were uncovered, they were missing both skulls and tailbones, suggesting a removal to another location for further processing and use. Researchers dug a pit in order to understand the site's stratigraphy. This was enlarged in 1945 and was followed by additional pits in the following years.

Unfortunately, in the 1970s, one of the more important dig sites in the draw became a garbage dump, destroying some of the research value. Additional pits in the draw would go to provide additional geological and stratigraphic information, including signs of a climatic shift toward drier, warmer weather, before they too became dump sites. The site was revisited and investigated in 1977, at which time the extent of the kill bed was enlarged. The collected materials have led to the suggestion that the site was repeatedly used as a kill site.

Visitor Information

This site is closed to the public, and the address is restricted.

These finds have also shed light on the butchering techniques of the prehistoric hunters. Some of the old bone bed was intact, but it took removing 9 feet of garbage and other debris. The location has not been investigated systematically since that time; however, because of what it has revealed about shifting life patterns, bison evolution, and environmental transformations, the site remains significant and represents a divide between the Paleoindian times and the Archaic period that followed.

Terms You May Need to Know

A

adobe: A kind of clay used as a building material, typically used as sun-dried bricks.

alcove: A recess in the wall of a room or in a garden.

Angus: Any of a breed of usually black hornless beef cattle originating in Scotland.

antebellum: Occurring or existing before a particular war, especially when referring to the American Civil War (pre-1861).

aqueduct: An artificial channel for conveying water, typically in the form of a bridge across a valley or some other gap.

art deco: This was the predominant decorative art style of the 1920s and 1930s. It is characterized by precise and boldly delineated geometric shapes and strong colors. It was used most notably in household objects (from furniture to clocks) and in architecture.

atmospheric theater: A type of movie palace design popular starting in the late 1920s. They were designed to evoke the feeling of a particular time and place through the use of projectors, lighting, architectural elements, and ornamentation that evoked a sense of being outdoors and being a more active participant in the setting. The most successful promoter of the style was John Eberson.

B

baroque ornamentation: A style of art and architecture developed in Europe from the early seventeenth to mid-eighteenth centuries. It emphasizes a dramatic, often-strained effect and is typified by bold, curving forms; elaborate ornamentation; and overall balance of disparate parts.

barque: A type of sailing vessel with three or more masts having the foremasts and mainmasts rigged square and only the mizzen (the aftmost mast) rigged fore and aft.

barracks: A building or group of buildings used to house soldiers or specific groups of people (e.g., laborers or prisoners) in austere conditions. These are typically furnished with multiple rows of bunks for sleeping arrangements.

battle stars: A small bronze star worn on a campaign ribbon by members of organizations taking part in certain battles or other wartime operations.

billet: A place, usually a civilian's house or other nonmilitary facility, where soldiers are lodged temporarily.

bioremediation: An ecologically sound and state-of-the-art technique utilizing natural biological processes to completely eliminate toxic contaminants. The process uses microorganisms, fungi, green plants, or their enzymes to return the natural environment altered by contaminants to its original condition.

bison kill site: Kill sites on the North American plains are well-studied archeological and anthropological examples of human communal hunting and mass killing of large ungulates, such as bison, whose bones from these sites are dominated by the remains of prime adult bison.

blaxploitation: The exploitation of Black people, especially with regard to stereotyped roles in movies. There was a wave of independently produced genre films of the early 1970s, predominately made by Black crews for Black audiences, with common subjects being crime, sex, drugs, and racial tensions.

boll weevil: A small and grayish or brown weevil (type of beetle) that feeds on the fibers of the cotton boll; a major pest of the American cotton crop.

bracero: A Mexican laborer allowed into the United States for a limited time as a seasonal agricultural worker. They typically worked along the US-Mexican border on farms and railroads in order to ease labor shortages during World War II.

Brahman: An ox of a humped breed originally domesticated in India that is tolerant of heat and drought and now kept widely in tropical and warm-temperate regions.

brevet (rank identifier): A former type of military commission conferred especially for outstanding service, by which an officer was promoted to a higher rank without the corresponding pay.

Butterfield Overland Mail Route: A stagecoach route operating from 1857 to 1861. It served as a conduit for the passengers and mail from terminals in the east (Memphis and St. Louis), both of which met at Fort Smith, Arkansas, then continued through Indian Territory, Texas, New Mexico, and Arizona Territories and ended in San Francisco.

C

caliche: A sedimentary rock; a hardened natural cement of calcium carbonate that binds other materials—such as gravel, sand, clay, and silt.

campanile: A bell tower, especially a freestanding one.

Cape-style home: Cape Cod–style homes are houses that originated in colonial America and later became recognized as a specific class of homes defined by certain architectural elements (e.g., simple homes of one or one and a half stories with wide clapboard siding, wooden shutters that could be closed against a storm, a central chimney, and a steep-pitched roof, among other details). The English colonists first constructed these houses and were inspired by the half-timbered houses of England.

cavalry: Soldiers who fought on horseback (in the past); it now refers to modern soldiers who fight in armored vehicles.

cenotaph: A monument to someone buried elsewhere. Typically used to commemorate people who died in a war.

chaparral: Vegetation consisting chiefly of tangled shrubs and thorny bushes.

Chili Queens: Latino women who sold stew they called chili made with dried red chilies and beef from open-air stalls at the Military Plaza Mercado. It was generally made at home, loaded onto colorful chili wagons, and transported to the plaza, where it was heated over mesquite fires on the square.

chipichil: Generally used as flooring in jacals; packed and hardened dirt, or, among those with the means, a mixture of lime, sand, and gravel mixture and an alternative to packed and hardened dirt.

City Beautiful movement: This American urban-planning movement was led by architects, landscape architects, and reformers. It flourished between the 1890s and the 1920s. Washington, DC, in 1902, became the first city to carry out such a design. The intent was to introduce beautification and monumental grandeur in cities in an effort to remedy poor living conditions in major cities and provide aesthetic value to residents.

Civilian Conservation Corps (CCC): A public work relief program that operated from 1933 to 1942 in the United States, generally for unemployed, unmarried men ages seventeen to twenty-three. It was one of the earliest New Deal programs and was established to relieve unemployment. Projects included everything from planting trees to fighting forest fires.

clapboard exterior: A narrow board used to cover the outside walls of a building by laying one board over part of the one already attached below it.

Clovis: In comparison to Folsom, this relates to a widely distributed prehistoric culture of North America characterized by leaf-shaped flint projectile points having fluted faces.

commissary: A restaurant in a movie studio, military base, prison, or other such institution.

contributing building: In regard to historic preservation and historic districts, a contributing property or resource is any building, object, or structure that adds to the historical integrity, or architectural qualities that make the historic district significant.

convento: The residence of a parish priest in Spanish America or the Philippines.

co-op: Short for "cooperative farm demonstration," it is a jointly owned commercial enterprise (in this case, organized by farmers) that produces and distributes goods and services and is run for the benefit of its owners' cooperative commercial enterprise.

cruisers: A relatively fast warship larger than a destroyer and less heavily armed than a battleship.

cupola: A small dome adorning a roof or ceiling.

customhouse: The office at a port or frontier post where customs duty is collected. It traditionally houses the offices for a jurisdictional government, whose officials oversaw the functions associated with importing and exporting goods.

D

Defense Reserve Fleet: A fleet composed of ships acquired and maintained by the Maritime Administration for use in mobilization or emergency situations.

despacho: A prayer bundle or offering. Typically used by high shamans in a ceremony for a wide variety of occasions, such as births and death, expressions of gratitude, to heal physical and emotional ailments, to restore balance and harmony, or for when there is a specific request of the spirit world.

Distinguished Flying Cross: A US or British military decoration for heroism or distinguished achievement while on aerial duty.

Dixiecrats: Any of the southern US Democrats who seceded from the Democratic Party in 1948 in opposition to its policy of extending civil rights.

dogtrot: Typically found in southern US architecture, a dogtrot is an open-ended passage that runs through the center of a house, flanked by two enclosed living spaces.

dragoons: Originally meant mounted infantry, who were trained in horse riding as well as infantry fighting. This usage changed over time, and during the eighteenth century, dragoons had evolved into light cavalry units and personnel.

dreadnought: A battleship that has big guns all of the same caliber.

E

edifice: A building or wall, especially a large, imposing one.

El Camino la Bahía: La Bahía Road was one of the first overland routes used by European explorers of Texas. It was originally an Indian trail in southeastern Texas and Louisiana. It is likely older than El Camino Real and was possibly used as early as 1685 by French explorer La Salle.

El Camino Real de los Tejas: Historic trail extending 2,580 miles from Northwest Louisiana at Natchitoches, across Texas to the Rio Grande, then continuing to Mexico City. This *camino real*, or royal road, served as a vital artery for Native Americans, missionaries, and soldiers who traveled the routes and built missions and presidios, bringing exploration, trade, migrations, settlement, war, independence, and statehood to the region. The Spanish began using the trail in 1690.

esplanade: A long, open, level area, typically beside the sea, along which people may walk for pleasure.

Essex-class aircraft carriers: A class of aircraft carriers of the US Navy. Constituted the twentieth century's most numerous class of heavy warships, with twenty-four built.

European modernism: A cultural movement that spread across Europe in the nineteenth and twentieth centuries. It refers to a wide range of experimental and avant-garde trends in literature and the arts and was a major influence on current Western literature, film, and the arts.

expeditionary force: An armed force organized to achieve a specific objective in a foreign country. The American Expeditionary Force was the US armed forces contingent that was sent to fight in Europe during World War I, the first time in the history of America that the US sent troops overseas.

F

farm-to-market road: In the US, a farm-to-market (FM) or ranch-to-market (RM) road is a state highway or county road that connects rural or agricultural areas to market towns. They are better quality roads, usually a highway, that farmers and ranchers use to transport products to market towns or distribution centers.

floatplanes: An aircraft equipped with floats for landing on water; a seaplane.

Folsom points: The Folsom were a Paleoindian culture of North and Central America, dated to about 10,500–8,000 years ago; the culture is distinguished by fluted stone projectile points or spearheads.

forecastle: The forward part of a ship below the deck, traditionally used as the crew's living quarters; a raised deck at the bow of a ship.

Franciscan friar: A member of a Roman Catholic religious order founded by St. Francis of Assisi in 1209 and dedicated to the virtues of humility and poverty. It is now divided into three independent branches; the missions in San Antonio were established by Franciscan friars.

fresco: A painting done rapidly in watercolor on wet plaster on a wall or ceiling, so that the colors penetrate the plaster and become fixed as it dries.

friary: A building or community occupied by or consisting of friars.

G

Garden City movement: This is a method of urban planning that was initiated in 1898 by Sir Ebenezer Howard in the UK. Garden cities were intended to be planned, self-contained communities surrounded by greenbelts, or parks, and containing proportionate areas of residences, industry, and agriculture.

garrison: Troops stationed in a fortress or town to defend it.

granary: A storehouse for threshed grain.

Greek Revival: This neoclassical style of architecture is inspired by and incorporates features of Greek temples from the fifth century BCE. It was popular in the US and Europe in the first half of the nineteenth century.

grotto: A small, picturesque cave, especially an artificial one in a park or garden.

H

HemisFair: This was the 1968 World's Fair, held April 6 through October 6. The theme was "The Confluence of Civilizations in the Americas," and the event was held to coincide with the 250th anniversary of San Antonio's 1718 founding.

Herefords: Any of a breed of hardy, red-coated beef cattle of English origin with white faces and markings.

hipped roof: A roof with the ends inclined, as well as the sides.

Houston Ship Channel: This is part of the Port of Houston, one of the busiest seaports in the world. The channel is a widened and deepened natural watercourse created by dredging the Buffalo Bayou and the Galveston Bay.

I

indentured workers (Mexican-American War era): Required by contract to work for another person for a certain period of time; such as a person who came to America during the colonial period.

Independence class: A class of littoral combat ships built for the US Navy; built from 2008 to the present. Littoral combat ships are relatively small surface vessels designed for operations near shore by the navy and are envisioned to be networked, agile, and stealthy—they are often compared to the corvettes of the navy.

infirmary: A place in a large institution for the care of those who are ill.

insurgent: A person who revolts against civil authority or an established government.

Italian Renaissance Revival: This mid-Victorian architectural style adapts the classical forms of fifteenth- and sixteenth-century Italian architecture, especially palace architecture, usually characterized by blocklike massing, with refined, classic-sized decorative detail around regularly organized windows.

J

James Webb Space Telescope: A joint NASA-ESA-CSA space telescope that is the successor to the Hubble Space Telescope as NASA's flagship astrophysics mission. It provides improved infrared resolution and sensitivity over Hubble and enables a broad range of investigations, including observing some of the most distant events and objects in the universe.

joint base: A base of the US armed forces utilized by multiple military services, hosting one or more other services as tenants on the base. It originated during the Base Realignment and Closure process in 1993. As bases closed, twenty-six bases were combined into twelve and renamed as joint bases, such as Joint Base San Antonio.

Jumano: A small Indian nation known for its members' tattooed or painted bodies; mentioned in a few Spanish documents as early as the late sixteenth century. These mobile hunter-gatherers lived in areas of the southern plains but by the eighteenth century had joined forces with former bitter enemies, the Apache, and eventually faded from history.

L

land grant: A grant of public land, especially used in the case of an institution or organization, or to particular groups of people. It could be given as an incentive, a means of enabling work, or as a reward to individuals and companies as incentives to develop unused land in relatively unpopulated areas.

Latino: A person, especially in the United States, of Latin American origin or descent (e.g., South America, Central America, or Mexico). The term was first identified in use in the 1940s.

light aircraft carrier: A carrier that is smaller than the standard carriers of a navy; the precise definition of the type varies by country, but they generally have a complement of aircraft only one-half to two-thirds the size of a full-size "fleet" carrier.

lintel: A horizontal support of timber, stone, concrete, or steel across the top of a door or window.

longhorn cattle: Long-horned brown and white breed of beef cattle originating from Craven in the north of England. They have a white patch along the line of their spine and under their bellies. They are typically associated with the cattle of Texas.

Louann Salt: This is a widespread evaporite formation that formed in the Gulf of Mexico in the mid-Jurassic. It formed as a rift as the South and North American plates separated. It underlies much of the northern Gulf coast from Texas to the Florida Panhandle and extends beneath wide swatches along the coastal plain of Mississippi, Louisiana, and Texas. One of its many salt domes derived from this was the site of the Spindletop oil strike.

Louisiana Purchase Exposition: Informally known as the St. Louis World's Fair, it was an international exposition held in St. Louis, Missouri, from April 30 to December 1, 1904. A number of architects, city movements, and inventions filtered out of the world's fair that year, including the City Beautiful movement.

M

magazine (militaria—forts): An item or place, generally a storehouse or drum, within which ammunition or other explosive material is stored.

manos: A handheld stone or roller for grinding corn or other grains on a metate, or flat stone.

Marianas Turkey Shoot: Another name for the Battle of the Philippine Sea by American pilots on June 19–20, 1944. It was the Japanese navy's attempt to hold the Marianas Islands and resulted in heavy losses on the part of the Japanese in men, planes, and carriers and was a decisive American victory.

Marianists (see Mission Concepción): A worldwide family of Catholic brothers, priests, sisters, and committed lay people encouraging them to reflect on Jesus's passion, the role of Mary, and the ongoing mission of the church.

McCarthyism: A campaign against alleged Communists in the US government and other institutions carried out under Senator Joseph McCarthy from 1950 to 1954. Many of those accused were blacklisted or lost their jobs, although most of them did not in fact belong to the Communist Party.

Mediterranean Spanish style: Generally, the style is meant to create a relaxing retreat connecting the homeowner with nature. It has many cultural influences and is also referred to as Mediterranean architecture, Spanish Colonial, Moroccan, mission revival, neo-Mediterranean, and other terms. Generally, buildings of this style will feature a white exterior and a red-tiled roof.

midget sub: A small submarine usually consisting of a small crew (typically two but up to six or nine) and carrying a single torpedo for use in surprise attacks.

militia: A military force that is raised from the civil population to supplement a regular army in an emergency, or a military force that engages in rebel or terrorist activities in opposition to a regular army.

mission revival: A popular style of architecture in the southwest US and Florida from about 1890 to 1930 and beyond. It is similar to the earlier mission-style architecture but is generally simpler because of the absence of sculptural ornamentation.

mission style: This architectural style was most popular between 1880 and 1930, with features such as having a smooth stucco, stone, or brick exterior with a red tile roof. Often combined with elements from other movements, such as the prairie-style or craftsman-style homes.

N

nave: The central part of a church building, intended to accommodate most of the congregation.

New York class: This class of battleship was the fifth series of two dreadnought battleships of the US Navy and served during both world wars. It represents the first use of the 14-inch naval gun. The battleships were designed in 1910 and launched in 1912. They underwent overhauls in the interwar period, improved their anti-aircraft batteries, and would go on to serve both in the Atlantic and Pacific theaters. They were decommissioned following the war; USS *New York* was used as a target for atomic testing and eventually sunk, while USS *Texas* became a museum ship.

niche: A shallow recess, especially one in a wall, typically used to display a statue or other ornament.

noncontributing buildings: A building, structure, object, or site that does not reinforce the cultural, architectural, or historical significance of the historic district in which it is located.

O

Old Three Hundred, the: The 297 grantees who purchased 307 parcels of land from Stephen F. Austin in Mexican Texas. By 1825, the colony they established had a population of 1,790, including 443 slaves, and covered an area that ran from the Gulf of Mexico on the south, to near present-day Jones Creek in Brazoria County, Brenham in Washington County, Navasota in Grimes County, and La Grange in Fayette County.

P

Paleoindian: One of the early American hunting people of Asian origin, extant in the Late Pleistocene.

parade ground: A large area of hard and flat ground, in modern usages usually of concrete or tarmac, where soldiers practice routine marching maneuvers (or parades).

paramilitaries: An unofficial force organized similarly to a military force. Also known as guerrillas, mercenaries, or partisan soldiers.

parapet: A low protective wall along the edge or a roof, bridge, or balcony. It can also be earthen and placed along the top of a trench or other place for the concealment of troops.

pergola: An archway in a garden or park consisting of a framework covered with trained climbing or trailing plants.

petrochemical: A chemical obtained, or relating to, the refining and processing of petroleum or natural gas. An example would be that plastics are a type of petrochemical.

petroglyphs: A rock carving, especially a prehistoric one.

picket guard: A soldier, or small unit of soldiers, placed on a defensive line forward of a friendly position to provide timely warning and screening against an enemy advance.

pictographs: A pictorial symbol for a word or phrase. It is the earliest known form of writing, with examples dating back thousands of years.

pit-house structures: A shelter built mostly belowground, with an entrance and ladder at the top.

plaza: A public square, marketplace, or similar open space in a built-up area.

Plaza de Armas: The main square in many Latin American cities. In San Antonio, this is a building on the historic Military Plaza and is a set of four historic structures dating to the 1880s and 1890s that were combined into one large office complex in 1979.

poor farm: A farm that houses, supports, and employs the poor at public expense.

portico: A structure consisting of a roof supported by columns at regular intervals and typically attached as a porch to a building.

presidio: In Spain and Spanish America, this is a fortified military settlement.

proscenium arch: An arch framing the opening between the stage and the auditorium in some theaters.

Protohistoric: The study of human beings in the times that immediately antedate recorded history; the period between prehistory and history, during which a culture or civilization has not yet developed writing, but other cultures have already noted their existence in their own writings.

punitive expedition: A military journey undertaken to punish a political entity or any group of persons outside the borders of the punishing state or union. It's generally undertaken in response to disobedient or morally wrong behavior, thus applying strong diplomatic pressure without a formal declaration of war.

Q

quadrangle: A square or rectangular space or courtyard enclosed by buildings.

quarter horse: A horse of small, stocky breed noted for agility and speed over short distances.

quartermaster: A military officer responsibility for providing quarters, rations, clothing, and other supplies. In the navy, it is a naval petty officer responsible for steering and symbols.

Queen Anne: This generally refers to English baroque from the reign of Queen Anne (1702–14) or, more commonly in the United States, a revived form popular in the last quarter of the nineteenth century and early twentieth century known as Queen Anne Revival. These buildings are characterized by red brick, modified forms of classical architecture, and simple, elegant, and stately ornamentation.

R

radiocarbon dating: The determination of the age or date of organic matter from the relative proportions of the carbon isotopes carbon-12 and carbon-14 that it contains. The ratio between them changes as radioactive carbon-14 decays and is not replaced by exchange with the atmosphere.

rejoneado: Patterned large and small stones used as building materials.

rejoneador: The name given to a bullfighter who fights the bull on horseback, spearing it with lances.

resaca: A dry riverbed, a former channel of the Rio Grande, generally found in the southern half of Cameron County, Texas, and deep into the northeast portions of the state of Tamaulipas, Mexico.

rotunda: A round building, or room, especially one with a dome.

S

sacristy: A room in a church where a priest prepares for a service, and where vestments and other things used in worship are kept.

salt dome: A type of structural dome formed when a thick bed of evaporite minerals (generally salt or halite) found at depth intrude vertically into surrounding rock strata, forming a diapir, or domed rock formation.

sanctuary: The inmost recess, or holiest part, of a temple or church; the part of the chancel of a church containing the high altar.

Santa Gertrudis cattle: Found in tropical areas of South Texas on the King Ranch. It is a famous breed and recognized by the USDA. It was first found in 1940 and is known as the first breed found in the United States.

seawall: The seawall in Galveston was built following the 1900 hurricane in anticipation of protection from future hurricanes. Construction began in September 1902, and the initial segment was completed on July 29, 1904. From 1904 to 1963, the seawall was extended from 3.3 miles to over 10 miles.

secession: The action of withdrawing formally from membership of a federation or body, especially a political state; prior to the American Civil War, it was the withdrawal of eleven southern states from the Union in 1860.

secularization: The seizure by laymen or by the state of all or part of a permanent endowment of church property; the historical process in which religion loses social and cultural significance and retains little power.

seminary: A college or private school that trains students to be priests, rabbis, or ministers.

shaman: A person regarded as having access to and influence in the world of good and evil spirits, especially among some of the peoples of northern Asia and North America. Typically, shamans enter a trance state during a ritual and practice divination and healings.

shorthorns: Any of a breed of red, roan, white, or red and white short-horned beef cattle originating in northern England and including good milk-producing strains.

signal corps: A military unit in charge of signal communications and information, especially for the branch of the US Army established in 1860 for this purpose. Throughout its history it had the initial responsibility for portfolios and new technologies that would eventually be transferred to other US government entities, including military intelligence, weather forecasting, and aviation.

sillar: Building material consisting of large blocks cut from a natural deposit such as lava, tuff, limestone, or compact clay.

Spanish alcalde: The Spanish form of mayoral representation.

Spanish Colonial Revival: A variant of the American Colonial Revival that drew from the buildings of former Spanish colonies. Typical features are adobe (or adobe-like) materials, a covered porch or arcade, balconies, unadorned stucco or plaster walls, and glazed or unglazed wall tiles. This was most common starting in 1915 and continues to be a popular style in the modern era.

Spanish Province: Generally used here when talking about Spanish Texas, situated on the border of Spain's vast North American empire. This province lay above the Nueces River to the east of the Medina River headwaters and extended into Louisiana. Over time, Texas was a part of four provinces in the Viceroyalty of New Spain (colonial Mexico).

Spanish viceroy: The governor of a country or province who rules as the representative of a Spanish king or sovereign.

stage fly grid system: A rigging system in a theater of rope lines, block (pulleys), counterweights, and related devices that enable a stage crew to quickly, quietly, and safely fly (or hoist) components such as curtains, lights, scenery, stage effects, and sometimes people.

streamline moderne: An international style of art deco architecture and design that emerged in the 1930s. It is inspired by aerodynamic design and emphasizes curving forms, long horizontal lines, and sometimes elements. It can also be found throughout industrial design, such as in railroad locomotives, toasters, vehicles, appliances, and other items, to give the impression of sleekness and modernity.

stucco: Fine plaster used for coating wall surfaces or molding into architectural decorations.

T

Tejano: A Mexican American inhabitant of southern Texas.

terra-cotta: Unglazed, typically brownish-red earthenware; used chiefly as an ornamental material and in modeling.

terrazzo: Flooring material consisting of marble or granite set in concrete and polished to give a smooth surface.

Texian: Generally used to describe a citizen of the Anglo-American section of the province of Coahuila and Texas or of the Republic of Texas. After annexation, Texian was commonly replaced by Texan.

Treaties of Velasco: On April 21, 1836, the forces of the Mexican army under Gen. Santa Anna were handed a decisive defeat by the Texans at San Jacinto. Dressed as a common soldier, Santa Anna attempted to flee but was taken prisoner. In order to obtain his freedom, he signed the "public agreement" and a "secret treaty" that ended the war and were signed in Velasco, Texas (now Surfside Beach).

Tuscan columns: A column that is plain, without carvings and ornamentation; it represents one of the five orders of classical architecture and is a defining detail of today's neoclassical-style building.

U

US Army Air Corps: The aerial warfare service component of the US Army between 1926 and 1941.

US Army Air Service: A brief precursor of the US Air Force and, before that, the Army Air Corps. It was created during World War I by President Wilson after America entered the war in April 1917, since the increasing military use of airplanes and aviation was readily apparent as the war continued to its climax. The service had a turbulent history trying to take off following the war and was reorganized to become the US Army Air Corps in 1926.

V

vaudeville: A type of entertainment popular in the United States in the early twentieth century. It featured a mixture of specialty acts such as burlesque comedy, song, and dance.

Victorian architecture: This series of architectural styles was utilized in the mid- to late nineteenth century, with "Victorian" referring to the reign, or era, of Queen Victoria (1837–1901). Many elements of this style of architecture did not become popular until later in the period, and it is used often as a term for American and British Empire styles and buildings. It is characterized by massive construction and elaborate ornamentation.

view corridor: An area that affords views of lakes, mountains, or other scenic amenities normally enjoyed.

W

wattle and daub: A material formerly or traditionally used in building walls, consisting of a network of interwoven sticks and twigs covered with mud and clay.

Bibliography

Books

Adovasio, James, and David Pedler. *Strangers in a New Land: What Archaeology Reveals about the First Americans*. Richmond Hill, ON: Firefly Books, 2016.

Alexander, Benjamin F. *The New Deal's Forest Army: How the Civilian Conservation Corps Worked*. Baltimore: Johns Hopkins University Press, 2018.

Alexander, Thomas E., and Dan K. Utley. *Faded Glory: A Century of Forgotten Texas Military Sites, Then and Now*. College Station: Texas A&M University Press, 2012.

Anderson, David G., and Robert C. Mainfort, eds. *The Woodland Southeast*. Tuscaloosa: University of Alabama Press, 2002.

Armstrong County Historical Association. *A Collection of Memories: A History of Armstrong County, 1876–1965*. Hereford, TX: Pioneer, 1965.

Arnn, John W., III. *Land of the Tejas: Native American Identity and Interaction in Texas, A.D. 1300–1700*. Austin: University of Texas Press, 2012.

Associated Press. *The Torch Is Passed: The Associated Press Story of the Death of a President*. New York: Associated Press, 1963.

Aston, B. W., and Ira Donathon Taylor. *Along the Texas Forts Trail*. Denton: University of North Texas Press, 1997.

Aten, Lawrence E. *Indians of the Upper Texas Coast*. New York: Academic Press, 1983.

Aten, Lawrence E., and Charles N. Bollich. *Early Ceramic Sites of the Sabine Lake Area, Coastal Texas and Louisiana*. Texas Archeological Research Laboratory Studies in Archeology 43. Austin: University of Texas, 2011.

Aten, Lawrence E., Charles K. Chandler, Al B. Wesolowsky, and Robert M. Malina. *Excavations at the Harris County Boys' School Cemetery: Analysis of Galveston Bay Area Mortuary Practices*. Texas Archeological Society Special Publication 3. Dallas: Texas Archeological Society, 1976.

Baker, Lindsay. *Ghost Towns of Texas*. Norman: University of Oklahoma Press, 1986.

Barkley, Mary Starr. *A History of Central Texas*. Austin: Austin Printing, 1970.

Barnstone, Howard. *The Galveston That Was*. New York: Macmillan, 1966.

Barr, Alwyn. *Texans in Revolt: The Battle for San Antonio, 1835*. Austin: University of Texas Press, 1990.

Barr, Juliana. *Peace Came in the Form of a Woman: Indians and Spaniards in the Texas Borderlands*. Chapel Hill: University of North Carolina Press, 2007.

Bastrop Historical Society. *In the Shadow of the Lost Pines: A History of Bastrop County and Its People*. Bastrop, TX: Bastrop Advertiser, 1955.

Bauer, Jack K. *The Mexican War, 1846–1848*. New York: Macmillan, 1974.

Bixel, Patricia Bellis. *Sailing Ship Elissa*. College Station: Texas A&M University Press, 2011.

Blair, Jayne E. *The Essential Civil War: A Handbook to the Battles, Armies, Navies and Commanders*. Jefferson, NC: McFarland, 2006.

Bolton, Herbert Eugene. *Texas in the Middle Eighteenth Century: Studies in Spanish Colonial History and Administration*. Austin: University of Texas Press, 1970.

Borch, Frederic L., and Daniel Martinez. *Kimmel, Short, and Pearl Harbor: The Final Report Revealed*. Annapolis, MD: Naval Institute Press, 2005

Boyd, Carolyn E. *Rock Art of the Lower Pecos*. College Station: Texas A&M University Press, 2003.

Boyd, Carolyn E. *The White Shaman Mural: An Enduring Creation Narrative in the Rock Art of the Lower Pecos*. Austin: University of Texas Press, 2016.

Brands, H. W. *Lone Star Nation: The Epic Story of the Battle for Texas Independence, 1835*. New York: Random House, 2005.

Brunson, Billy Ray. *The Texas Land and Development Company*. Austin: University of Texas Press, 1970.

Bugliosi, Vincent. *Reclaiming History: The Assassination of President John F. Kennedy*. New York: Norton, 2007.

Burrough, Bryan, Chris Tomlinson, and Jason Stanford. *Forget the Alamo: The Rise and Fall of an American Myth*. New York: Penguin, 2021.

Burton, Harley True. *A History of the JA Ranch*. New York: Argonaut, 1966.

Byfield, Patsy Jeanne. *Falcon Dam and the Lost Towns of Zapata*. Austin: Texas Memorial Museum, 1971.

Calore, Paul. *The Texas Revolution and the U.S.-Mexican War: A Concise History*. Jefferson, NC: McFarland, 2014.

Calvert, Robert A., and Arnoldo De León. *The History of Texas*. Arlington Heights, IL: Harlan Davidson, 1990.

Caro, Robert. *The Years of Lyndon Johnson: Master of the Senate*. New York: Alfred A. Knopf, 2002.

Caro, Robert. *The Years of Lyndon Johnson: Means of Ascent*. New York: Alfred A. Knopf, 1990.

Caro, Robert. *The Years of Lyndon Johnson: The Passage of Power*. New York: Alfred A. Knopf, 2012.

Caro, Robert. *The Years of Lyndon Johnson: The Path to Power*. New York: Alfred A. Knopf, 1982.

Carson, Paul. *Deep Time and the Texas High Plains: History and Geology*. Lubbock: Texas Tech University Press, 2005.Carter, R. G. *On the Border with Mackenzie*. Washington, DC: Enyon, 1935.

Castañeda, Carlos E., comp. *The Mexican Side of the Texas Revolution [1836] by the Chief Mexican Participants*. Austin, TX: Graphic Ideas, 1970.

Castañeda, Carlos E. *Our Catholic Heritage in Texas*. 7 vols. New York: Arno, 1976.

Catton, Bruce. *The Centennial History of the Civil War*. Vol. 3, *Never Call Retreat*. Garden City, NY: Doubleday, 1965.

Champagne, Anthony. *Congressman Sam Rayburn*. New Brunswick, NJ: Rutgers University Press, 1984.

Champagne, Anthony. "John Nance Garner." In *Masters of the House: Congressional Leadership over Two Centuries*. Edited by Raymond W. Smock and Susan W. Hammond, 144–80. New York: Routledge, 1998.

Champagne, Anthony. *Sam Rayburn: A Bio-bibliography*. Westport, CT: Greenwood, 1988.

Chariton, Wallace O. *Exploring the Alamo Legends*. Dallas: Republic of Texas Press, 1990.

Chemerka, William H., and Allen J. Wiener. *Music of the Alamo*. Houston: Bright Sky, 2009.

Chipman, Donald. *Spanish Texas, 1519–1821*. Austin: University of Texas Press, 1992.

Choate, Mark. *Nazis in the Pineywoods*. Lufkin, TX: Best of East Texas, 1989.

Civil War Preservation Trust. *Civil War Sites: The Official Guide to the Civil War Discovery Trail*. 2nd ed. Guilford, CT: Globe Pequot, 2007.

Clark, John W., Jr. *The Woodlands: Archeological Investigations at the Sam Houston Home, Huntsville, Walker County, Texas*. Reports of Investigations 4. Austin, TX: Prewitt, 1980.

Coker, Caleb. *News from Brownsville: Helen Chapman's Letters from the Texas Military Frontier, 1848–1852*. Austin: Texas State Historical Association, 1992.

Conger, Roger, Rupert Norval Richardson, Harold B. Simpson, et al. *Frontier Forts of Texas*. Waco, TX: Texian, 1966.

Conkling, Roscoe P., and Margaret B. Conkling. *The Butterfield Overland Mail, 1857–1869*. 3 vols. Glendale, CA: Clark, 1947.

Conn, Stetson, Byron Fairchild, and Rose C. Engelman. *7—the Attack on Pearl Harbor: Guarding the United States and Its Outposts*. Washington, DC: Center of Military History, United States Army, 2000.

Connor, Seymour V., and Odie B. Faulk. *North America Divided: The Mexican War, 1846–1848*. New York: Oxford University Press, 1971.

Connor, Seymour V., Donald M. Yena, J. B. Frantz, et al. *Battles of Texas*. 3rd ed. Waco: Texian Press, 1967 (3rd ed., 1980).

Cotner, Robert C. *The Texas State Capitol*. Austin: Pemberton, 1968.

Crisp, James E. *Sleuthing the Alamo*. New York: Oxford University Press, 2005.

Cruz, Gilberto R. *The San Antonio Missions National Historical Park: A Commitment to Research*. San Antonio, TX: Lebco Graphics, 1983.

Cypher, John. *Bob Kleberg and the King Ranch: A Worldwide Sea of Grass*. Austin: University of Texas Press, 1996.

Dallek, Robert. *Flawed Giant: Lyndon Johnson and His Times, 1961–1973*. Oxford: Oxford University Press, 1998.

Dallek, Robert. *Lone Star Rising: Lyndon Johnson and His Times, 1961–1973*. Oxford: Oxford University Press, 1991.

Daniel, Jean, Price Daniel, and Dorothy Blodgett. *The Texas Governor's Mansion*. Austin: Texas State Library, 1984.

Davis, William C. *Lone Star Rising: The Revolutionary Birth of the Texas Republic*. New York: Free Press, 2004.

Davis, William C. *Three Roads to the Alamo: The Lives and Fortunes of David Crockett, James Bowie, and William Barret Travis*. New York: HarperCollins, 1998.

de la Teja, Jesús F. *A Revolution Remembered: The Memoirs and Selected Correspondence of Juan N. Seguín*. Austin, TX: State House Press, 1991.

de la Teja, Jesús F. *San Antonio de Béxar: A Community on New Spain's Northern Frontier*. Albuquerque: University of New Mexico Press, 1995.

Dempsey, Charles A. *Air Force Aerospace Medical Research Laboratory: 50 Years of Research on Man in Flight*. Wright-Patterson Air Force Base, OH: US Air Force, 1985.

Fort Richardson, Texas (1867–1878) and the Mackenzie Trail. Jacksboro, TX: William Weatherford Dennis, 1964.

Dibble, David S., and Dessamae Lorraine. *Bonfire Shelter: A Stratified Bison Kill Site, Val Verde County, Texas*. Texas Memorial Museum Miscellaneous Papers 1. Austin: University of Texas Press, 1968.

Donovan, James. *The Blood of Heroes: The 13-Day Struggle for the Alamo—and the Sacrifice That Forged a Nation*. New York: Little, Brown, 2012.

Dorough, C. Dwight. *Mr. Sam*. New York: Random House, 1962.

Doyle, Gerry. *A Picture Book Introduction to the San Jacinto Museum of History*. Houston: San Jacinto Museum of History Association, 2021.

Duffield, Lathel, and Edward B. Jelks. *The Pearson Site*. University of Texas Department of Anthropology Archaeology Series 4. Austin: University of Texas Press, 1961.

Ebers, Paul. *San Antonio: The Metropolis and Garden Spot of Texas and Fort Sam Houston*. San Antonio, TX: San Antonio Printing, 1909.

Edmondson, J. R. *The Alamo Story: From History to Current Conflicts*. Plano, TX: Republic of Texas Press, 2000.

Eisenhower, Virginia. *The Strand of Galveston*. Galveston, TX: Virginia Eisenhour, 1974.

Evinger, William R. *Directory of Military Bases in the US*. Phoenix: Oryx, 1991.

Fagin, Stephen. *Assassination and Commemoration: JFK, Dallas, and the Sixth Floor Museum at Dealey Plaza*. Norman: University of Oklahoma Press, 2013.

Faulk, Odie B. *The Last Years of Spanish Texas, 1778–1821*. The Hague: Mouton, 1964.

Federal Writers Project. *Texas: A Guide to the Lone Star State*. New York: Hastings House, 1940.

Ferguson, John C. *Historic Battleship Texas: The Last Dreadnought*. Military History of Texas 4. Abilene, TX: State House Press, 2007.

Field, Ron. *Forts of the American Frontier, 1820–91: The Southern Plains and Southwest*. Oxford: Osprey, 2006.

Fish, Jean Y. *Zapata County Roots Revisited*. Edinburg, TX: New Santander, 1990.

Fisher, Lewis F. *River Walk: The Epic Story of San Antonio's River*. San Antonio, TX: Maverick, 2007.

Ford, Gus L., ed. *Texas Cattle Brands*. Dallas: Cockrell, 1936.

Ford, John Salmon, and Stephen Oates. *Rip Ford's Texas (Personal Narratives of the West)*. Austin: University of Texas Press, 1987.

Fort Sam Houston Museum. *A Pocket Guide to Historic Fort Sam Houston*. San Antonio, TX: Fort Sam Houston, 2003.

Fort Sam Houston Museum. *A Pocket Guide to the Staff Post*. San Antonio, TX: Fort Sam Houston, 2006.

Fort Sam Houston Museum. *Commodious Homes for the Troops: A Centennial History of the Cavalry and Light Artillery Addition, Fort Sam Houston, Texas, 1905–2005*. San Antonio, TX: Fort Sam Houston, 2006.

Fort Sam Houston Museum. *The Post at San Antonio: 1845–1879*. San Antonio, TX: Fort Sam Houston, 2002.

Fort Sam Houston Museum. *The Quadrangle: Hub of Military Activity in Texas; An Outline History*. San Antonio, TX: Fort Sam Houston, 2009.

Frazer, Robert W. *Forts of the West*. Norman: University of Oklahoma Press, 1965.

Friedman, Norman. *U.S. Battleships: An Illustrated Design History*. Annapolis, MD: Naval Institute Press. 1986.

Gailey, Harry A. *War in the Pacific: From Pearl Harbor to Tokyo Bay*. Novato, CA: Presidio, 1997.

Galloway, Diane, and Kathy Matthews. *The Park Cities: A Walker's Guide and Brief History*. Dallas: Southern Methodist University Press, 1988.

Gannon, Michael V. *Pearl Harbor Betrayed*. New York: Henry Holt, 2001.

Gardiner, Robert. *Conway's All the World's Fighting Ships, 1947–1982*. Part 1, *The Western Powers*. Annapolis, MD: Naval Institute Press, 1983.

Graham, Don. *The Kings of Texas: The 150-Year Saga of an American Ranching Empire*. New York: Wiley, 2004.

Graves, Lawrence L., ed. *A History of Lubbock*. Lubbock: West Texas Museum Association, 1962.

Graves, Lawrence L., ed. *Lubbock: From Town to City*. Lubbock: West Texas Museum Association, 1986.

Groneman, Bill. *Alamo Defenders: A Genealogy, the People and Their Words*. Austin: Eakin Press, 1990.

Groneman, Bill. *Battlefields of Texas*. Plano, TX: Republic of Texas Press, 1998.

Groneman, Bill. *Eyewitness to the Alamo*. Plano, TX: Republic of Texas Press, 1996.

Groves, Helen Kleberg. *Bob and Helen Kleberg of King Ranch*. San Antonio, TX: Trinity University Press, 2017.

Guffee, Eddie Joe. *The Plainview Site*. Plainview, TX: Llano Estacado Museum, 1979.

Hafen, LeRoy R. *Overland Mail, 1849–1869*. Cleveland, OH: Clark, 1926.

Hafertepe, Kenneth. *Abner Cook: Master Builder on the Texas Frontier*. Austin: Texas State Historical Association, 1992.

Haley, J. Evetts. *Charles Goodnight*. Norman: University of Oklahoma Press, 1949.

Haley, J. Evetts. *Fort Concho and the Texas Frontier*. Virginia: Borodino Books, 2018.

Hall, Joan Upton, and Stacey Hasbrook. *Grand Old Texas Theaters That Won't Quit*. Plano, TX: Republic of Texas Press, 2002.

Hamilton, Allen Lee. *Sentinel of the Southern Plains: Fort Richardson and the Northwest Texas Frontier, 1866–1878*. Fort Worth: Texas Christian University Press, 1988.

Handy, Mary Olivia. *History of Sam Houston*. San Antonio, TX: Naylor, 1951.

Hanson, Todd, ed. *The Alamo Reader: A Study in History*. Mechanicsburg, PA: Stackpole Books, 2003.

Hardin, Stephen L. *Texian Iliad: A Military History of the Texas Revolution*. Austin: University of Texas Press, 1994.

Hardin, Stephen L., and Angus McBride. *The Alamo 1836: Santa Anna's Texas Campaign*. Oxford: Osprey, 2001

Hayes, Charles Waldo. *Galveston: History of the Island and the City*. 2 vols. Austin, TX: Jenkins Garrett, 1974.

Haynes, Robert V. *A Night of Violence: The Houston Riot of 1917*. Baton Rouge: Louisiana State University Press, 1976.

Henderson, Timothy J. *A Glorious Defeat: Mexico and Its War with the United States*. New York: Hill and Wang, 2008

Hendrickson, Robert. *The Road to Appomattox*. New York: John Wiley & Sons, 2000.

Hoffman, David, comp. *Fort Concho National Historic Landmark: A Master Plan for Development*. Austin, TX: Bell, Klein, and Hoffman, 1980.

Hoffman, Scott L. *A Theatre History of Marion, Ohio: John Eberson's Palace and Beyond*. Charlotte, NC: History Press, 2015.

Hone, Thomas C., and Trent Hone. *Battleline: The United States Navy, 1919–1939*. Annapolis, MD: Naval Institute Press, 2006.

Houston County Historical Commission. *History of Houston County, Texas, 1687–1979*. Tulsa, OK: Heritage, 1979.

Houston County Historical Commission, Preservation Committee. *Houston County (Texas) Cemeteries*. 3rd ed. Crockett, TX: Houston County Historical Commission, 1977.

Hunt, Jeffrey Wm. *The Last Battle of the Civil War: Palmetto Ranch*. Austin: University of Texas Press, 2000.

Jackson, Jack. *Los Mesteños: Spanish Ranching in Texas, 1721–1821*. Centennial Series of the Association of Former Students, Texas A&M University 18. College Station: Texas A&M University Press, 2006.

Johnson, Eileen, ed. *Lubbock Lake*. College Station: Texas A&M University Press, 1987.

Jones, Jerry W. *Battleship Texas*. Annapolis, MD: Naval Institute Press, 1998.

Keegan, John. *The American Civil War: A Military History*. New York: Alfred A. Knopf, 2009.

Kegley, George. *Archeological Investigations at Hueco Tanks State Park*. Austin: Texas Parks and Wildlife Department, 1980.

Keim, Norman O. *Our Movie Houses: A History of Film and Cinematic Innovation in Central New York*. Syracuse, NY: Syracuse University Press, 2014.

Kelin, John. *Praise from a Future Generation: The Assassination of John F. Kennedy and the First Generation Critics of the Warren Report*. San Antonio, TX: Wings, 2007.

Kennedy, Frances H., ed. *The Civil War Battlefield Guide*. 2nd ed. Boston: Houghton Mifflin, 1998.

Kesselus, Kenneth. *History of Bastrop County, Texas, 1846–65*. Austin, TX: Jenkins, 1987.

Kesselus, Kenneth. *History of Bastrop County, Texas, before Statehood*. Austin, TX: Jenkins, 1986.

Kirkland, Forrest, and William W. Newcomb Jr. *The Rock Art of Texas Indians*. Austin: University of Texas Press, 1967.

Knox, Orion, et al. *Preservation Plan and Program for Fort Richardson State Historical Park*. Austin: Texas Parks and Wildlife Department, 1975.

Lane, Ann J. *The Brownsville Affair*. Port Washington, NY: National University Publications / Kennikat, 1971.

Lea, Tom. *The King Ranch*. 2 vols. Boston: Little, Brown, 1957.

Ledbetter, Barbara Neal. *Fort Belknap Frontier Saga: Indians, Negroes and Anglo-Americans on the Texas Frontiers*. Burnet, TX, Eakin, 1982.

Lindley, Thomas Ricks. *Alamo Traces: New Evidence and New Conclusions*. Lanham, MD: Republic of Texas Press, 2003.

Long, Jeff. *Duel of Eagles: The Mexican and U.S. Fight for the Alamo*. New York: William Morrow, 1990.

Lorrain, Dessamae. *Archaeological Excavations in the Fish Creek Reservoir*. Southern Methodist University Contributions in Anthropology 4. Dallas: Southern Methodist University, 1969.

Lowry, Chris, ed. *Archaeological Investigations of the Hot Well and Sgt. Doyle Sites, Fort Bliss, Texas: Late Formative Period Adaptations of the Hueco Bolson*. Fort Bliss Cultural Resource Report 94–18. Fort Bliss, TX: Directorate of Environment, Conservation Division, United States Army Air Defense Artillery Center and Fort Bliss, 2005.

Lozano, Ruben Rendon. *Viva Texas: The Story of the Tejanos, the Mexican-Born Patriots of the Texas Revolution*. San Antonio, TX: Alamo Press, 1985.

Macrae, James Burr Harrison. *Pecos River Style Rock Art: A Prehistoric Iconography*. College Station: Texas A&M University Press, 2018.

Madsen, Daniel. *Resurrection: Salvaging the Battle Fleet at Pearl Harbor*. Annapolis, MD: US Naval Institute Press, 2003.

Malinowski, Sharon, and Anna Sheets. *Gale Encyclopedia of Native American Tribes*. Vol. 2, *Great Basin, Southwest, Middle America*. Farmington Hills, MI: Gale / Cengage Learning, 1997.

Manchester, William. *The Death of a President: November 20–November 25, 1963*. New York: Harper & Row, 1967.

Manguso, John. *Fort Sam Houston*. Images of America. Charleston, SC: Arcadia, 2012.

Manning, Thomas. *History of Air Education and Training Command, 1942–2002*. Randolph Air Force Base, TX: Office of History and Research, Headquarters, AETC, 2005.

Martinez de Vara, Art. *Tejano Patriot: The Revolutionary Life of Jose Francisco Ruiz, 1783–1840*. Austin: Texas State Historical Association Press, 2020.

Matovina, Timothy M. *The Alamo Remembered: Tejano Accounts and Perspectives*. Austin: University of Texas Press, 1995.

Matthews, James T. *Fort Concho: A History and a Guide*. Austin: Texas State Historical Association, 2013.

Maxwell, Ross A. *Geologic and Historic Guide to the Texas State Parks*. Austin: Bureau of Economic Geology, University of Texas, 1970.

McComb, David G. *Galveston: A History*. Austin: University of Texas Press, 1986.

McCoy, Dorothy Abbott. *Texas Ranchmen*. Austin, TX: Eakin, 1987.

McDonald, David. *Jose Antonio Navarro: In Search of the American Dream in Nineteenth-Century Texas*. Austin: Texas State Historical Association, 2011.

McKinley, Fred B., and Greg Riley. *Black Gold to Bluegrass: From the Oil Fields of Texas to Spindletop Farm of Kentucky*. Austin, TX: Eakin, 2005.

Meltzer, David J. *First Peoples in a New World: Colonizing Ice Age America*. Berkeley: University of California Press, 2009.

Metz, Leon C. *El Paso Chronicles: A Record of Historical Events in El Paso, Texas*. El Paso, TX: Mangan Books, 1993.

Metz, Leon C. *El Paso: Guided through Time*. El Paso, TX: Mangan Books, 1999.

Miller, George Oxford. *Texas Parks and Campgrounds: Central, South, and West Texas*. Austin: Texas Monthly Press, 1984.

Miller, Myles R., Nancy A. Kenmotsu, and Melinda Landreth, eds. *Significance and Research Standards for Prehistoric Archaeological Sites at Fort Bliss*. Fort Bliss Historic and Natural Resources Report 05–16. Fort Bliss, TX: Environmental Division, Fort Bliss Garrison Command, 2009.

Miller, Ray. *Ray Miller's Texas Parks: A History and Guide*. Houston, TX: Cordovan, 1984.

Moore, Richard R. *West Texas after the Discovery of Oil*. Austin, TX: Pemberton, 1971.

Moore, Stephen L. *Eighteen Minutes: The Battle of San Jacinto and the Texas Independence Campaign*. Plano, TX: Republic of Texas Press, 2004.

Moorhead, Max L. *The Presidio: Bastion of the Spanish Borderlands*. Norman: University of Oklahoma Press, 1975.

Morison, Samuel Eliot. *History of United States Naval Operations in World War II: The Rising Sun in the Pacific, 1931–April 1942*. Champaign: University of Illinois Press, 2001.

Nance, Joseph Milton. *Attack and Counterattack: The Texas-Mexican Frontier, 1842*. Austin: University of Texas Press, 1965.

Neidinger, Adriane Askins. *Envision, Design, Train: A Pictorial History of the U.S. Army Medical Department Center & School, 1920–2010*. Fort Sam Houston, TX: Borden Institute, 2013.

Nofi, Albert. *The Alamo and the Texas War for Independence*. Conshohocken, PA: Combined Books, 1992.

Nofi, Albert A. *The Alamo and the Texas War of Independence, September 30, 1835, to April 21, 1836: Heroes, Myths, and History*. Conshohocken, PA: Combined Books, 1992.

O'Connor, Kathryn Stoner. *Presidio La Bahía Del Espiritu Santo De Zuniga: 1721 to 1846*. Austin, TX: Von Boeckmann-Jones, 1966.

O'Laughlin, Thomas C. *The Keystone Dam Site and Other Archaic and Formative Sites in Northwest El Paso*. El Paso Centennial Museum Publications in Anthropology 8. El Paso: University of Texas at El Paso, 1980.

Olien, Diana, and Roger Olien. *Oil in Texas: The Gusher Age, 1895–1945*. Austin: University of Texas Press, 2002.

Ormsby, Waterman L. *The Butterfield Overland Mail*. San Marino, CA: Huntington Library, 1955.

Ousley, Clarence, ed. *Galveston in 1900*. Atlanta: Chase, 1900.

Patenaude, Lionel V. *Texans, Politics, and the New Deal*. New York: Garland, 1983.

Peattie, Mark R. *Sunburst: The Rise of Japanese Naval Air Power, 1909–1941*. Annapolis, MD: Naval Institute Press, 2001.

Perttula, Timothy K. *The Caddo Nation: Archaeological and Ethnohistoric Perspectives*. Austin: University of Texas Press, 1992.

Perttula, Timothy K., ed. *The Prehistory of Texas*. College Station: Texas A&M University Press, 2004.

Petite, Mary Deborah. *1836 Facts about the Alamo and the Texas War for Independence*. Mason City, IA: Savas, 1999.

Pohl, James W. *The Battle of San Jacinto*. Austin: Texas State Historical Association, 1989.

Powers, Hugh. *Battleship Texas*. College Station: Texas A&M University Press, 1993.

Poyo, Gerald E., and Gilberto M. Hinojosa, eds. *Tejano Origins in Eighteenth-Century San Antonio*. San Antonio, TX: Institute of Texan Cultures, 1991.

Prange, Gordon W. *At Dawn We Slept*. New York: McGraw-Hill, 1981.

Prange, Gordon W. *December 7, 1941: The Day the Japanese Attacked Pearl Harbor*. New York: McGraw-Hill, 1988.

Prange, Gordon W. *Pearl Harbor: The Verdict of History*. New York: McGraw-Hill, 1986.

Prange, Gordon William, Donald M. Goldstein, and Katherine V. Dillon. *December 7, 1941: The Day the Japanese Attacked Pearl Harbor*. New York: McGraw-Hill. 1998.

Pruett, Jakie, and Everett Cole. *The History and Heritage of Goliad County*. Austin, TX: Eakin / Goliad County Historical Commission, 1983.

Ramos, Raul A. *Beyond the Alamo: Forging Mexican Ethnicity in San Antonio, 1821–1861*. Chapel Hill: University of North Carolina Press, 2008.

Reid, Stuart. *The Secret War for Texas*. Elma Dill Russell Spencer Series in the West and Southwest. College Station: Texas A&M University Press, 2007.

Rienstra, Ellen Walker, Jo Ann Stiles, and Judith Walker Linsley. *Giant under the Hill: A History of the Spindletop Oil Discovery at Beaumont, Texas, in 1901*. Austin: Texas State Historical Association, 2008.

Roberts, Robert B. *Encyclopedia of Historic Forts: The Military, Pioneer, and Trading Posts of the United States*. New York: Macmillan, 1988.

Robertson, Pauline D., and R. L. Robertson. *Cowman's Country: Fifty Frontier Ranches in the Texas Panhandle, 1876–1887*. Amarillo, TX: Paramount, 1981.

Roell, Craig. *Matamoros and the Texas Revolution*. Denton, TX: Texas State Historical Association, 2013.

Roell, Craig. *Remember Goliad!: A History of La Bahía*. Austin: Texas State Historical Association, 1994.

Ryan, Cornelius. *The Longest Day: 6 June 1944*. New York: Simon & Schuster, 1959.

Schoelwer, Susan Prendergast, and Tom W. Gläser. *Alamo Images: Changing Perceptions of a Texas Experience*. Dallas: DeGolyer Library and Southern Methodist University Press, 1985.

Scobee, Barry. *Old Fort Davis*. San Antonio, TX: Naylor, 1947.

Scobee, Barry. *The Story of Fort Davis: Jeff Davis County and the Davis Mountains*. Fort Davis, TX: Marvin Hunter, 1936.

Scott, Robert. *After the Alamo*. Plano, TX: Republic of Texas Press, 2000.

Shafer, Harry, and Jim Zintgraff. *Ancient Texans: Rock Art and Lifeways along the Lower Pecos*. Austin: Texas Monthly Press, 1986.

Shafer, Harry J. *Painters in Prehistory: Archaeology and Art of the Lower Pecos Canyonlands*. San Antonio, TX: Trinity University Press, 2013.

Spearing, Darwin. *Roadside Geology of Texas*. Missoula, MT: Mountain, 1991.

St. Clair, Kathleen E., and Clifton R. St. Clair, eds. *Little Towns of Texas*. Jacksonville, TX: Jayroe Graphic Arts, 1982.

Staff, Department of Urban Planning, City of Dallas. *West End Historic District*. Dallas: Department of Urban Planning, City of Dallas, 2016.

Steely, James W. *Parks for Texas: Enduring Landscapes of the New Deal*. Austin: University of Texas Press, 1999.

Steely, James Wright, comp. *A Catalog of Texas Properties in the National Register of Historic Places*. Austin: Texas Historical Commission, 1984.

Stille, Mark E. *Tora! Tora! Tora! Pearl Harbor 1941*. Osprey Raid Series 26. Oxford: Osprey, 2011.

Thompson, Frank. *The Alamo: A Cultural History*. Dallas: Taylor Trade, 2001.

Thompson, Josiah. *Six Seconds in Dallas: A Micro-study of the Kennedy Assassination*. New York: Bernard Geis, 1967.

Timmons, Bascom N. *Garner of Texas*. New York: Harper, 1948.

Todish, Timothy J., Terry Todish, and Ted Spring. *Alamo Sourcebook, 1836: A Comprehensive Guide to the Battle of the Alamo and the Texas Revolution*. Austin, TX: Eakin, 1998.

Trask, Richard B. *Pictures of the Pain: Photography and the Assassination of President Kennedy*. Danvers, MA: Yeoman, 1994.

Utley, Robert M. *Fort Davis National Historic Site*. Washington, DC: National Park Service, 1965.

Ward, Geoffrey C., and Kenneth Burns. *The Civil War*. New York: Knopf, 1990.

Weaver, John. *The Brownsville Raid*. New York: Norton, 1970.

Weber, David. *The Spanish Frontier in North America*. New Haven, CT: Yale University Press, 1992.

Weddle, Robert. *San Juan Bautista: Gateway to Spanish Texas*. Austin: University of Texas Press, 1991.

Wertz, Jay, and Edwin C. Bearss. *Smithsonian's Great Battles and Battlefields of the Civil War*. New York: William Morrow, 1997.

Winders, Richard Bruce. *Sacrificed at the Alamo: Tragedy and Triumph in the Texas Revolution*. Austin, TX: State House Press, 2004.

Winfrey, Dorman. *Six Missions of Texas*. Waco, TX: Texian, 1965.

Winsor, Bill. *Texas in the Confederacy: Military Installations, Economy, and People*. Hillsboro, TX: Hill Junior College Press, 1978.

Wiper, Steve, and Tom Flowers. *USS Texas BB-35*. Warship Pictorial 4. Tucson, AZ: Classic Warships, 2006.

Wohlstetter, Roberta. *Pearl Harbor: Warning and Decision*. Stanford, CA: Stanford University Press, 1962.

Wooster, Robert. *Fort Davis: Outpost on the Texas Frontier*. Austin: Texas State Historical Assn., 2014.

WPA Writers Program. *Houston*. Houston, TX: Anson Jones, 1942.

Yergin, Daniel. *The Prize: The Epic Quest for Oil, Money & Power*. New York: Simon & Schuster, 1991.

Zimm, Alan D. *Attack on Pearl Harbor: Strategy, Combat, Myths, Deceptions*. Havertown, PA: Casemate, 2001.

Zintgraff, Jim, and Solveig Turpin. *Pecos River Rock Art: A Photographic Essay*. San Antonio, TX: Sandy McPherson, 1991.

Handbook of Texas Online

"A Tejano Statesman's Home." *Handbook of Texas Online*. Texas Historical Commission. https://www.thc.texas.gov/historic-sites/casa-navarro/history/Tejano-statesmans-home. Accessed April 21, 2021.

"Alamo Cenotaph." *Handbook of Texas Online*. Texas State Historical Association. 1952; updated June 17, 2020. https://www.tshaonline.org/handbook/entries/alamo-cenotaph. Accessed November 1, 2021.

Alcott, Edward B. "Brooks Air Force Base." *Handbook of Texas Online*. Texas State Historical Association. Updated July 28, 2020. https://www.tshaonline.org/handbook/entries/brooks-air-force-base. Accessed April 18, 2021.

Anderson, H. Allen. "Fort Concho National Historic Landmark." *Handbook of Texas Online*. Texas State Historical Association. January 1, 1995; updated October 22, 2020. https://www.tshaonline.org/handbook/entries/fort-concho-national-historic-landmark. Accessed April 14, 2021.

Anderson, H. Allen. "Fort Concho National Historic Landmark." *Handbook of Texas Online*. Texas State Historical Association. January 1, 1995; updated October 22, 2020. https://www.tshaonline.org/handbook/entries/fort-concho-national-historic-landmark. Accessed February 10, 2021.

Anderson, H. Allen. "JA Ranch." *Handbook of Texas Online*. Texas State Historical Association. 1952; updated April 14, 2021. https://www.tshaonline.org/handbook/entries/ja-ranch. Accessed June 23, 2021.

Ashton, John, and Edgar P. Sneed. Revised by Bob Kinnan. "King Ranch." *Handbook of Texas Online*. Texas State Historical Association. 1976; updated December 10, 2014. https://www.tshaonline.org/handbook/entries/king-ranch. Accessed November 1, 2021.

Bishop, Eliza H. "Fort Brown." *Handbook of Texas Online*. Texas State Historical Association. Updated September 21, 2021. https://www.tshaonline.org/handbook/entries/fort-brown-2.

Brown, Timothy M. Revised by Lane Bourgeois. "Randolph Air Force Base." *Handbook of Texas Online*. 1976; updated February 13, 2018. https://www.tshaonline.org/handbook/entries/randolph-air-force-base. Accessed March 21, 2021.

Champagne, Anthony, and Floyd F. Ewing. "Rayburn, Samuel Taliaferro (1882–1961)." *Handbook of Texas Online*. Texas State Historical Association. 1976; updated January 11, 2020. https://www.tshaonline.org/handbook/entries/rayburn-samuel-taliaferro. Accessed November 28, 2020.

Christian, Garna L. "Brownsville Raid of 1906." *Handbook of Texas Online*. Texas State Historical Association. Updated November 30, 2020. www.tshaonline.org/handbook/entries/brownsville-raid-of-1906. Accessed November 28, 2021.

Clayton, Lawrence. "Fort Davis." *Handbook of Texas Online*. Texas State Historical Association. January 1, 1995. https://www.tshaonline.org/handbook/entries/fort-davis. Accessed July 12, 2021.

Daniel, Wayne, and Carol Schmidt. "Fort Concho." *Handbook of Texas Online*. Texas State Historical Association. 1952; updated October 3, 2019. https://www.tshaonline.org/handbook/entries/fort-concho. Accessed February 8, 2021.

Davenport, Elizabeth Perrit. "Fort Brown." *Handbook of Texas Online*. Texas State Historical Association. January 1, 1995. www.tshaonline.org/handbook/entries/fort-brown. Accessed February 2, 2021.

Davenport, Harbert, and Craig H. Roell. "Goliad Massacre." *Handbook of Texas Online*. Texas State Historical Association. March 22, 2018. https://www.tshaonline.org/handbook/entries/goliad-massacre. Accessed April 16, 2021.

Davis, Charles G. "Camp Charlotte." *Handbook of Texas Online*. Texas State Historical Association. 1976; updated September 5, 2019. https://www.tshaonline.org/handbook/entries/camp-charlotte. Accessed April 17, 2021.

Davis, Charles G. "Fort Chadbourne." *Handbook of Texas Online*. Texas State Historical Association. 1952; updated January 1, 1995. https://www.tshaonline.org/handbook/entries/fort-chadbourne. Accessed March 23, 2021.

Davis, Charles G. "Belknap, TX." *Handbook of Texas Online*. Texas State Historical Association. November 1, 1994. https://www.tshaonline.org/handbook/entries/belknap-tx. Accessed April 21, 2021.

"Davis Mountains." *Handbook of Texas Online*. Texas State Historical Association. 1952; updated June 22, 2019. https://www.tshaonline.org/handbook/entries/davis-mountains. Accessed July 12, 2021.

Draves, Tim. "Spanish Governor's Palace [Comandancia]." *Handbook of Texas Online*. Texas State Historical Association. 1976; updated January 11, 2017. https://www.tshaonline.org/handbook/entries/spanish-governors-palace-comandancia. Accessed June 17, 2021.

Duke, Escal F. "San Angelo, TX." *Handbook of Texas Online*. Texas State Historical Association. 1952; updated February 1, 1996. https://www.tshaonline.org/handbook/entries/san-angelo-tx. Accessed February 12, 2021.

Green, Walter Elton. "Capitol." *Handbook of Texas Online*. Texas State Historical Association. 1976; updated February 7, 2019. https://www.tshaonline.org/handbook/entries/capitol. Accessed July 1, 2021.

Hamilton, Allen Lee. "Fort Richardson." *Handbook of Texas Online*. Texas State Historical Association. 1952; updated June 29, 2018. https://www.tshaonline.org/handbook/entries/fort-concho-national-historic-landmark. Accessed March 8, 2021.

Hardin, Stephen L. "Battle of the Alamo." *Handbook of Texas Online*. Texas State Historical Association. 1952; updated July 29, 2020. https://www.tshaonline.org/handbook/entries/alamo-battle-of-the. Accessed April 18, 2021.

Hoffman, Michael P. "Universal City, TX." *Handbook of Texas Online*. Texas State Historical Association. 1952; updated February 14, 2021. https://www.tshaonline.org/handbook/entries/universal-city-tx. Accessed November 1, 2021.

Hunt, Jeffrey William. "Battle of Palmito Ranch." *Handbook of Texas Online*. Texas State Historical Association. 1952; updated April 20, 2020. https://www.tshaonline.org/handbook/entries/palmito-ranch-battle-of. Accessed July 8, 2021.

Kohout, Martin Donell. "Fort Davis, TX." *Handbook of Texas Online*. Texas State Historical Association. 1976, updated October 22, 2020. https://www.tshaonline.org/handbook/entries/fort-davis-tx. Accessed July 12, 2021.

Kozlowski, Gerald F. "Porter Farm." *Handbook of Texas Online*. Texas State Historical Association. May 1, 1995. https://www.tshaonline.org/handbook/entries/porter-farm. Accessed July 22, 2021.

Leatherwood, Art. "Battle of Resaca de la Palma." *Handbook of Texas Online*. Texas State Historical Association. 1952; updated August 4, 2020. https://www.tshaonline.org/handbook/entries/alamo-cenotaph. Accessed September 1, 2021.

Leckie, William H. "Tenth United States Cavalry." *Handbook of Texas Online*. Texas State Historical Association. July 1, 1995; updated March 10, 2021. https://www.tshaonline.org/handbook/entries/tenth-united-states-cavalry. Accessed February 25, 2021.

Lintz, Christopher. "Antelope Creek Phase." *Handbook of Texas Online*. Texas State Historical Association. 1952; updated February 25, 2021. https://www.tshaonline.org/handbook/entries/antelope-creek-phase. Accessed October 1, 2021.

Manguso, John. "Fort Sam Houston." *Handbook of Texas Online*. Texas State Historical Association. 1976; updated May 16, 2018. https://www.tshaonline.org/handbook/entries/fort-sam-houston. Accessed August 22, 2021.

McChristian, Douglas C. "Fort Davis." *Handbook of Texas Online*. Texas State Historical Association. 1976; updated October 22, 2020. https://www.tshaonline.org/handbook/entries/fort-davis-qbf15. Accessed July 12, 2021.

McChristian, Douglas C. "Fort Davis National Historic Site." *Handbook of Texas Online*. Texas State Historical Association. January 1, 1995; updated October 3, 2019. https://www.tshaonline.org/handbook/entries/fort-davis-national-historic-site. Accessed November 1, 2021.

McDonald, David R. "Casa Navarro State Historic Site." *Handbook of Texas Online*. Texas State Historical Association. January 31, 2014; updated April 6, 2016. https://www.tshaonline.org/handbook/entries/casa-navarro-state-historic-site. Accessed August 19, 2021.

Nall, Matthew Hayes. "Texas School Book Depository." *Handbook of Texas Online*. Texas State Historical Association. August 1, 1995; updated July 27, 2020. https://www.tshaonline.org/handbook/entries/texas-school-book-depository. Accessed February 8, 2021.

Neighbours, Kenneth F. "Fort Belknap." *Handbook of Texas Online*. Texas State Historical Association. January 1, 1995. https://www.tshaonline.org/handbook/entries/fort-belknap.

"Nolan Expedition [1877]." *Handbook of Texas Online*. Texas State Historical Association. 1952; updated March 6, 2021. https://www.tshaonline.org/handbook/entries/nolan-expedition-1877. Accessed February 10, 2021.

Nolan, Patrick B. "Sam Houston Memorial Museum." *Handbook of Texas Online*. Texas State Historical Association. 1996; updated February 5, 2019. https://www.tshaonline.org/handbook/entries/sam-houston-memorial-museum. Accessed November 1, 2021.

Richardson, Rupert. "Butterfield Overland Mail." *Handbook of Texas Online*. Texas State Historical Association. 1976; updated November 1, 1994. https://www.tshaonline.org/handbook/entries/butterfield-overland-mail. Retrieved March 5, 2021.

Richardson, T. C. "Goodnight–Loving Trail." *Handbook of Texas Online*. Texas State Historical Association. 1976; updated April 18, 2017. https://www.tshaonline.org/handbook/entries/goodnight-loving-trail. Accessed March 5, 2021.

Roell, Craig H., and Robert S. Weddle. "Nuestra Señora de Loreto de La Bahía Presidio." *Handbook of Texas Online*. Texas State Historical Association, 1976. https://www.tshaonline.org/handbook/entries/nuestra-senora-de-loreto-de-la-Bahía-Presidio. Accessed July 8, 2021.

Smyrl, Vivian Elizabeth. "Governor's Mansion." *Handbook of Texas Online*. Texas State Historical Association. 1976; updated July 20, 2017. https://www.tshaonline.org/handbook/entries/governors-mansion. Accessed June 28, 2021.

"Texas Centennial." *Handbook of Texas Online*. Texas State Historical Association. https://www.tshaonline.org/handbook/entries/texas-centennial. 1952; updated July 7, 2017. Accessed December 1, 2017.

Turner, Jeri Robison. "Goliad, TX." *Handbook of Texas Online*. Texas State Historical Association. December 2, 2019. https://www.tshaonline.org/handbook/entries/goliad-tx.

Ward, William A. "*Elissa*." *Handbook of Texas Online*. Texas State Historical Association. January 1, 1995; updated October 26, 2018. https://www.tshaonline.org/handbook/entries/*Elissa*. Accessed November 1, 2020.

Wiley, Nancy. "State Fair of Texas." *Handbook of Texas Online*. Texas State Historical Association. 1976; updated April 6, 2019. http://www.tshaonline.org/handbook/online/articles/lks02. Accessed August 16, 2021.

Wooster, Robert, and Christine Moor Sanders. "Spindletop Oilfield." *Handbook of Texas Online*. Texas State Historical Association. 1976, updated April 2, 2019. https://www.tshaonline.org/handbook/entries/spindletop-oilfield. Accessed May 11, 2021.

Wooster, Robert. "Lucas, Anthony Francis (1855–1921)." *Handbook of Texas Online*. Texas State Historical Association. 1952, Updated July 21, 2016. https://www.tshaonline.org/handbook/entries/lucas-anthony-francis. Accessed February 8, 2021.

Magazines & Journals

Arneson, Edwin P. "Early Irrigation in Texas." *Southwestern Historical Quarterly* 25, no. 2 (October 1921): 121–30.

Black, Craig C., ed. "History and Prehistory of the Lubbock Lake Site." *Museum Journal* 15 (1974). Lubbock: West Texas Museum Association.

Boyd, Douglas K. "Prehistoric Agriculture on the Canadian River of the Texas Panhandle: New Insights from West Pasture Sites on the M-Cross Ranch." *Plains Anthropologist* 53, no. 205 (2008): 33–57. https://doi.org/10.1179/pan.2008.004.

Brown, Norman D. "Garnering Votes for 'Cactus Jack': John Nance Garner, Franklin D. Roosevelt, and the 1932 Democratic Nomination for President." *Southwestern Historical Quarterly* 104, no. 2 (2000): 149–88.

Carter, George F. "Caves of the Upper Gila and Hueco Areas in New Mexico and Texas. C. B. Cosgrove." *Quarterly Review of Biology* 23, no. 2 (1948): 191. https://doi.org/10.1086/396400.

Chapman, Carol Flake. "The Rocks That Speak." *Texas Parks & Wildlife Magazine*, September 2004, 41–45.

Chapman, John. "Fort Concho . . ." *Southwest Review* 25, no. 3 (April 1940): 258–86.

Christian, Garna L. "The Brownsville Raid's 168th Man: The Court-Martial of Corporal Knowles." *Southwestern Historical Quarterly* 93, no. 1 (July 1989): 45–59.

Crook, Wilson W., and R. K. Harris. "A Pleistocene Campsite near Lewisville, Texas." *American Antiquity* 23, no. 3 (1958): 233–46. https://doi.org/10.2307/276304.

Earl, John. "Landscape in the Theatre: Historical Perspective." *Landscape Research* 16, no. 1 (1991): 21–29.

Graham, Roy Eugene. "Federal Fort Architecture in Texas during the Nineteenth Century." *Southwestern Historical Quarterly* 74, no. 2 (October 1970): 165–88.

Hafertepe, Kenneth. "The Romantic Rhetoric of the Spanish Governor's Palace, San Antonio, Texas." *Southwestern Historical Quarterly* 108, no. 2 (October 2003): 239–77.

Hanyok, Robert J. "How the Japanese Did It." *Naval History Magazine* 23, no. 6 (September 2019): 44–50.

Herzog, Charlotte. "The Movie Palace and the Theatrical Sources of Its Architectural Style." *Cinema Journal*, Spring 1981, 15–37.

Hendrickson, Kenneth E., Jr. "Replenishing the Soil and the Soul of Texas: The Civilian Conservation Corps in the Lone Star State as an Example of State-Federal Work Relief during the Great Depression." *The Historian* 65, no. 4 (Summer 2003): 801–16.

Hutchins, Wells A. "The Community Acequia: Its Origins and Development." *Southwestern Historical Quarterly* 31, no. 3 (January 1928): 261–84.

Hughes, Jack T. "Prehistoric Cultural Developments on the Texas High Plains." *Bulletin of the Texas Archeological Society* 60 (1989): 1–56.

Jones, Kathryn. "Brownsville to Laredo on U.S. 83 and Mexico Highway 2." *Texas Monthly*, May 1, 2002. https://www.texasmonthly.com/travel/brownsville-to-laredo-on-u-s-83-and-mexico-highway-2-2/. Accessed November 11, 2020.

Kurtz, Henry I. "Last Battle of the War." *Civil War Times Illustrated* 1, no. 1 (April 1962): 32–33.

Lowery, Jack. "Fort Concho: Outpost on the Texas Frontier." *Texas Highways*, March 1989.

Marvel, William. "Last Hurrah at Palmetto Ranch." *Civil War Times*, June 12, 2006.

Miles, Robert W. "Hueco Tanks: Desert Oasis." *Password* 29, no. 2 (Summer 1984): 64–72.

Pinkard, Tommie. "The Stars Shine Again at the Majestic." *Texas Highways*, January 1983, 22.

Pollard, R. M. "The Evolution of a Great State's Capitol." *Illustrated American* 21, no. 362 (January 1897): 108–09.

Preddy, Jane. "The Greater Majestic Theatre." *Marquee: Journal of the Theatre Historical Society of America* 20 (1988): 5–10.

Richardson, Rupert N. "Some Details of the Southern Overland Mail." *Southwestern Historical Quarterly* 29, no. 1 (July 1925): 1–18.

Rivera, José A. "Restoring the Oldest Water Right in Texas: The Mission San Juan Acequia of San Antonio." *Southwestern Historical Quarterly* 106, no. 3 (January 2003): 367–96.

Schuler, Edgar A. "The Houston Race Riot, 1917." *Journal of Negro History* 29, no. 3 (1944): 300–38. https://doi.org/10.2307/2714820.

Simek, Peter. "A Scathing Look at Fair Park's History and Why Dallas Needs to Finally Fix the Park." *D Magazine*. August 3, 2017. https://www.dmagazine.com/frontburner/2017/08/a-scathing-look-at-fair-parks-history-and-why-dallas-needs-to-finally-fix-the-park/. Accessed June 3, 2021.

Simek, Peter. "The Long, Troubled, and Often Bizarre History of the State Fair of Texas." *D Magazine*, September 26, 2019. https://www.dmagazine.com/frontburner/2019/09/the-long-troubled-and-often-bizarre-history-of-the-state-fair-of-texas/. Accessed August 27, 2020.

Smith, Griffin, Jr. "Forgotten Places." *Texas Monthly* 71 (August 1975): 64–71, 94.

Southworth, Herbert R. "The Later Years of Seaman A. Knapp." *West Texas Historical Association Year Book* 10 (1934): 88–103.

Spennemann, Dirk H. R. "The Naval Heritage of the US Space Programme: A Case of Losses." *Journal for Maritime Research* 7, no. 1 (2005): 170–214. https://doi.org/10.1080/21533369.2005.9668350.

Stewart, A. J. "Those Mysterious Midgets." *United States Naval Institute Proceedings*, December 1974, 55–63.

Sullivan, Christina. "Survivors." *Texas Architect Magazine*, November 5, 2019.

Sutherland, Kay, PhD. "Rock Paintings at Hueco Tanks State Historical Park." *Texas Parks & Wildlife Magazine*. Austin: Texas Parks & Wildlife Department, 1996. https://tpwd.texas.gov/publications/pwdpubs/media/pwd_bk_p4501_0095e.pdf. Accessed August 21, 2021.

Williams, J. W. "The Butterfield Overland Mail Road across Texas." *Southwestern Historical Quarterly* 61, no. 1 (July 1957): 1–19.

National Park Service Nomination/Application Forms

Adams, George R. *National Register of Historic Places Nomination: Fort Sam Houston, Béxar County, Texas*. Nashville: American Association for State and Local History, 1974.

Adams, George R. *National Register of Historic Places Nomination: Hangar Nine, Béxar County, Texas*. Nashville: American Association for State and Local History, 1976.

Adams, George R. *National Register of Historic Places Nomination: U.S.S. Texas, Harris County, Texas*. Nashville: American Association for State and Local History, 1976.

Adams, George R., and Ralph Christian. *National Register of Historic Places Nomination: John Nance Garner House, Uvalde County, Texas*. Nashville: American Association for State and Local History, 1976.

Alexander, Cathay A., Ralph Christian, and George R. Adams. *National Register of Historic Places Nomination: Samuel "Sam" T. Rayburn House; "The Home Place," Fannin County, Texas*. Nashville: American Association for State and Local History, 1976.

Bell, M. Wayne, and Larry J. Kennedy. *National Register of Historic Places Nomination: The Strand Historic District, Galveston County, Texas*. Austin: Texas Historical Survey Committee, 1969.

Bell, Wayne, and Gary Hume. *National Register of Historic Places Nomination: The Sam Rayburn House, Fannin County, Texas*. Austin: Texas State Historical Survey Committee, 1972.

Bell, Wayne, and Gary Hume. *National Register of Historic Places Nomination: Roma Historic District, Starr County, Texas*. Austin: Texas State Historical Survey Committee, 1972.

Bell, Wayne, and Roxanne Williamson. *National Register of Historic Places Nomination: Hangar Nine, Béxar County, Texas*. Austin: Texas State Historical Survey Committee, 1970.

Bell, Wayne, and Roxanne Williamson. *National Register of Historic Places Nomination: José Antonio Navarro House Complex, Béxar County, Texas*. Austin: Texas State Historical Survey Committee, 1971.

Bell, Wayne, and Roxanne Williamson. *National Register of Historic Places Nomination: Spanish Governor's Palace, Béxar County, Texas*. Austin: Texas State Historical Survey Committee, 1970.

Bell, Wayne, and Roxanne Williamson. *National Register of Historic Places Nomination: Texas State Capitol, Travis County, Texas*. Austin: Texas State Historical Survey Committee, 1970.

Brooker, Hallie. *National Register of Historic Places Nomination: U.S.S. Lexington, Nueces County, Texas*. Washington, DC: National Historic Landmarks Survey, National Park Service, 2001.

Butowsky, Harry A. *National Register of Historic Places Nomination: Apollo Mission Control Center, Harris County, Texas*. Washington, DC: National Park Service, Division of History, 1984.

Butowsky, Harry A. *National Register of Historic Places Nomination: Space Environment Simulation Laboratory (SESL), Harris County, Texas*. Washington, DC: Division of History, National Park Service, 1984.

Chambers, Allen. *National Register of Historic Places Nomination: The Governor's Mansion, Austin County, Texas*. Washington, DC: Office of Archeology and Historic Preservation, National Park Service, 1974.

Cook, Jody, and John H. Sprinkle Jr. *National Register of Historic Places Nomination: Randolph Field Historic District, Béxar County, Texas*. Atlanta: Southeast Regional Office, National Park Service, 2001.

Delgado, James P. *National Register of Historic Places Nomination: Elissa, Galveston County, Texas*. Washington, DC: National Park Service, 1990.

Delgado, James P. *National Register of Historic Places Nomination: HA. 19 (Japanese Midget Submarine), Monroe County, Florida*. Washington, DC: National Park Service, 1988.

Ferguson, John C. *National Register of Historic Places Nomination: Texas State Capitol, Travis County, Texas*. Austin: Texas Historical Commission, 1985.

Heintzelman, Patricia. *National Register of Historic Places Nomination: The Alamo, Béxar County, Texas*. Washington, DC: Landmark Review Project, Historic Sites Survey, 1975.

Heintzelman, Patricia. *National Register of Historic Places Nomination: Espada Aqueduct and Acequia, Béxar County, Texas*. Washington, DC: Landmark Review Project, Historic Sites Survey, National Park Service, 1975.

Heintzelman, Patricia. *National Register of Historic Places Nomination: Lucas Gusher, Spindletop Oil Field, Jefferson County, Texas*. Washington, DC: Division of Historic and Architectural Surveys, 1979.

Heintzelman, Patricia. *National Register of Historic Places Nomination: Palo Alto Battlefield, Cameron County, Texas*. Washington, DC: Landmark Review Project, Historic Sites Survey, National Park Service, 1975.

Heintzelman, Patricia. *National Register of Historic Places Nomination: Resaca de la Palma Battlefield, Cameron County, Texas*. Washington, DC: Landmark Review Project, Historic Sites Survey, National Park Service, 1975.

Heintzelman, Patricia, and Cecil McKithan. *National Register of Historic Places Nomination: Presidio Nuestra Señora de Loreto de La Bahía, Goliad County, Texas*. Washington, DC: Landmark Review Project, Historic Sites Survey, National Park Service, 1977.

Heintzelman, Patricia, and Charles W. Snell. *National Register of Historic Places Nomination: Spanish Governor's Palace, Béxar County, Texas*. Washington, DC: Landmark Review Project, Historic Sites Survey, National Park Service, 1975.

Hunt, Conover, and James H. Charleton. *National Register of Historic Places Nomination: Dealey Plaza Historic District, Dallas County, Texas.* Dallas: Dallas County Historical Foundation, 1991.

Jones, W. Dwayne. *National Register of Historic Places Nomination: Highland Park Shopping Village, Dallas County, Texas.* Austin: Texas Historical Commission, 1997.

Jones, W. Dwayne, and Susan Allen Kline. *National Register of Historic Places Nomination: Highland Park Shopping Village, Dallas County, Texas.* Austin: Texas Historical Commission, 2000.

Landon, Marie D., and Joe R. Williams. *National Register of Historic Places Nomination: East End Historic District, Galveston County, Texas.* Austin: Texas Historical Commission, 1975.

Levy, Benjamin, and Betty McSwain. *National Register of Historic Places Nomination: Presidio Nuestra Señora de Loreto de La Bahía, Goliad County, Texas.* Washington, DC: Landmark Review Project, Historic Sites Survey, National Park Service, 1977.

Levy, Benjamin, and Betty McSwain. *National Register of Historic Places Nomination: Sam Houston House "Woodland," Walker County, Texas.* Washington, DC: Division of Historic and Architectural Surveys, 1973.

Levy, Benjamin, and Betty McSwain. *National Register of Historic Places Nomination: Sam Houston House "Woodland," Walker County, Texas.* Washington, DC: Landmark Review Project, Historic Sites Survey, National Park Service, 1979.

McAllen, Mary Margaret. *National Register of Historic Places Nomination: Majestic Theatre, Béxar County, Texas.* San Antonio: Las Casas Foundation, 1992.

Mendinghall, Joseph S. *National Register of Historic Places Nomination: J A Ranch, Armstrong County, Texas.* Washington, DC: Landmark Review Project, Historic Sites Survey, National Park Service, 1978.

Mendinghall, Joseph Scott. *National Register of Historic Places Nomination: Fort Belknap, Young County, Texas.* Washington, DC: Landmark Review Project, Historic Sites Survey, National Park Service, 1983.

Mendinghall, Joseph S. *National Register of Historic Places Nomination: Fort Richardson, Jack County, Texas.* Washington, DC: Landmark Review Project, Historic Sites Survey, National Park Service, 1978.

Mendinghall, Joseph Scott. *National Register of Historic Places Nomination: Porter Farm, Kaufman County, Texas.* Washington, DC: Landmark Review Project, Historic Sites Survey, National Park Service, 1979.

Moore, David, Terri Myers, and Matt Goebel. *National Register of Historic Places Nomination: Palmito Ranch Battlefield, Cameron County, Texas.* Austin: Hardy-Heck-Moore & Associates, 1992.

Muckelroy, Duncan G., and Joe Williams. *National Register of Historic Places Nomination: Majestic Theatre, Béxar County, Texas.* Austin: Texas Historical Commission, 1975.

Myers, Terri, Edwin C. Bearss, and James H. Charleton. *National Register of Historic Places Nomination: Palmito Ranch Battlefield, Cameron County, Texas.* Austin: Hardy-Heck-Moore & Associates, 1994.

Myers, Terri, and Marlene Elizabeth Heck. *National Register of Historic Places Nomination: Treviño-Uribe Ranch, Zapata County, Texas.* Austin: Hardy-Heck-Moore & Associates, 1997.

Newlan, Ralph Edward, James W. Steely, Susan Begley, and Ethan Carr. *National Register of Historic Places Nomination: Bastrop State Park, Bastrop County, Texas.* Washington, DC: National Park Service, 1997.

Pitcaithley, Dwight. *National Register of Historic Places Nomination: Fort Davis, Jeff Davis County, Texas.* Santa Fe, NM: National Park Service, 1977.

Pitts, Carolyn. *National Register of Historic Places Nomination: East End Historic District, Galveston County, Texas.* Washington, DC: Historic Sites Survey, National Park Service, 1976.

Pitts, Carolyn. *National Register of Historic Places Nomination: The Strand Historic District, Galveston County, Texas.* Washington, DC: Landmark Review Project, Historic Sites Survey, National Park Service, 1993.

Snell, Charles W. *National Register of Historic Places Nomination: Mission Concepción (Nuestra Señora de la Purísima Concepción de Acuña Mission), Béxar County, Texas.* Washington, DC: National Park Service, 1968.

Snyder, Stephen G., and James H. Charleton. *National Register of Historic Places Nomination: Texas Centennial Exposition Buildings (1936–37), Dallas County, Texas.* Johnson City, TX: Lyndon B. Johnson National Historical Park, 1985.

Thomason, Philip J. M. *National Register of Historic Places Nomination: Randolph Field Historic District, Béxar County, Texas.* Nashville: Thomason and Associates, Preservation Planners, 1993.

Weitze, Karen J., Michael R. Corbett, and James H. Charleton. *National Register of Historic Places Nomination: Roma Historic District, Starr County, Texas.* Austin: Dames & Moore, Inc., 1993.

Westerhoff, Bruce. *National Register of Historic Places Nomination: Fort Brown, Cameron County, Texas.* Denver, CO: National Park Service, 1985.

Westerhoff, Bruce. *National Register of Historic Places Nomination: King Ranch, Nueces, Kenedy, Kleberg, and Willacy Counties, Texas.* Denver, CO: National Park Service, 1985.

Williams, Joe R., and David Moore. *National Register of Historic Places Nomination: Elissa, Galveston County, Texas.* Austin: Texas Historical Commission, 1978.

Williamson, Roxanne, and Martha Doty. *National Register of Historic Places Nomination: The Governor's Mansion, Austin County, Texas.* Austin: Texas State Historical Survey Committee, 1970.

Newspapers

Flick, David. "47 Years after JFK Assassination, Sixth Floor Museum Adapts to New Era." *Dallas News*, Nov. 22, 2010. https://www.dallasnews.com/news/2010/11/22/47-years-after-jfk-assassination-sixth-floor-museum-adapts-to-new-era.

Harmon, Dave. "Past the Ashes." *Austin American-Statesman*, November 24, 2011, 1–7.

"It's True: Texas Capitol Stands Taller Than Nation's." *Orlando Sentinel*, January 14, 1999. https://www.orlandosentinel.com/news/os-xpm-1999-01-14-9901140152-story.html.

Jackson, Anthony. "Rio Vista Farm in Socorro Nominated for National Historic Landmark." *El Paso Times*, October 15, 2021. https://www.elpasotimes.com/story/news/2021/10/15/rio-vista-farm-socorro-nominated-national-historic-landmark/8457437002/. Accessed October 20, 2021.

Martin, Deborah. "Majestic Now Can Be Proud as Peacock." *San Antonio Express News*, March 19, 2017, 1.

Rice, Harvey. "Galveston's Tall Ship *Elissa* No Longer Seaworthy." *Houston Chronicle*, July 11, 2011. Accessed July 25, 2021.

Schutze, Jim. "The Fair Park Plan Is Dead! Long Live the Fair Park Plan." *Dallas Observer*, October 17, 2016. http://www.dallasobserver.com/news/the-fair-park-plan-is-dead-long-live-the-fair-park-plan-8807438. Accessed August 30, 2021.

Schutze, Jim. "New Report Tells Sordid Past of Fair Park, State Fair of Texas—but Offers Hope." *Dallas Observer*, August 3, 2017. http://www.dallasobserver.com/news/new-report-explains-how-state-fair-screwed-up-dallas-fair-park-9723989. Accessed May 28, 2021.

Wolff, Henry. "A Trip on *Elissa*." *Victoria Advocate*, March 31, 1989. Accessed December 22, 2014.

Online Resources

"Apollo Mission Control Center—Aviation: From Sand Dunes to Sonic Booms; A National Register of Historic Places Travel Itinerary." National Parks Service. Archived from the original on May 1, 2008. Accessed Nov. 13, 2008. https://web.archive.org/web/20080501221321/http:/www.nps.gov/nr/travel/aviation/apo.htm.

"Briscoe-Garner Museum." Dolph Briscoe Center for American History. July 30, 2021. https://live-briscoe-v2.pantheonsite.io/visit/briscoe-garner-museum.

"Cabot II (CVL-28)." Naval History and Heritage Command. April 7, 2020. https://www.history.navy.mil/content/history/nhhc/research/histories/ship-histories/danfs/c/cabot-ii.html.

Davis, Domini. "It's State Fair of Texas Season—Here's What You Need to Know." *KERA News*, September 26, 2019. Accessed October 24, 2019. https://www.keranews.org/post/its-state-fair-texas-season-heres-what-you-need-know.

"Fort Richardson State Park, Historic Site & Lost Creek Reservoir State Trailway." Texas Parks and Wildlife Department. Accessed July 5, 2021. https://tpwd.texas.gov/state-parks/fort-richardson/park_history.

Gutro, Rob. "NASA Readies Famous 'Chamber A' to Welcome the James Webb Space Telescope." NASA, January 23, 2013. Accessed July 28, 2021. https://phys.org/news/2013-01-nasa-readies-famous-chamber-james.html

Hutchinson, Lee. "NASA's Restored Apollo Mission Control Is a Slice of '60s Life, Frozen in Amber." Ars Technica, June 28, 2019. Accessed April 12, 2020. https://arstechnica.com/science/2019/06/behind-the-scenes-at-nasas-newly-restored-historic-apollo-mission-control/.

Kalthoff, Ken. "Dallas Leaders Praise New Fair Park Plan." NBC DFW, September 3, 2014. Retrieved January 18, 2017. https://www.nbcdfw.com/news/local/dallas-leaders-praise-new-fair-park-plan/2098535/.

"Las Casas Foundation: About Us." Las Casas Foundation. Accessed December 21, 2020. https://www.lascasasfoundation.org/about-us-2. (Information now available at https://www.themajesticempirefdn.org/about-us/.)

Lavine, Pat, and Mark Spier. "Changing of the Guard at Resaca de La Palma." National Park Service, September 1, 2011. https://www.nps.gov/paal/learn/news/changing-of-the-guard-at-resaca-de-la-palma.htm.

"Lexington V (CV-16)." Naval History and Heritage Command, July 29, 2015. https://www.history.navy.mil/research/histories/ship-histories/danfs/l/lexington-cv-16-v.html.

"Lyndon B. Johnson National Historical Park to Temporarily Close Texas White House and Pool House." Lyndon B. Johnson National Historical Park, August 2, 2018. https://www.nps.gov/lyjo/learn/news/texas-white-house-closure.htm.

"Lyndon B. Johnson State Park & Historic Site." Texas Parks and Wildlife. Accessed June 16, 2021. https://tpwd.texas.gov/state-parks/lyndon-b-johnson.

"Majestic Theatre: History." Charline McCombs Majestic Theatre & Empire Theatre, 2013. https://www.majesticempire.com/info/history.

Martinez, Krystina. "From The Newsroom: Fair Park's Future; Making Dallas a Smart City." KERA News, November 18, 2015. Accessed January 18, 2020. https://www.keranews.org/texas-news/2015-11-18/from-the-newsroom-fair-parks-future-making-dallas-a-smart-city.

Moorhead, Gerald, et al. "Jesús Treviño Fort (Treviño-Uribe Rancho)." *SAH Archipedia*. https://sah-archipedia.org/buildings/TX-01-SM1. 2020. Accessed November 1, 2021.

"NASA Names Mission Control for Legendary Flight Director Christopher Kraft." NASA, April 14, 2011. Accessed September 6, 2013. https://www.nasa.gov/people/christopher-c-kraft-jr/#:~:text=On%20April%204%2C%202011%2C%20NASA,in%20support%20of%20space%20missions.

"NASA Sends Historic Apollo Mission Control Consoles to Be Restored." NASA, January 25, 2018. Accessed February 21, 2021. http://www.collectspace.com/news/news-012518a-apollo-mission-control-consoles-restoration.html.

"Resaca de La Palma Battlefield—American Latino Heritage: Discover Our Shared Heritage Travel Itinerary." National Park Service. Accessed August 15, 2021. https://www.nps.gov/nr/travel/american_Latino_heritage/resaca_de_la_palma_battlefield.html.

"Resaca de La Palma Battlefield—Palo Alto Battlefield National Historical Park." National Park Service. Accessed August 26, 2021. https://www.nps.gov/paal/learn/historyculture/resacadelapalma.htm.

"Rio Vista Farm." National Trust for Historic Preservation, 2016. Accessed November 1, 2021. https://savingplaces.org/places/rio-vista#.YYBG4m3MLIU.

"San Antonio Missions National Historical Park." National Park Service. Accessed September 3, 2016. https://www.nps.gov/saan/index.htm.

"Texas State Parks: Bastrop and Buescher State Parks Interpretive Guide." Texas State Parks, Texas Parks and Wildlife Department, 2019. https://tpwd.texas.gov/publications/pwdpubs/media/pwd_br_p4505_0043p.pdf.

"The Collection." Friends of the Governor's Mansion, June 3, 2018. https://txfgm.org/the-collection.

"The First Fort Davis: 1854–1862." Fort Davis National Historic Site, National Park Service, January 4, 2018. https://www.nps.gov/foda/learn/historyculture/firstfortdavis.htm.

"USS *Cabot* (CVL-28)." National Park Service, August 29, 2018. https://www.nps.gov/subjects/nationalhistoriclandmarks/uss-cabot.htm.

Valadez, Alejandra. "Rio Vista Farm Closer to National Historic Landmark Designation." *Socorro Initiative*. October 30, 2021. https://socorroinitiative.org/rio-vista-farm-closer-to-national-historic-landmark-designation/. Accessed November 1, 2021.

Wells, B. A., and K. L. Wells. "Oil Reigns at King Ranch." American Oil and Gas Historical Society, April 29, 2014. Accessed July 20, 2021. https://aoghs.org/oil-almanac/king-ranch-oil.

About the Author

Tristan Smith is an independent historian living in the suburbs of Houston, Texas. He has worked for museums and nonprofits in Kansas, Missouri, and Texas for more than twenty-five years in marketing, curatorial, educational, volunteer, management, and administrative capacities. Museums he's been involved with have featured natural history/science, the 1950s, fine art, community history, a sunken steamboat found in a Kansas cornfield, a US president, and fire history. He has also consulted with organizations and municipalities in historic preservation.

Smith is the author of *Images of America: Houston Fire Department* (Arcadia, 2015), *A History Lover's Guide to Houston* (History Press, 2020), *Historic Cemeteries of Houston & Galveston* (History Press, 2023), and *The History Lover's Guide to Galveston* (History Press, 2024). He is also a beat writer covering the Houston Astros for LastWordOnSports.com and writes features for the statewide heritage magazine *Authentic Texas*.